MS-DOS User's Guide

Chris DeVoney

Que Corporation
Indianapolis

88 87 86 85 84   8 7 6 5 4 3

Interpretation of the printing code: the rightmost double-digit number is the year of the book's printing; the rightmost single-digit number, the number of the book's printing. For example, a printing code of 83-4 shows that the fourth printing of the book occurred in 1983.

Editorial Director
David F. Noble, Ph.D.

Editors
Diane F. Brown, M.A.
Virginia D. Noble, M.L.S.
Pamela Fullerton

Managing Editor
Paul L. Mangin

About the Author

Chris DeVoney is the vice-president, Technology, for Que Corporation. He received his B.S. degree from the University of Gloucester. Mr. DeVoney has been employed in the microcomputer industry since it began in 1975. He founded Marcum Consulting and, prior to joining Que, served as technical consultant to two retail computer stores. President of the Indianapolis Small Systems Group, Mr. DeVoney has been active in forming other computer professional organizations and has conducted workshops for IBM Product Center personnel on operating systems and the IBM Personal Computer. He has written and edited numerous books and articles about microcomputers. Mr. DeVoney is author of *IBM's Personal Computer,* first and second editions, and *PC DOS User's Guide* and co-author of *Introducing IBM PCjr,* all published by Que Corporation.

Acknowledgments

The author of this book wishes to thank the following people:

George Eberhardt of Computer Innovations, Inc., Red Bank, New Jersey

Mark Tyson of IBM Entry Systems Division, Boca Raton, Florida

Tom Fenwick of Manx Software Systems, Inc., Shrewsbury, New Jersey

Chris Larson and Don Immerwahr of Microsoft, Inc., Bellevue, Washington, for their invaluable assistance

Tony Barge of Victor Data Products, Inc., Indianapolis, Indiana

Foreword

I received my first copy of the DOS V2.0 documentation in late 1982. After reading it for several hours, I was both excited and confused. I like the UNIX operating system. It has several features I wish were on more microcomputer systems. The prospect of an operating system that combined the friendliness and performance of Microsoft's MS-DOS Version 1 with some of the powerful features of Bell Laboratories' UNIX operating system was tantalizing. The idea of using hierarchical directories, I/O redirection, and piping on my Personal Computer was awesome. I poured through the manuals, imagining what it would be like to have DOS Version 2.

At first, I could not understand all the concepts and materials in the documentation. Not having a working copy of DOS V2.0 made my usual learning technique—understanding by trying—impossible. IBM, one of the first manufacturers to implement DOS V2.0, did not announce V2.0 until March, 1983. I had to wait until April, 1983, before I could use DOS V2.0.

In April, 1983, I was writing the second edition of *IBM's Personal Computer*. I thought it would be appropriate to use the XT while I wrote the book because a major part of the book covered the XT and the differences between it and the PC. That XT still resides on a table in my office.

In the second edition, I tried to explain all about DOS V2.0 in less than 30 pages, a feat I did not feel I accomplished. Although the book is excellent, I felt that someone needed to cover DOS V2.0 in more detail.

After I finished the book, I took a short break. While on that vacation, I walked into a book store and counted more than 35 titles on the IBM Personal Computer. Although several books covered PC DOS, Version 1, no books covering PC DOS or MS-DOS Version 2 were available.

Having gone through the experience of learning a new version of an operating system, I felt that others should not have to suffer through the experience the same way—the hard way. This book is the result.

DOS V2 is not very hard to learn, but more time is needed to learn how to use its new features and functions. I made several "near fatal" mistakes while becoming familiar with DOS V2. Most of them were unimportant, but two almost wiped out all the information on my 10-megabyte hard disk.

That is why I wrote this book. One of Murphy's sayings is, "Experience is directly proportional to the amount of equipment ruined." I changed that saying to, "Computer experience is directly proportional to the number of disk files ruined." I am a very experienced DOS V2 user!

This book is a user's guide to DOS V2 for the novice-to-intermediate computer user. The book discusses the philosophy and concepts behind DOS V2, the way the computer operates, and the commands. Examples are provided for most of the commands. Often, you see on the page exactly what happens on the video screen.

But this book is more than just a user's guide. It is also an excellent DOS V2 reference book. The Command Summary section lists the purpose, syntax, rules, and exit codes for the major DOS V2 commands. Many commands also have examples or sample sessions as well as additional background notes. The commands are alphabetized for easy reference. This feature allows anyone, including the advanced user, to locate a command quickly, find the information needed to make it work, and continue working.

Throughout this book, hints, suggestions, and occasional warnings appear, stemming from my experience with DOS V2. As I wrote this book, I attempted to exercise DOS to its limits. What would DOS allow? What would it find objectionable? Occasionally, DOS would accept an improperly phrased command and do the completely unexpected. Actually, DOS did exactly what it was instructed to do, which was not always what I wanted. Sometimes I ran into genuine bugs with DOS. The known bugs (only two real bugs for DOS V2.0) are listed in Appendix A. Fortunately, the version of DOS V2.0 that you receive will probably not have these bugs.

Don't be intimidated by DOS V2. I have never met a person who learned how to ride a bicycle just by reading a book. The same is true for computers. Try the examples. Experiment. Be daring occasionally. However, be sure to experiment with practice disks (diskettes that do not contain valuable information) until you become comfortable with DOS. There are very few "dangerous" commands in DOS. (FORMAT, ERASE, and DISKCOPY are the major ones.) If you make a mistake, look at what you typed. Most often, you simply mistyped a word. Try to find out what you did wrong and try the command again. The Commands Section of the book will help you determine what might be wrong. DOS is friendly once you get to know it.

This book is not identical to my *PC DOS User's Guide*. The *MS-DOS User's Guide* was written for "vanilla" (generic) MS-DOS, as provided by Microsoft. Although many examples were created on an IBM PC XT, the examples and discussions are relevant to any MS-DOS computer, such as Altos, DEC, NEC, Texas Instruments, Wang, Victor, or Zenith. Many examples were created on the NEC APC, the Victor 9000, and the Texas Instruments Professional.

My best wishes to you. I hope your experience with DOS V2 is painless and enjoyable.

Introduction

What You Should Know

Before you start reading this book, you should have handy the DOS manual that came with your computer. You will need to know some information in this manual: the control and DOS editing keys, the EDLIN line-editing program, and any program needed to set up your hard disk, if your computer uses one.

The control keys and DOS editing keys are used to type commands to DOS and to edit or correct typing mistakes. Learn the control keys as soon as possible; they are important. The DOS editing keys, on the other hand, may be learned at any time. Both kinds of keys are covered in Chapter 3.

The EDLIN program is a *text editor*. It allows you to record and edit text into a disk file, but is only half of a word-processing program. (The other half is the printing process.) As a limited, line-oriented text editor, EDLIN is not as good as many other programs, such as PMATE, VEDIT, WordStar, etc.

You will need a text editor later in this book, starting with the discussion of batch files in Chapter 10. If you decide to use EDLIN, read the information in your DOS manual and experiment with EDLIN before reading Chapter 10.

You may use a different text editor or word-processing program. If you choose a word-processing program, use its programming, or non-document, mode. With some word processors, such as WordStar, the characters are manipulated and stored differently by the document and nondocument modes. Text to be used by DOS should always be created under the word processor's nondocument mode.

If your computer has a hard disk, it may need some preparation before it can be used. Your dealer might already have configured your hard disk for you. If not, either contact your dealer for this service (possibly for a fee) or check your DOS manual for instructions on setting up the hard disk.

What You Should Have

Starting in Chapter 2, you will need the following items:

- Your computer system, connected and working

- The diskettes provided with DOS V2.0, your DOS master diskettes

- Several blank diskettes, with the accompanying protective envelopes, and blank labels

Throughout this book, you will be asked to try a command or sequence of commands on your computer system. To work these exercises, you will need your working computer, the DOS diskettes, and several blank diskettes.

What Will Be Covered

Chapter 1 presents the basic history of DOS and its role in the computer system. Chapter 2 is an introduction to your computer system and covers the CPU, memory, peripherals, and modems.

Chapter 3 is a hands-on session during which you prepare blank diskettes, copy diskettes and files, and are introduced to basic DOS concepts. Chapter 4 offers facts about disk drives and diskettes as well as some useful tips.

Chapter 5 discusses the inner workings of DOS and its major sections. Chapter 6 covers device and disk drive names. Chapter 7 handles disk files and file names, and also introduces some of the conventions used in this book.

The new features of DOS 2 are covered in Chapters 8 and 9. Chapter 8 covers two important DOS V2 features: redirection and piping. Chapter 9 introduces the hierarchical directory system.

Chapter 10 introduces batch files and their new and unique sub-commands. Chapter 11 covers the new CONFIG.SYS file that allows you to tailor DOS to your needs with little effort.

Old and new DOS commands that have changed from Version 1 to Version 2 are discussed in Chapter 12. This chapter also discusses the new RECOVER and FC (file compare) programs.

Chapter 13 provides more facts about DOS V2, offers advice and tips for hard disk users, and suggests additional sources of information.

Three appendixes are included in this book. Appendix A lists some of the known bugs of DOS V2.00, the first release of V2. This brief list should be outdated by the time you read this book. The differences between DOS V2.00 and DOS V2.10 are briefly discussed in this appendix. Appendix B is an example of a disk, showing the hierarchical directory structure, and Appendix C is an ASCII character chart. A detailed index rounds out the book.

What Is Not Covered

No book can cover DOS completely. There are so many aspects of this operating system that no one book can serve as a tutorial on learning DOS, a DOS reference guide, a system programmer's guide, etc. For this reason, several subjects were omitted from this book:

- Control and DOS editing keys
- The EDLIN (line editor), DEBUG (assembly language debugger), and LINK (program linker) programs
- The ANSI terminal control codes
- The DOS function calls
- Writing device drivers
- Similar technical details about DOS
- Manufacturer-specific programs

Most of this information is important to programmers. If you do not program, or program only in BASIC-86 or GW BASIC, the lack of this information will not matter to you. If you'd like more information on the programming aspects of DOS, read your DOS manual.

This book discusses the generic version of MS-DOS. Not covered are programs that have been written for your computer by the computer's manufacturer. Your DOS manual will be the best source of information on operating programs specific to your system.

Read, try, learn, and enjoy. After all, the computer is a servant. All you have to do is be comfortable in your role as user.

Table of Contents

1
DOS and You

DOS is the acronym for disk operating system. An operating system is a collection of programs that direct and aid in the management of the computer's resources. A *disk* operating system also controls the use of disk drives for the storing and loading of programs and data.

Anyone who uses a personal computer with one or more disk drives should have some knowledge of DOS. What you need to know depends on what you want to do with your computer. You may want to know only how to turn on the computer, start DOS, and issue one or two commands. On the other hand, you may use your computer so much that you need to know all the commands and how they work. Most people fall somewhere in between.

What should you know about DOS? There is no exact answer to this question, but you must know some commands and facts. The most basic commands cover how to format a disk, place a copy of the operating system on the diskette, copy and erase disk files, get a list of the files on a disk, and perform other fundamental operations of DOS. Everyone who operates a computer should know these commands.

If you use your computer extensively, you will need to know even more. Knowing how disk files are actually stored, finding the amount of free space on a disk, establishing and using the hierarchical directories, or using redirected I/O will be important to you. If you fall into this "heavy-user" category, be sure to read about all the features and commands.

DOS has many useful functions and features. You don't have to use all of them, nor are you obligated to learn everything about each command you use. The first time through, just try to remember the basic functions of each command. Later, you can return to this book or your DOS reference manual and learn more about the commands and functions of DOS.

At times, learning about DOS can be a circular process. You may need to know one thing before you can go on to something else. When this problem occurs, you do not need to be alarmed, because DOS is not really complicated.

The Origin of MS-DOS

The following is a "fairy tale" description of the origin and evolution of MS-DOS.

In the beginning (1972), there were microprocessors: computers, each on its own silicon chip. This chip had replaced many different chips, but the microprocessors were without software, the instructions that told these computers-on-a-chip what to do.

So engineers from such companies as Intel™ Corporation began to write software. But they found that writing software was difficult. Each instruction had to be entered by hand as a number, not an English-like word or phrase. So the engineers designed assemblers, programs that took pidgin English-like commands (*mnemonics*) and transformed them into instructions the microprocessors could understand. After assemblers came debuggers, programs that helped engineers find problems in other programs.

A convenient way to get the programs into the microprocessors was still needed. In those early days, the mighty paper tape punch and reader were the standard. They were slow, however, and handling paper tape was difficult.

The engineers then began to write new operating systems that used a new device called a disk drive. One was partially developed at IBM. A circular piece of flexible plastic, eight inches in diameter and coated with iron ferrite, was placed in a cardboard jacket. This *floppy diskette* was inserted into the disk drive, and a special board in the computer controlled the actions of the disk drive. The floppy disk drive was exciting because it could hold 246,784 bytes of information, the equivalent of over a mile of paper tape. The new operating system that handled the placing, reading, and organizing of information on the diskette was called a *disk operating system.*

In 1975 a new company displayed its new board that used floppy disk drives and floppy diskettes. The software used to "control" the new board was called Control Program for Microcomputers, or CP/M™. Dr. Gary Kildall was the co-author of this early disk operating system.

And so CP/M became a standard for the microcomputers that used microprocessors from Intel (the 8080 and later 8085 CPU) and a new company called Zilog Corporation (the Z80 CPU). As time passed, CP/M was improved and gained popularity.

Soon (1978) Intel Corporation announced a new and improved version of its microprocessor, the 8086 CPU. It worked faster and could immediately use more RAM memory than its predecessors. Because of some differences between the systems, the software that worked with the older Intel microprocessors would not work with the new 8086 CPU.

Later, Intel developed a sister microprocessor to the 8086 CPU, the 8088 CPU. It worked like the 8086, and both could use the same software, but the 8088 "talked" only half as well to memory and the outside world as the 8086: in units of 8 bits at a time as opposed to 16 bits, respectively. (A *bit* is a *b*inary dig*it,* the smallest unit of storage in the computer. Eight bits make up one *byte,* the basic unit of storage that holds one character.)

After the 8086, but before the 8088, a small company in Seattle, Washington, wrote a new disk operating system for the 8086 CPU. The author was Tim Paterson, a co-owner of Seattle Computer Products. The firm had developed a computer that used the 8086 CPU and needed a disk operating system for it. In 1979, Tim Paterson wrote 86-DOS. It was patterned after the CP/M operating system. However, Paterson added some changes to 86-DOS. He wanted the operating system to work quickly and take advantage of the new features offered by disk drives and other computer equipment. He also wanted a friendly operating system, and one whose internal workings were different (and better) than CP/M's.

Meanwhile, the world's largest computer maker, International Business Machines, was considering making a personal computer. IBM decided that it was important to have a BASIC programming language available for its computer. The logical choice was to use BASIC from Microsoft, Inc., a company located in Bellevue, Washington. Microsoft had written the most popular version of this programming language, one which, at that time, was running on more than 500,000 computers.

Bill Gates, then president of the company and one of the two authors of Microsoft BASIC, met with IBM. Microsoft began to work on a special version of its 8086 BASIC language. (Microsoft's BASIC-86 made its debut in 1979.)

At the same time, IBM began talking to Digital Research, Inc., the Pacific Grove, California, company that wrote CP/M. The two firms did not come to an agreement. IBM began to look elsewhere for an operating system for its new personal computer.

Microsoft quickly acquired the rights to distribute Tim Paterson's 86-DOS and began talking to IBM about using this new operating system. An agreement was made, and Microsoft's MS-DOS became one of the operating systems for the new IBM Personal Computer.

Prior to this agreement, Microsoft had acquired the rights to rewrite and distribute Bell Laboratories' UNIX™ operating system. Microsoft called its version of UNIX, XENIX™. The company believed that XENIX would be the best operating system for the new generation of microcomputers that used the new, more powerful microprocessors. The impact of this decision will become apparent later in this story.

In April, 1981, IBM announced the IBM Personal Computer, which uses the 8088 CPU and the IBM Personal Computer Disk Operating System. The microcomputer industry nicknamed the new operating system PC DOS. PC DOS—really MS-DOS with some program additions from IBM—quickly became the most popular operating system for the Personal Computer. Soon many other companies began marketing computers that used MS-DOS. Companies such as Zenith Data Systems, Wang Laboratories, Digital Equipment Corporation, Texas Instruments, and Victor Technology made computers with the 8088 or 8086 CPU that ran the MS-DOS operating system.

Microsoft began to work on a new version of its operating system: a hybrid that would combine features of both the current MS-DOS and the XENIX operating system. Microsoft believed that the current version of MS-DOS was well suited for one person doing one thing at a time on one computer. However, the new computers allowed more than one person at a time (multiple users) to run more than one program at a time (multiple tasks). MS-DOS Version 2 was written to start the transition.

Microsoft took some of the features of its XENIX operating system and incorporated them into MS-DOS Version 2. As a result, features that had not been available before on microcomputers became available through MS-DOS V2. One of the biggest changes was the use of hierarchical directories. (This concept is discussed in Chapter 9.) The popularity of larger, faster disk drives made the change necessary. The hard disk drive could hold twenty to forty times more information than a floppy disk. In addition, the XENIX method of organizing information on the disks was more attractive than the old method.

Almost two years after IBM announced the Personal Computer, the Personal Computer XT made its debut. The XT came with a 10-million-byte hard disk drive. Although IBM could have modified DOS Version 1 to handle the hard disk, the need to organize information on the hard disk with the new XENIX method was important. IBM announced PC DOS Version 2.0, the IBM/Microsoft implementation of MS-DOS V2, for the Personal Computer XT. Today every IBM XT owner uses PC DOS V2.0. Old and new Personal Computer owners are also buying and using DOS V2.0.

Other computer companies followed IBM's example. This explains why you have DOS on your computer system.

Because some computer companies are either based overseas or sell their computers to foreign countries, Microsoft wrote a slightly different version of DOS V2 called 2.10. Version 2.10 works the same way as version 2.00, except that the messages DOS produces for the operator to read are organized into certain places in the programs. This organization facilitates changing programs for use with foreign languages. DOS V2.10 is sometimes called the *international* version of DOS V2.

What Did This Story Tell You?

The origin of MS-DOS is closely linked to Tim Paterson of Seattle Computer Products and to IBM. Microsoft acquired 86-DOS because of IBM. Initially, the only difference between 86-DOS and MS-DOS was the name. MS-DOS is a trademark of Microsoft; the company has improved MS-DOS since the first version. Tim Paterson worked for Microsoft for a year to help perfect MS-DOS. The first published version of PC DOS was V1.0, which was MS-DOS V1.10. Microsoft corrected several problems with MS-DOS, and it finally evolved into MS-DOS V1.25. This version became PC DOS V1.1, which also incorporated the routines for handling the new double-sided floppy disk drives. In the latter part of 1982, Microsoft wrote MS-DOS V2.0. It was adopted by IBM and became PC DOS V2.0. IBM and Microsoft use PC DOS V2.1 and MS-DOS V2.1 respectively. V2.1 is the most current version of DOS.

MS-DOS V2 represents a transition in operating systems: a directory on the disk stores the list of the files on that disk. The old Version-1 method for handling the directory worked well for floppy diskettes, but hard disk drives posed a new problem. A different method was needed to handle the directory. Microsoft used the UNIX-style hierarchical directories to solve the directory problem. This method allowed many more files to be stored and retrieved. Microsoft also added the UNIX abilities to redirect I/O and pipe information between programs, along with the necessary DOS system calls. It is not important to know all the terms that were just mentioned. They are discussed in detail in later chapters. The point to remember is that MS-DOS V2 deliberately resembles the UNIX operating system.

Chapter 2 introduces you to the major parts of your computer system, and Chapter 3 explains how DOS works with your system.

2

Your Computer System

Take a look at your computer system. You can easily see several key parts. The computer is usually in a box, which may contain one or more disk drives. You may have a separate video screen and keyboard or use a *CRT,* which is a video terminal that includes both the video screen and the keyboard in one unit. Your computer system may have all of these parts built into the box.

Regardless of what components are visible, each computer system can be broken down into several important elements. This chapter discusses the key parts of your computer system and how each component works with the others. Because disk drives are especially important, they are covered separately in Chapter 4.

We will start with the CPU, the heart of a computer system.

The CPU

Inside every computer system is a *CPU,* a central processing unit. It is to the computer what the brain is to the human body.

A microcomputer's CPU has two main functions: computation and control. Usually, it is the CPU that adds, subtracts, multiplies, divides, and compares numbers and characters. The CPU also regulates and controls the flow of information among the parts of the computer.

The choice of CPU for your computer is important. Currently, to run MS-DOS, your computer must use one of the Intel family's 8086 CPUs or one of Motorola's 68000s. In late 1984 MS-DOS may become available on other CPUs.

Some CPUs are similar; others are different. The 8086 family from Intel Corporation is one example of similar CPUs. It includes the 8086, 8088, iAPX 186, and iAPX 188 CPUs.

To understand the similarity and differences among CPUs, you will need to know a few computer buzz words. For example, *bit* is the shorthand buzz word for *b*inary dig*it*. A bit is a single on or off switch and the smallest unit of storage in a computer system. Everything in a computer system is based on the binary digit and binary notation. Most numbers associated with a computer can eventually be broken down into a power of two (2^x).

The second buzz word you need to know is *byte*. Eight bits grouped together form 1 byte, the next smallest unit of storage and the basic unit of measurement for your computer system. With eight on or off bits, a byte can hold 2^8, or 256, different combinations of on or off bits. Each byte holds one character. For example, the word "byte" takes up 4 bytes in your computer, one for each character. The RAM memory and disk storage in a computer system is rated in bytes.

K is another frequently used designation. It represents 1,024 (2^{10}) bytes. A 128K system usually contains 128 * 1,024 bytes of RAM memory, or 131,072 bytes. You don't have to remember exactly what a K is; just keep in mind that each K contains more than 1,000 bytes.

Your computer usually works with groups of bytes. The most frequently used grouping is a *pair,* which is 2 bytes, or 16 bits.

An 8-bit microprocessor uses 8 bits (1 byte) at a time. It moves the byte between itself and the computer's memory. Most 8-bit processors use a 16-bit number when specifying (addressing) a memory location. Therefore, the maximum amount of memory an 8-bit processor can use without help is 65,536 (2^{16}) bytes, or 64K.

A 16-bit microprocessor uses 16 bits at a time. Because the computer frequently uses 2 bytes in computations, a 16-bit microprocessor works faster than a comparable 8-bit microprocessor and can also handle more memory, usually between 1 and 16 million bytes.

MS-DOS was written for 16-bit microprocessors. Computers with 8-bit CPUs can never run MS-DOS.

The most popular CPUs for computers that run MS-DOS are the Intel 8086 and 8088. The 8086 is a 16-bit processor. It thinks in pairs of bytes and talks to the computer's memory in units of 16 bits at a time. The 8088 functions like the 8086 with one exception: it talks to the computer's memory 1 byte at a time. The 8088 should actually be called an 8-/16-bit CPU. Internally, the 8088 thinks in terms of 16 bits. When talking to the "outside world," however, the 8088 talks only in 8-bit units. It is slower than the 8086.

The iAPX 186 and the iAPX 188 are two other members of the Intel 8086 family. The former is simply an 8086 CPU with many of the support circuits needed to use the 8086 built into the CPU itself. The iAPX 188 is the 8088 version of the iAPX 186. The iAPX 186 or 188 CPU can take the place of the 8086 or 8088 CPU and about 30 other integrated circuits. Computer manufacturers can therefore make smaller, less expensive computers by using the 186 or the 188.

The four Intel CPUs discussed here are *software compatible:* programs that work with any one of the four CPUs will work with the other three as well. However, these CPUs cannot use software written for any other CPU, nor can software for the Intel 8086 family work with any other CPU.

Note: For a machine to be IBM compatible (a popular topic these days), the computer must use one of the four members of the 8086 family. The IBM PC uses the 8088 CPU. A computer attempting to be IBM compatible must use the 8086, 8088, iAPX 186, or iAPX 188 CPU. Using the right CPU, however, is only the beginning of fitting into the IBM mold. (IBM compatibility is discussed in Chapter 5.)

The Motorola 68000 family also runs MS-DOS, and, like the Intel 8086 family, has several versions. A major difference between the 8086 and 68000 is that the latter can be considered a 32-bit processor. Internally, 68000 CPUs use 4 bytes (32 bits) at a time. The individual members of the 68000 family differ in the number of bits they use when communicating with the rest of the computer.

The 68000 CPU talks to the outside world in units of 16 bits at a time and is therefore a 16-/32-bit processor. The 68008 is an 8-/32-bit CPU. Internally, it's a 32-bit CPU, but it talks to the rest of the computer in units of only 8 bits (1 byte) at a time. Like the 68000, the 68010 is a 16-/32-bit processor, but it uses a concept called *virtual memory* (to be discussed later). The 68020 is the true 32-bit version that talks to the computer's memory in units of 32 bits at a time. Currently, the 68000 CPU is the most widely used of its family. At the time I wrote this book, Motorola was just begining to mass produce the 68010 and had schedled the 68020 for mass production in mid-1984. The 68008 is not widely used.

There are other differences among 68000 family members. Programs written for the 68000 CPU will work on the 68010 and 68020. However, the operating systems (not your programs) will need to be changed to handle the new features of the 68010 and 68020. Most publishers will want to rewrite their programs to take advantage of these features, which can make programs more powerful. Software written especially for the 68010 or 68020 won't work with the 68000.

The 68000 family is *upward compatible*. Programs written for the lower members of the family generally will work with the higher members, but not vice versa. This is not unique to the 68000 family. The Intel iAPX 286, a 32-bit version of the 8086 family to be produced in 1984, is upward compatible with the 8086; but software written for the 286 will not work with the 8086.

Two other families you will hear more about in the next two years are the Zilog Z8000 and the National Semiconductor 16000 families. They have 16-bit, 16-/32-bit, and 32-bit CPUs that may be able to run MS-DOS in the next year or so.

Which CPUs Are Better?

Comparing CPU performance is difficult, but two good guidelines can help: the number of bits handled at one time, and system clock speed. First, the more bits the CPU can handle at one time, the faster the CPU should work and the more work it should be able to do. This is a guideline, not a hard rule. Generally, a 16-bit CPU works faster than an 8-bit, and a 32-bit CPU functions faster than a 16-bit, but some computer systems with 8-bit Z80 processors work faster than systems that use 16-bit CPUs.

Second, CPUs with fast system clocks function faster than CPUs with slow ones. A major factor in CPU performance is the *system clock,* the timing signal that coordinates the activity in a computer system. This clock is rated in millions of cycles per second or MHz (megahertz). The limiting factor for the system clock is usually the CPU, which is rated to perform at some maximum clock rate. The 4.5-MHz 8088 is one example.

Each CPU has its own rating. Companies may produce different versions of the same CPU with different system clock ratings. For example, Motorola produces versions of the 68000 CPU for system clocks that range from 4 MHz to 12.5 MHz. Most microcomputer systems today use a system clock that operates between 4 MHz and 8 MHz.

Generally, the faster the system clock, the faster the CPU will work. A CPU with an 8-MHz system clock should work twice as fast as the same CPU using a 4-MHz version.

Which CPU is the best? Every microprocessor manufacturer can produce test results which indicate that his CPU is the best. These performance tests don't prove much. The best thing to do is to choose a CPU with a fast system clock and find out whether the programs you want to run will work with that CPU.

Remember, the faster the CPU, the more your computer can do in the same amount of time. A computer system with a fast CPU clock is therefore helpful.

Software, however, can be the deciding factor. If you want to use a program that runs on only the 8086 family, there is no sense in picking a computer system with a 68000 CPU. The software you select should determine your choice of computer.

Coprocessors

Some computers use more than one microprocessor. Is each microprocessor a CPU? No! A computer usually has only one central processing unit. Any additional microprocessors are used to take some of the workload off the CPU. These additional microprocessors are called *coprocessors* or *auxiliary processors*.

The Intel 8087 numeric processor is one example. It's often called the *math coprocessor* because its purpose is to perform mathematical calculations swiftly.

Most CPUs are fast when working with integers in a range from -32,768 to +32,767. These numbers can be held in 16-bit units. Many of the numbers you work with, such as dollars and cents, scientific notation, sine, cosine, and others, are not so easily handled because a CPU must be specially programmed to manipulate them.

This is not true of the 8087, whose sole purpose in life is to "crunch" numbers. The 8087 has built-in instructions for handling these types of numbers and can perform math operations 10 to 100 times faster than the 8086 or 8088 CPU. With the proper software, your computer, using the 8087, can typically run math-oriented programs 5 to 25 times faster.

There is one hitch. Your software must be written to use the 8087 coprocessor, rather than the normal CPU, for math. If your software is not written for the 8087, you have no advantage.

Other auxiliary microprocessors can relieve the CPU of regulating and controlling terminals, keyboards, video screens, disk drives, and other devices. The entire computer system can run faster if several processors share the workload.

An exception to the "one-CPU-per-system" rule exists. Some computers use a combination of an 8-bit and a 16-bit CPU. For example, DEC's Rainbow 100 and the Xerox 8/16 Professional use an 8088 and a Z80 CPU. The Zenith Z-100 uses an Intel 8085 instead of the Z80. Technically, these are coprocessors; actually, each is a CPU. Most of the time, the 16-bit CPU handles the computer. When you use the 8-bit CPU, the Z80 or the 8085 runs your programs, and the 8088 runs the rest of the computer. When this happens, the difference between a CPU and a coprocessor blurs, but the arrangement works, and that is all that matters. Because MS-DOS does not run on 8-bit computers (the Z80 and the 8085 use CP/M), this subject will not be discussed in more detail.

Memory

CPUs, coprocessors or auxiliary microprocessors, and CPU performance all affect a computer's speed; but other items can be just as important. Memory is one example.

Every computer system has memory. It holds programs and computer-processed information. Memory size can greatly affect your computer's performance and manageability.

ROM and RAM

Memory can be divided into two major classes: ROM and RAM. The CPU does not distinguish between them; it views them the same way. Both ROM and RAM are necessary in a computer.

ROM, or *read-only memory,* holds permanent programs and information. They are electrically fixed into the chip. A computer system's ROM holds the programs—basic startup programs, for example—that make a computer somewhat intelligent. When you turn on the computer, the enduring programs in ROM are executed immediately.

RAM is the abbreviation for *random-access memory.* It is volatile memory: whatever is in it is lost when the computer is turned off. RAM should really be called R/WM, or read-write memory. It is the blackboard for your computer system. You can put information (write) on the blackboard, take information (read) from the blackboard, erase all or part of the blackboard, and start over again. Your computer needs this blackboard-type memory to process your programs and information.

RAM is a misnomer. All memory, including ROM, is "randomly accessible." Your CPU can access two nonadjacent memory locations, one after the other. For example, you do not have to plow through memory locations 0 through 5 to get to memory location 6.

From the user's standpoint, having more ROM and RAM memory can be important. The more ROM memory you have, the more programs are permanently available right in your computer. For instance, IBM devotes 40K to ROM memory, 32K of which is the BASIC programming language. Most of the BASIC language, therefore, is built into the computer system.

More RAM memory is also a benefit. The RAM memory is your workplace. You can do more work, and faster, with a larger workplace. RAM memory size greatly affects both your computer's performance and friendliness.

Some programs need as much memory as possible. Electronic spreadsheets, such as VisiCalc®, SuperCalc™, and 1-2-3™ can use all the RAM memory available in a computer. A large spreadsheet requires a large amount of RAM memory. Programs that sort information work faster when more RAM memory is available. Some of the new performance features of MS-DOS work best with a large amount of RAM memory.

Usually, making a program friendly increases the size of the program, thereby requiring more RAM memory. A friendly program gives the operator readable prompts and messages. It handles most errors without giving up (aborting). The best programs let you select an activity from a menu or just type your choice.

Other popular uses for RAM memory include printer spoolers and RAM disks drives. A *print spooler* is a program that buffers, or contains temporarily, in RAM memory the information you send to the printer. By sending into a RAM buffer information to be printed, the computer is freed sooner to continue with the same or a different task.

RAM disk drives are programs that trick the computer into seeing a portion of the RAM memory as a disk drive. Because data moves faster between the CPU and RAM memory than between the CPU and the disk drives, RAM disks are 10 to 100 times faster than their mechanical counterparts.

How Much RAM Is Enough?

The programs you use will determine how much RAM you need. The following guidelines should help you calculate how much RAM you should have.

Never have less than 64K of RAM. MS-DOS V2 does not work well on any system with less than 64K because MS-DOS itself takes up between 20K and 40K, which does not leave much room for your programs.

DOS and your programs can usually coexist comfortably in 128K. Most programs will use a maximum of 96K to 128K.

If you plan to use an electronic spreadsheet program to create very large models, make sure that you have 256K or more of memory. Most spreadsheet programs will not use more than 256K, although some— spreadsheets like 1-2-3, for example—can use all the RAM memory you may have (more than 512K).

Most printer spoolers use between 2K and 32K of RAM memory. RAM disk drive programs will use as much RAM as you can spare, from a minimum of 32K to a maximum of 360K. If you plan to use these types of programs, adjust the guidelines accordingly.

Generally, 128K to 256K is the right amount of RAM memory for your computer. Less than 128K makes your computer less efficient. Some programs won't run at all without 128K of memory. Having more than 256K of RAM may be overinvesting in your computer, unless your programs can use this additional memory.

Peripherals

The core of your computer system is comprised of the CPU; the coprocessor(s), if any; and ROM and RAM memory. Technically, they are the computer, and everything else is a peripheral. A *peripheral* is a part of the computer system that is connected to the CPU and memory. The major peripherals of your computer system are the video display and keyboard or terminal, disk drives, printers, and modems. Without these peripherals, your computer would be deaf and mute. Peripherals can be connected to your computer in several ways: through buses, boards, slots, adapters, and interfaces.

Connecting Peripherals

Buses and Boards

Computers use a *bus* or bus lines. Just as bus lines move people from one place to another, a computer's bus lines move data. They connect the CPU to the RAM memory and the computer's peripherals.

All computers use their bus lines for the same purpose, but the buses may vary between computers. Bus lines used by S-100 computers are one example. They use a main board (or *motherboard*) that has 100 lines. (S-100 stands for the *standard 100* lines of the bus.) In turn, boards that contain the CPU, memory, and other circuits for the peripherals are plugged into the motherboard. Each board uses the motherboard's bus lines to talk with the rest of the computer system.

The most popular form of computer buses for MS-DOS computers is the *system board,* which holds the CPU, RAM memory, circuits for some of the peripherals, and also the connectors for other boards. The circuits on the board connect the computer to other peripherals. Most MS-DOS computers, such as DEC, IBM, Victor, Wang, and Zenith use this configuration. The main board is called the system board because it houses most of the electronics for the computer.

Slots and Boards

An S-100-based computer or a system board computer has several slots for plug-in boards. Because these boards enhance or increase a computer's capability, their slots are called *expansion slots.* The plug-in board can hold more RAM memory for the computer or connect it to a printer, modem, or terminal. Most systems also use a board to connect disk drives to the computer system.

Each board plugs into a slot in the computer. The boards you will need, as well as the number of slots, depend on the standard equipment that came with your computer. For example, the Victor 9000 system board has everything necessary for 128K of RAM memory, the keyboard, video display, a printer, a modem, and a disk drive. In this case, most of the expansion capabilities are built into the computer.

If your computer system does not have many built-in connections for more RAM memory or additional peripherals, you will need expansion boards. The number of slots in your computer will become important. You may find that your computer is at a dead-end if you cannot expand it the way you wish. Generally, five to eight expansion slots are enough.

You should also find out how many expansion slots are already taken when you buy the computer system. The Zenith Z-100 has five S-100 expansion slots, but one is used by a board for the floppy disk drives, and another may be used for the board that connects the hard disk to the computer. Only three are left. Are they enough? Probably. The Zenith Z-100 has the built-in capability for 256K of RAM and connections for the keyboard, video display, a printer, a modem, and another device. Because the "standard equipment" is comprehensive, three slots leave ample room for growth.

When you buy a computer system, plan on expanding it. I have not yet met anyone who did not add to his computer system. If yours has only 64K and you cannot add more memory without adding another board, plan on using one slot for the RAM memory you will add. Each device you add—printer, modem, etc.—may require its own board and one expansion slot. That's just a guideline. You may find that one board will handle several different items. These *multifunction boards* (some include RAM memory) are very popular with the IBM PC and S-100 computers and are usually worth the money when you begin to run low on expansion slots.

Remember, if you add a board, you will need a slot. Run out of expansion slots, and you run out of room to grow.

Interfaces

Interface is the technical name for the physical connection and electronic circuits that connect your computer to a peripheral. *Adapter* is another name for interface. Every peripheral uses an interface, whether it is a purchased expansion board or is built into the system board.

Interfaces can be divided into two groups—parallel and serial—based on how the device talks to the computer. In a *parallel* interface or connection, all 8 bits of the byte are transmitted simultaneously. This means that a parallel connection uses a minimum of eight separate lines, one for each bit in the byte. Most parallel cables have between 20 and 50 lines; and most of the additional lines are used to coordinate the moving of information between the device and the computer.

In *serial* connections, the byte's 8 bits are broken up and sent one at a time. Serial cables use a maximum of 25 lines; most connections use only between three and seven separate lines. Two lines handle the actual data: one line sends data, and the second line receives it. The other lines coordinate the movement of information between the computer and the device. Additional bits of information are sent with the bytes to help the receiving device find the begining and end of the byte.

Disk drives and printers are the popular users of parallel interfaces. Printers, terminals, and modems are usually serial devices.

Parallel interfaces can transmit information at a higher rate than serial interfaces, but serial cables can be longer than parallel cables. Longer cables allow you to place a device, like a noisy printer, farther away from the computer.

It really does not matter which type of device you use. What does matter is having the right interface for your device. A parallel device needs a parallel interface, and a serial device requires a serial interface. A parallel device cannot use a serial interface, nor will a serial device work with a parallel interface.

Modems and computers with terminals require serial interfaces. Some printers use a parallel connection, and others use a serial one. If you use a printer, be sure to have the appropriate interface. Newer printers, such as the Centronics 353, have both a parallel and serial interface built in.

Keyboards, Video Displays, and Terminals

Keyboards, video displays, and terminals are all peripherals. Your computer may use a keyboard and a video display. They may be separate units connected to the computer or built in. If you don't use a keyboard and video display, then you use a terminal, a box with a built-in CRT (cathode ray tube) display and keyboard. DPers call terminals "tubes" because of their TV-like screen. All of these devices allow you to "talk" to your computer.

There is almost no difference between a keyboard/video display combination and a terminal. Both allow you to type characters to, and see messages and information from, the computer. The major difference is that a terminal needs a serial interface to talk to your computer. This interface is usually provided with the computer.

Computers without a terminal use a keyboard unit and video display. One, both, or neither can be built into the computer.

Most computers have built-in circuits for the keyboard. Some also have built-in circuit connections for a video display; others do not. In the latter case, a separate interface or adapter board, which takes up one expansion slot, is purchased and plugged into the computer.

All keyboards, video displays, and terminals are not alike. If you look at three or more different computer systems, you can spot the differences.

Keyboards

Every keyboard has the QWERTY keys, the common alphanumeric keys found on a typewriter. A variety of keys are added to this foundation. A standard IBM Selectric typewriter has about 50 keys, whereas a Victor 9000 keyboard has 99 keys. What do these additional keys do?

The *escape key* is unique to computers. It is normally used to prefix a command to the printer, video screen, or modem.

The *control key* is also unique to computers. It acts like a supershift key. When you hold the control key down and tap a letter key, you can produce 27 unique computer characters.

Alt is another unique computer key, used to type an "alternate" set of characters or words. Because computer manufacturers have not agreed on what Alt should do, its use may vary among computers.

The four keys with arrows pointing up, down, left, and right are the cursor-control keys. The *cursor* is the flashing underline or box on the terminal or video screen. The cursor shows you where the next character will be placed on the screen. With the right software, the cursor-control keys can move the cursor anywhere on the screen for editing or creating pictures. If you have a key marked *Home,* it is another cursor-control key. It moves the cursor to the leftmost side of the top line, called the *home position.*

Keys labeled *Ins* and *Del* are editing keys that allow you to insert or delete characters. Your computer may have several keys that perform different editing functions.

The keys marked F1, F2, etc., are special-function keys you or your programs can use to answer questions, select items from a menu, or type a line of characters into the computer. All of these things can be accomplished by pressing one particular key. As with the Alt key, the use of special-function keys can vary from computer to computer and from program to program.

Some keyboards have a separate, calculator-style keypad, which allows numbers to be typed rapidly for accounting or spreadsheet programs. Some computers use the same keypad for the cursor-control keys. Usually, another key shifts these dual-purpose keypads between the numeric and the cursor-control mode. Sharing a set of keys can be confusing or plain annoying. If you have a choice, use a keyboard with separate numeric and cursor-control keypads.

If you are intimidated by a church-organ-like keyboard, you may wonder if all of these additional keys are (1) necessary, (2) useful, (3) helpful, or (4) unnecessary.

The alphanumeric keys are required. So are the control, escape, and alternate keys. The cursor-control keys are useful if your software uses them. The numeric keypad is helpful for accounting and spreadsheets.

Special-function keys can range from unnecessary to very useful, depending on the software you use. If your software takes advantage of the special-function keys, they can be powerful allies. If your software ignores them, however, these keys are "dead weight."

Your computer's hardware is the foundation of your system, but the software makes the hardware useful. This is especially true for keyboards. If your software takes advantage of your keyboard, typing can be easier and faster. The hardware provides the basic capabilities, but without the appropriate software, these features are wasted.

Video Displays

There are several types of keyboards and many kinds of video displays. Your computer may use a built-in video screen, a television, or a video monitor. The screen may be black and white, green and white, or color. You may have purchased the display separately, or it may have been included with your computer. What your computer provides dictates the display you use.

Displays can be broken down into three groups:

1. *Televisions,* which you use with an *RF modulator* that changes the video signal from the computer into a channel your TV can receive. Televisions are good for displaying 40 characters or less on a line but work poorly if you try to use 80 characters on a line.

2.   *Monochrome video monitors,* or a one-color display. Black and white monitors have only one active color—white. The dark color (black) appears where nothing is displayed.

Commercial monochrome video monitors use a composite video signal. You will notice a circular connector on the back of the computer or monitor for the cable.

Special monochrome monitors use a multiple-pin plug for the connection. These monitors are provided with computer systems from DEC, IBM, Victor, and Wang and generally have a sharper picture than commercial video monitors that use a composite video signal.

A popular trend in computers is to use a green and white screen rather than a black and white or green one. These green screens use a green phosphor, industry code number P-39. P-39 is a wonderfully slow phosphor. The image on the screen does not break up (you see flashing streaks of light) when scrolling (as the lines move up on the screen). Unfortunately, P-39 screens don't support light pens or graphics well because the screen image changes too slowly. However, P-39 screens are excellent for word processing and spreadsheets.

3.   *Color video monitors* are good for graphics. There are two types of color monitors: composite video and RGB. The former uses the computer's composite video signal. *RGB* monitors need a separate video signal for the red, green, and blue colors. RGB monitors are more expensive than composite video color ones. However, most composite video color monitors don't display 80-character lines crisply. In fact, most composite color monitors only work with computers that display 40-character lines. Most MS-DOS computers, if they use a color monitor, need the more expensive RGB monitor.

Some computer systems allow more than one type of display. If you have this option, here's a good guideline. Use a monochrome display if you have no need for color graphics. Some computers can produce high-resolution graphics on their special monochrome displays. This is usually sufficient. Color with word processing and spreadsheets is nice, but not a necessity. Most other programs do not use color graphics, and a color monitor is therefore unnecessary.

If you need color graphics and can afford a color display, get an RGB monitor. I have one on my PC XT and am pleased with the results. The displayed characters, however, do not look as sharp or as crisp as they do on the Compaq, DEC, or Victor monochrome displays.

Memory-Mapped Video

You may not know that the computer handles the video screen in different ways. If you use a terminal, the computer sends characters to your screen down a serial connection. The rate can vary from 30 characters per second (300 baud), 120 characters per second (1200 baud), 960 characters per second (9600 baud), up to 1920 characters per second (19.2K baud). *Baud* is the number of bits sent each second. Divide the baud rate by 10 to find the approximate number of characters per second. The faster the baud rate, the faster your display will react. Obviously, high baud rates are desirable.

Some computers use a different concept. The contents of RAM memory are used to form the picture displayed on the monitor. When you "print" to the video display, the computer moves the appropriate pattern into a reserved section of RAM memory. You think you are printing one character at a time, as if the character were moving down the serial port to a terminal, but the computer is actually moving the character around in memory. This is called *memory-mapped video display*.

The RAM memory is the basis of the image you see on the screen. Information can move very quickly within RAM. That's why programs like Wordstar® and Lotus' 1-2-3 "fly around" the screen much faster on a Victor or IBM PC than on computer systems that use a terminal. These programs shove the characters directly into the video display's RAM memory, where the picture is instantly displayed. Displays based on memory-mapped video can change in 1/60th of a second. A minimum of one second is needed to change the display completely on a terminal. That's why some programs "work" faster than others. With memory-mapped video, the screen can be changed faster than the monitor can react. If you use a spreadsheet program, it probably exploits your computer's memory-mapped video.

Control Codes

Although this chapter is devoted to hardware, let's turn briefly to some software that is related to the video display. Every display can position the cursor at a certain place on the screen, erase a line, erase the entire screen, and so forth. Most programs use control codes to do this (unless the program works with the RAM memory for memory-mapped displays).

A *control code* is a sequence of one or more characters that your terminal or computer recognizes. The sequence tells the terminal or computer to manipulate the video screen. When your program prints these control codes to the video screen or terminal, it grabs these characters and follows the established directions.

Just as many computers are different, so are the control codes for video screens and terminals. Authors of programs must confront this problem. Their programs must accommodate the many different sets of terminal or video-screen control codes that a computer uses.

One benefit of DOS V2 is the incorporation of the ANSI terminal control codes. ANSI is the American National Standards Institute, an organization that publishes standards for various industries, including the computer industry. ANSI has established a set of control codes for terminals. Because DOS incorporates a set of standardized codes, one version of a program can work with many different computers that use DOS. The advantage for your computer system, should it have DOS, is that more software becomes available faster.

This benefit does not apply to programs that use memory-mapped video displays. These programs must be rewritten for each different computer system.

Printers and Plotters

Printers are another important peripheral for your computer system. The printer is your system's paper or *hard-copy* device.

Plotters are also hard-copy devices. Plotter prices have decreased in the last few years, so more plotters have appeared on microcomputer systems.

Printers

Printers can be divided into three major classes: daisywheel, dot-matrix, and high-density dot-matrix.

Daisywheel printers were invented in the 1970s. These printers have a metal or plastic wheel (or, with NEC printers, a thimble) that revolves on a movable platform. Each wheel contains petals or fingers that contain one or two characters. As the appropriate petal or finger moves into place, a hammer strikes the petal, which strikes the ribbon that makes the character on the paper. These printers produce fully formed characters and are often called *letter-quality* printers because their print is the same quality as a typewriter's. They can also print graphics, but very slowly.

Dot-matrix printers use a series of pins to form a character. The pins strike the ribbon and leave a pattern of dots. Some printers use a multicolored ribbon that allows the printing of color graphics. Although the characters have a computer-like appearance, dot-matrix printers are popular because they are fast. Letter-quality printers usually print between 10 and 55 characters per second, whereas dot-matrix printers can print between 30 and 250 characters per second.

High-density dot-matrix printers are a recent development (about 1980). They have two modes: a normal, high-speed dot-matrix mode; and a slower, correspondence-quality mode. In the slower mode, the printer prints each character several times. The additional printings are usually one dot higher or to the right of the first printing. The shift fills in the gaps between the dots and improves the quality of the type. In addition, most of these printers can produce high-resolution graphs and charts. Nevertheless, the character quality of high-density dot-matrix printers is not as good as that of daisywheel and thimble printers; therefore, high-density dot-matrix printers cost less.

Other printing technologies you may see include the following:

1. *Electrostatic.* A silvery paper is zapped by electricity to form a dot-matrix character. Electrostatic printers have marginal quality and use more expensive paper that turns black after a period of time.

2. *Thermal.* Hot pins in the printer's head move across a specially treated paper. Thermal printers also use a dot-

matrix-like character. They are very quiet but slow (30 characters per second), and the paper they use is somewhat expensive.

3. *Ink-jet*. Thin jets of ink are sprayed on the paper. These printers also produce a dot-matrix-like character, although some of the more expensive ink-jet printers can produce almost letter-quality characters. These printers can print at speeds of 200 characters per second and more. Recently, ink-jet printers have decreased in price; they now cost less than $3,000. Their popularity should increase in the next year.

4. *Line dot-matrix*. The printer uses 44 to 132 sets of dots to produce one line of print at a time. Don't be confused by some manufacturers who claim that they have a dot-matrix line printer. A printer that has a single printhead and prints only one character at a time is not a line printer.

Line dot-matrix printers can usually produce graphics and bar codes. The speed of these machines is measured in lines per minute, usually 150 to 600+, the equivalent of 330 to 1,320 characters per second. These printers are higher priced, generally starting in the $5,000 to $6,000 range.

5. *Band*. A metal band is struck to form the characters on a line. Generally, band printers are used for their speed, not their character quality. They are rated in lines per minute, from 150 to 24,000+. Needless to say, these printers start at $5,000 and go into the $50,000 range, not quite accessible for most microcomputer owners.

6. *Laser*. A laser burns the characters on normal, untreated sheets of paper. This technology promises higher speed and quality and may eventually dominate the entire field of printing. Laser printers are also graphics-capable. Machines in the $5,000 range can print 6 to 12 pages a minute. Some models can cost $100,000 and more. These printers, not exactly recommended for a computer that costs less than half a million dollars, print 20,000 to 30,000+ lines a minute. I have actually seen a laser printer, whose cover was left open, stack paper up to the top of a ceiling eight feet high.

Many companies are experimenting with laser-technology printers, and the appearance of an under-$5,000 model is very possible within the next two years.

Printer prices have decreased dramatically in the past five years. Printers with more and more features are becoming available. The selection can be bewildering. If you can afford only one printer and don't plan to print letters, a dot-matrix printer is the best choice. If you can afford it, a high-density dot-matrix printer capable of graphics is an even better choice. If the quality of your letters is important, a daisywheel or thimble printer is ideal. Printers for computers can range in price from $200 to $3,000. Speed, type of printing (daisywheel, dot-matrix, etc.), and printer features (underlining, different character sets, graphics, etc.) account for the differences in cost.

Plotters

Graphics, or color graphics, are becoming a standard microcomputer feature. The increase in their popularity has boosted the popularity of plotters.

Plotters generally use a set of two mobile arms and a pen. The arms provide up, down, left, and right mobility. The pen is dropped onto the paper to draw a chart, graph, or picture. Most plotters can use several pens, each with a different color ink. Under the control of the computer system, a sophisticated plotter can change pens automatically.

Larger plotters use a drum. The pen moves right and left, while the drum moves the paper. Some drum plotters can plot with multiple colors, but others cannot.

Until three years ago, the cheapest plotters cost $5,000 or more. Now, some multicolor plotters are available for less than $1,500. As demand increases for color graphics on paper, mass production for the consumer market may lower prices even more.

Other Printer/Plotter Issues

Regardless of what printer you select, it must be connected to your computer with the appropriate interface, either parallel or serial. The same is true for plotters.

The standard parallel connection is Centronics-compatible, named after the Centronics Data Products Corporation. Most parallel printers use this type of connection and interface.

Serial interfaces are another story. Too many standards exist. Some printers may use one or more serial connection lines for *handshaking,* the coordination (between computer and device) that prevents characters from "dropping into the bit bucket." *Hardware handshaking* occurs when a line from the computer coordinates the timing. Unfortunately, any combination of four different lines may be used.

Software handshaking uses certain control characters, such as the "stop, I'm not ready" and the "send me more" signals, sometimes called *software protocols*. Two different sets of two characters are used for software handshaking. Serial, letter-quality printers are the major users of software protocols.

To complicate matters, some printers and computers use both hardware handshaking and software signals. A further complication with serial printers is determining who should talk on what lines. Two standards are used: DTE (Date Terminal Equipment) and DCE (Data Communications Equipment). With DTE, the computer talks on line two, listens on line three, and says that it is ready to send characters on line four. With DCE, the device receives characters on line two, speaks on line three, and indicates that it is ready to receive characters on line five. (For completeness, line one is used for the frame ground.)

When both the computer and printer think they should be the DTE or DCE, they do not communicate successfully. Usually, the lines in the cable connecting the two devices are switched so that each talks and receives on different lines.

The easiest way to avoid headaches with printers is to have your local dealer hook up the printer to your computer and make sure the printer works. Another solution is to buy only the printers offered by the computer manufacturer. If you are more adventurous, you can buy any printer and try to hook it up yourself. You will probably need a soldering iron, pliers, some special tools, diagnostic equipment, and plenty of patience.

Software-protocol mismatches with computers present a different problem. You may need some skill in assembly language programming to make DOS talk to your printer. (You also will get a little more help when CONFIG.SYS is discussed in Chapter 11.)

Printer control codes can be potentially troublesome. Like the terminal control codes that manipulate the screen, printer control codes are special characters sent to your printer to turn special features on and off. Some of the more common features are special fonts, compressed or expanded characters, underlining, superscripts and subscripts, changeable number of lines printed per inch, and graphics.

Like terminals, few printers use the same special characters to control their special features. Unlike terminals, ANSI, the standards group, has no standards for printer control codes.

Before you buy a printer, check the software you will be using. Presumably, it will support the printer you select. If your software does not, you may waste some or all of your printer's special features.

Plotters suffer from the same problems as printers, but also have a greater problem: graphics software. If your printer can receive characters, it will at least print them. You may sacrifice some features, but you will get a printout of your work.

Plotters, however, don't understand characters. Plotters plot charts, graphics, and pictures. Unless you buy or create software to "drive" the features of your plotter, it will be a totally wasted piece of equipment. Before you buy a plotter, be sure that appropriate software is available.

One Last Word about Printers

Buying and using the right printer can be a harrowing experience. Price, features, speed, type of interface, handshaking, and other matters must be taken into account. The redeeming fact is that once you have purchased your printer and set it up properly, you have cleared the biggest hurdle. Your printer, once installed, should provide millions of carefree characters.

If you feel intimidated, ask for help from a friend, a local computer dealer, a user group, or any person who knows about computers and printers. Clearing the selection and connection hurdles can be tough, but using the printer is ordinarily easy.

Modems

Modem is the abbreviation for *mo*dulator-*dem*odulator, a device that changes your computer's ones and zeros into audible frequencies, and vice versa. The modem transmits computer information through a telephone line.

Most MS-DOS computers use two types of modems: a plug-in board and a box that connects to a serial interface. Another name for a plug-in is an *on-board* modem. One advantage to the plug-in board is that the modem is completely contained inside the computer system. A second advantage is that a serial interface is not used.

Computers that can't use an on-board modem use the traditional modems. They require a serial interface for your computer system.

Modem features vary. Some modems automatically dial a telephone number, answer the telephone, change baud rates "on the fly," and correct errors in received characters. The more features a modem has, the higher is its price.

Baud rates also vary. Most microcomputer modems transmit 30 to 120 characters per second, operating at 300 and 1,200 baud, respectively. The old standard for microcomputers was 110 (11 characters per second) and 300 baud. Mass consumption of 300/1200-baud modems has brought modem prices down. The 300/1200-baud modems cost $600 or less, depending on their features. Most 110/300-baud modems are available for $300 or less, also depending on their features.

Most modems use a small modular connector and plug into normal telephone jacks. This method usually works well at home. Unfortunately, some businesses don't use the modular plug, and you may have trouble using these types of modems at your office.

Looking Back

In this chapter the following hardware components were examined: the CPU, coprocessor, RAM, ROM, buses, interfaces, terminals, video screens, keyboards, printers, plotters, and modems. Almost every major piece of your computer's hardware was included. The importance of having the right software for optimal hardware use was also considered.

One piece of computer hardware was not discussed: disk drives. Disk drives are so important to DOS that all of Chapter 4 is devoted to them. Before you learn about them, however, you must learn how to use your computer system.

3

Starting Out

I am a firm believer in learning by doing. In this chapter you will use several DOS commands to copy a diskette, format a diskette, copy some files, and get a listing of the files on a disk. You'll also find out about some of the special keys on your keyboard.

I am also an eager person. I like to try new things as soon as I can. If you are like me and, in addition, are a newcomer to DOS, please read carefully each complete step before you try it. If you don't, you may miss some small detail that could make things work improperly.

Before you start, take a moment to become familiar with the notation used throughout this book. It will help you to distinguish what you type from what the computer displays. What you type on the computer appears **like this**. Anything the computer displays looks like this. For example, in the line

A:**DIR**

DOS printed the A:. You type the **DIR**. After you type **DIR**, you must hit the Enter key.

Your keyboard may use a key called "Enter" or "Return," or one with the international symbol (◀─┘). In the last chapter, I mentioned that all keyboards are not created equal. You can determine which key is the Enter key by looking at the manual that came with your computer. Whichever key it is, you must hit it after you finish typing a line.

Whenever DOS is ready for a command, you will see one of the following symbols:

```
A:
```

or

```
A>
```

This is called the *system prompt*. In all the examples, we'll use the colon after the letter. If your computer uses the greater than sign instead, don't worry. Just mentally change the > after the letter to the colon used in the examples.

We'll discuss the system prompt later in this book.

For this session, you will need the following:

1. Your computer system, plugged in and ready to go

2. The DOS Master Diskette(s) that come with your computer

3. Three blank diskettes, plus labels and write-protect tabs for the diskettes (These normally come in the box with the blank diskettes.)

If your computer has a hard disk, make sure that it is set up. If necessary, follow the instructions that are provided with your computer. To format the hard disk with the DOS FORMAT program, use the **/S** option. It will put DOS on your hard disk so that you can start your computer without using a floppy diskette.

A Few Important Keys

Before you start using your computer, first learn about some of its special keys. To do this, you'll need to look up some information in the DOS manual provided with your system.

Your computer system's keyboard may be completely different from the keyboard used by another system. Since generic MS-DOS is the subject of this book, I cannot tell you exactly which key or keys you will use for particular functions. For this information, refer to your DOS manual. It should tell you what keys to use in each case.

The keys are divided into two sets: control functions and editing functions. Control functions control the way your computer acts. Editing functions allow you to edit what you type into the computer.

The Control Keys

The most important key is the control or supershift key. This key is usually labeled "Ctrl" or "Control." To type a control character, hold down the control key and tap a lettered key. When you see the notation **Ctrl** , it means that you hold down the Ctrl key as you tap the next key. For example, **Ctrl-C** means that you hold down the Ctrl key as you tap the C key. When you type a control character, a caret (^) will appear in front of the letter you typed. For a Ctrl-C, you will see ^C.

The following list shows the control characters and what they mean to DOS. If your computer uses different keys for these functions, write the name of each key in the margin of this book so that you can refer to it later.

Key	Meaning
Enter	Signals DOS that you have finished typing and that DOS should act on your answer. Enter is the "go" key.

Ctrl-C	Tells DOS to stop a currently running program. Ctrl-C is the "abort" key.
Ctrl-H	Backs up the cursor one space and erases the character that was there. This key can be used to backspace and correct typing mistakes.
Ctrl-J	Moves the cursor down to the next line (a line feed). This key is used to type more than one line command to DOS. DOS will not execute the lines until you hit Enter.
Ctrl-N	Turns off the printing of the screen to the printer.
Ctrl-P	Turns on the printing of the screen to the printer. When you type a Ctrl-P, everything that is printed to the screen will also be "echoed" (printed) on the printer.
Ctrl-S	Freezes the video display. Tapping any key unfreezes the screen.
Ctrl-X	Cancels the line you are typing. DOS will place a backslash on the screen and drop to the next line.

Remember that the Enter key is the "go" key and may be labeled "Enter," "Return," or (◄─┘) on your keyboard.

The Enter key can also be thought of as the "point of no return." In many cases, once you have tapped Enter, you cannot reenter your answer to the computer's request. Before you hit the Enter key, take a moment to check that your typing is correct. After you become acquainted with DOS, you will know when typing mistakes are harmless and when they can cause trouble.

Several DOS commands need only a one-letter answer, such as a "Y" for yes or an "N" for no. In these cases, you don't need to hit Enter after you type your response. (The FORMAT program that you'll use in this chapter is one example.) For now, *always* finish what you type by tapping the Enter key.

Ctrl-C is the "stop what you are doing" command, sometimes called the *Control-Break* sequence. When you type it, you are telling DOS to stop immediately the program that was running, exit the program, and take control again.

Ctrl-C is a panic button for drastic situations. You can use it if the wrong diskette is in the drive, if you gave the wrong command, or if you used the wrong file. You may be able to stop the program by typing Ctrl-C, but not always. Later in this book you will learn why.

Ctrl-H, or the backspace key, may be labeled "backspace" or "bs," or may have an arrow (◄—). You use Ctrl-H when you make a mistake. Each time you tap this key, the cursor will back up one character and erase it. After you back up the cursor and erase the mistake, you can retype the rest of the line.

If you have made some major typing mistakes, you will need to use Ctrl-X, which is the cancel key. When you type Ctrl-X, DOS puts a backslash (\) on the screen and drops the cursor to the next line. DOS will ignore what you typed on the previous line and let you retype the entire line.

Ctrl-P echoes whatever is printed on the video screen to the printer. This echoing, however, is not the same as screen printing. Screen printing prints whatever is already on the video screen. Ctrl-P will echo only *new* information. To turn off the echoing, use Ctrl-N.

Ctrl-S freezes the video screen. This key lets you stop the screen to read information before it scrolls off the top of the screen. To unfreeze the screen, tap any key.

For now, the three keys you need to remember are Enter, Backspace, and Cancel. As you go through the examples, these keys will help you to enter commands and answers and to correct typing mistakes. You can experiment with the other keys at your leisure.

The Editing Keys

The DOS editing keys enable you you to type and correct commands and answers. To use the editing keys, you must know about the *template*, which is the last line you typed into the computer system. DOS always remembers the last line. By manipulating your previously typed line, you can easily edit it to correct mistakes or change it to type a new command with just a few keystrokes.

The following list shows the names of the DOS editing key functions. As with the control functions, a special key or control character can be used with these functions. A space is provided to the left for you to write which key your computer uses for these editing functions.

Key	Name	Function Key
	COPY1	Copies one character from the template to the new command line.
	COPYUPTO	Copies all characters from the template (up to the character you specify) into the new command line. The specified character is entered after you hit the COPY-UPTO key.
	COPYALL	Copies all the characters in the template into the new command line.
	SKIP1	Skips over one character in the template. You can use this function to delete (or remove) a character from the template.
	SKIPUPTO	Skips over all the characters in the template up to the character you specify after hitting the SKIPUP-TO key. This function deletes a series of characters from the template.
	VOID	Cancels any current editing you did to the command line, leaving the original line in the template unchanged.
	INSERT	Turns on the insert mode, which allows you to type additional characters into the command line without typing over characters to the right.

Key	Name	Function Key
	EXIT	Turns off the insert mode. Usually, this key is the same as the INSERT key. The first time you hit the INSERT key, you turn on the insert function. Hitting the INSERT key a second time turns off the insert function.
	NEWLINE	Moves the current command line, which you are typing, into the template. This function lets you move a line into the template to correct mistakes before the line goes to DOS for execution.

Remember that you don't need to memorize the editing keys now. Practice with them later. Once you have learned how to use them, the editing keys and template can help you to correct typing mistakes easily.

The Boot

Now let's start using your computer.

Put your DOS master diskette into the disk drive labeled "A:," "A>," or "0." This drive is usually the leftmost or upper disk drive. Close the door.

If your computer is turned off, turn it on. If your computer is on, turn it off, wait five seconds, and turn it on again.

The red light on the disk drive should come on. At this point you may see the message MS-DOS V2.00 and a copyright notice. This message, however, may not appear until after you have performed the next two steps.

Next, DOS will ask you for the current date and time. I wrote this chapter at 3:45 pm on August 27, 1983. This is how I answered both questions:

```
Current date is Tue  1-01-1980
Enter new date: 8-27-83<Enter>
Current time is 0:00:13.47
Enter new time: 15:45:27<Enter>
```

Notice how the current date and time were entered. The date is entered as numbers in the form **mm-dd-yy**, where **mm** is the month, **dd** is the day, and **yy** is the year. I used hyphens (-) between the numbers, but I could have used slashes (/) instead.

DOS is a little fussier about the time. You enter the time as **hh:mm:ss.xx**, where **hh** stands for the hour; **mm**, the minutes; **ss**, the seconds; and **xx**, the hundredths of a second. You must use a colon (:) between the hours and minutes and the minutes and seconds, but use a period (.) between the seconds and hundredths of a second.

DOS uses a 24-hour clock that is similar to military or universal clocks. You add 12 to the afternoon hours. For example, 3:00 p.m. becomes 15:00.

Enter the current date and the time now. (Don't bother entering the hundredths of a second, **xx**.) Be sure to hit the Enter key after you finish typing. The screen display should look like this:

```
Current date is Tue  1-01-1980
Enter new date: 8-27-83
Current time is 0:00:13.47
Enter new time: 15:45:27
```

Beneath this you should see the sign-on message MS-DOS, a version number, and a copyright notice. If the screen says something else or nothing at all, there is a problem. If you see the message Invalid Date or Invalid time on your screen, then you did not enter the number correctly. You may have typed a nonsense date or time, or you may have incorrectly punctuated the date or time. Until you successfully answer the request for the date and time, DOS will keep asking you to reenter them.

If the video screen looks like the example, DOS has successfully started and is in control of your computer system. This process is called *booting*. Now everything you type will be handled by DOS.

If the numbers after the decimal point are different from the example, don't worry. You have a later revision of DOS, which does not matter for now. (This difference is discussed in a later chapter.)

Copying a Diskette

Now that DOS is started, let's copy the DOS system diskette, which is the diskette in drive A.

If your computer system has just one floppy disk drive, or if your floppy disk drives are two different sizes (for example, one 8 inch and one 5 1/4-inch), read the next section and do the first example. Because you have only one disk drive (or two different sizes of floppy disk drives), your instructions will be different from those for users with two drives.

If you have two or more identical disk drives, place the new blank diskette into drive B, usually the right-hand drive. Close the door and type:

A:**FORMAT B:**

Then tap the Enter key. Follow the directions on your screen. If the program asks you for a volume label, just hit the Enter key. (Volume labels are discussed later.) When the program is finished, it will ask whether you want to format another diskette. Answer **N** to this question. You do not need to hit Enter in this case.

Now type the line

A:**DISKCOPY A: B:**

and then hit Enter. You have been using capital letters for your commands. In most cases, DOS does not care if you use upper- or lower-case letters, but sometimes the distinction between them is important.

The red light on the left-hand drive should come on briefly. Then the following message will appear:

```
Insert source diskette in drive A:
Insert target diskette in drive B:
Strike any key when ready.
_
```

If you have a single floppy drive system, you should see this message:

```
Insert the source diskette in drive A:
Strike any key when ready.
```

DOS is now waiting for you to hit any key. Type Ctrl-C.

If you are using a two-minifloppy disk drive system, you should now see the following message on your screen:

```
Insert source diskette in drive A:
Insert target diskette in drive B:
Strike any key when ready.
^C

A:_
```

If you have a one-floppy drive system, you won't see the "target diskette" line. Typing Ctrl-C initiates the "stop what you are doing" command, discussed earlier. I wanted you to try this now to see what happens when you type Ctrl-C.

When DOS gives the message Strike any key when ready, DOS really means that you should "strike *almost* any key when ready." Some keys are "absorbed" by your computer. The Shift and Caps Lock keys are two examples. If you tap one of these keys, DOS will appear to ignore it and continue to wait. Generally, the Enter key and the space bar are two good, large targets to use when DOS wants any key struck.

Two-Floppy Disk Drive DISKCOPY

If you have a one-floppy drive system or two floppy disk drives of different sizes, read the rest of this section, but don't do the examples. The next instructions for you follow this discussion.

For the copying process, the *source diskette* is the DOS master diskette that you put into drive A. The *target diskette* is the freshly formatted diskette that is still in drive B.

Type the following command line:

A:**DISKCOPY A: B:**

If you inserted the correct diskettes into the appropriate disk drives before you typed DISKCOPY, you may hit any key to start the copying process.

First, the light on the A: drive will go on. You may see a message about the number of sides and sectors that DOS will copy. In three to eight seconds, the light on the A: drive will go out, and the light on the B: drive will go on.

You will probably notice that the lights on the drives will go on and off again several times. The number of times this occurs depends on the amount of RAM memory in your computer.

After DISKCOPY has finished copying the diskette, you will see this message:

Copy another (Y/N)? _

DOS is asking if you want to copy another diskette. You don't, so you should answer **N**. The A: sign will reappear.

You have just made a copy of your DOS diskette. Find one of the labels for your diskettes, write "DOS V2 System Master" on the label, and put the label on the diskette. Always label a diskette after you perform a DISKCOPY to remind you that the diskette has something useful on it.

Now put your original DOS system diskette back into the envelope and place the copy you made into drive A.

One-Floppy Disk Drive DISKCOPY

If you have two floppy disk drives, skim this section, but don't try the example. If you have one floppy disk drive in your system, this section will show you how to DISKCOPY your DOS diskette. Type:

```
A:DISKCOPY A: A:
```

You will see the following message:

```
Insert the source diskette into drive A:

Strike any key when ready
```

The source diskette, which is the DOS master diskette, is already in drive A. Hit the space bar. The light on your floppy disk drive will go on. In a few seconds, you may see a message indicating the number of sides and sectors that are being copied. After a few more seconds, you should see this message:

```
Insert the destination diskette into drive A:

Strike any key when ready.
```

Take your DOS diskette out of the floppy disk drive, put the diskette you formatted earlier into the drive, close the door, and press a key. After a few seconds, you will see the following message:

```
Insert the source diskette into drive A:

Strike any key when ready.
```

Take out the second diskette and put your DOS diskette into the drive. Close the door and hit a key. After a few seconds, you will see this message:

```
Insert the destination diskette into drive A:

Strike any key when ready.
```

Change diskettes again, close the door, and hit a key. These messages may appear one or two more times. If they do, exchange diskettes each time and hit a key.

The message

```
Copy another (Y/N)? _
```

indicates that DISKCOPY has finished making the copy of the DOS master diskette. Answer **N** in response to this question. The A: sign should reappear.

Take out a label for the diskette and write "DOS V2 System Master Diskette" on the label. Take the diskette out of the drive and put the label on the diskette.

Formatting and Copying a Diskette

Everyone should try this exercise. Get the diskette you just made, labeled "DOS V2 System Master Diskette." Find one of the write-protect tabs that came with your diskettes. Put the tab over the notch on the upper left-hand edge of the diskette. If you are using 8-inch diskettes, uncover the write-protect notch. Once you have done this, put the disk into drive A.

Now we will format another blank diskette and put the DOS operating system on it. Type:

FORMAT A: /S

Notice how this command line is phrased. First, you type the name of the command, FORMAT, then the name of the disk drive you are using to format the diskette. Next, enter the switch **/S**. The **/S** tells DOS to put the operating system on the diskette you are formatting.

What is a *switch*? Most DOS commands have options that affect the way the command works. In the case of FORMAT, the two options copy the operating system to the newly formatted disk and place a volume label on it. To use these options, you must "pull the switch" when you use the command. When you pull the switch, you tell the command to do extra work or handle things in a different way. Most DOS commands have switches. To use a switch, type the switch character, which is a slash (**/**), followed by the appropriate switch letter. A switch is usually typed at the end of the DOS command line.

After you type the FORMAT command line, the red light on the disk drive will come on for a while. Then you will see the following message:

```
Insert the new diskette for drive A:

Strike any key when ready.
```

Take the DOS diskette out of drive A, put your blank diskette into the drive, then tap a key. The red light will come on again, and this message will appear:

```
Formatting...
```

After twenty to forty seconds, you will scc the following:

```
Formatting complete
```

The disk drive will keep spinning. After a few more seconds, you will see this message:

```
System transferred
```

Now DOS asks:

```
Volume label (11 characters, ENTER for none)? _
```

Type **My DOS disk**, then hit Enter.

The diskette will whirl, and then DOS will tell you how much information the disk can hold, how much space is being taken by DOS, and how much free space is available. For my IBM and Compaq computers, I usually see the following information:

```
362496 bytes total disk space
 40960 taken by system
321536 bytes free
```

362,496 bytes of total disk space is the maximum storage capacity of the disk or diskette. This capacity is equivalent to 360K. A *K* is 1,024 bytes. In dividing 362,496 by 1,204, you get 360K. This number tells me that I am using double-sided disk drives. If you are using single-sided disk drives, the amount of total disk space is 180K, or 183,240 bytes. The amount of free space shown on the screen should be 138,296 bytes.

The amounts you see may be different from these or the same, depending on your computer system. If you are using 8-inch disk drives, the numbers for total disk space and bytes available will be much larger. The numbers mentioned here are for typical minifloppy (5 1/4-inch) disk drives.

If you see the line bytes in bad sectors, DOS found some sectors on the diskette that are bad and cannot be used to hold information. Your total amount of free space will be reduced by the number at the front of this line. If you see this message, answer **Y** to the following question:

```
Format another (Y/N)? _
```

Take the disk partially out of the drive, reinsert the diskette, close the door, and tap a key. Some diskettes do not format correctly the first time but usually do the second time. If the disk does not format properly the second time, something is wrong with the disk drive or, more likely, the diskette. If there are still some bad sectors on the diskette, you can either take it back to the dealer for a replacement or simply live with the fact that you won't have all the storage space you should on that diskette.

FORMAT should now be asking this question:

```
Format another (Y/N)? _
```

Answer **N**, and the A: should reappear.

You have formatted a diskette that holds a copy of the DOS operating system. Now type **DIR**. You should see something like this:

```
A:DIR

   Volume in drive A is MY DOS DISK
   Directory of A:\

COMMAND    COM      17664  3-08-83  12:00p
           1 File(s)      321536 bytes free

A:_
```

You have just asked DOS to display a list of files on the diskette in drive A. That is the purpose of the DIR (directory) command. If you want to know what files are on a disk, use the DIR command.

The first line shown above is the *volume label* for the diskette. This label helps you to identify the diskette. DOS does not do anything with a volume label except show it with certain DOS commands.

The next line tells you what disk drive and directory path are being displayed. (These subjects are discussed in later chapters.)

You will see one line for every file on the disk. The only file here is COMMAND.COM. The line shows the root name of the file, the suffix, the length of the file in bytes, and the date and time that the file was first created or last updated (when the information in the file was changed).

The last line tells you the number of files displayed by the DIR command and the amount of free disk space. Again, the number of free bytes may vary because of either the type of disk drives you use or the bad sectors on your disk.

But something is wrong. The only disk file on the list, COMMAND.COM, is just 17,664 bytes. Didn't FORMAT tell us that more than 40,000 bytes were used by DOS?

The rest of the space is taken up by two files that you cannot see: IO.SYS and MSDOS.SYS. They are *system* files that hold the disk operating system. They do not show up when you ask for a directory (using the DIR command). These files are on this disk but are hidden from you.

If you have a two-floppy diskette drive system, take the diskette out of drive A and put it into drive B. Then put your copy of the DOS master diskette into drive A and type:

COPY A:*.* B: /V

Your disk lights will flash several times. The **/V** switch used here is different from FORMAT's /V switch (to be discussed later). Here it tells DOS to verify the copy and make sure that the copied information has been recorded properly. Many DOS commands use the same switch, but the switch may have a different meaning for each command. Watch out for this distinction.

Shortly, you will see the following message:

```
   23 file(s) copied
```

Then you will see the A:. You may also see a number other than 23, but don't worry. The number will vary from one computer manufacturer to another.

The message above indicates that you have just copied all the files from your copy of the DOS system diskette to the second diskette.

If you received two or more different DOS diskettes with different programs for your computer system, you may need to repeat the COPY command. Put the second DOS diskette into drive A and repeat the command.

Does your computer have a hard disk? If it does, follow the steps below. (If you already have a subdirectory called BIN, change BIN to DOS in all places in the directions where BIN is used.)

Make sure that your hard disk is set up properly, and then find out what letter you should use for your hard disk drive. Substitute the correct letter of your hard disk drive in C: if your hard disk drive is not C:. Drive C is used in these examples. Now type the command line

MD C:\BIN

to create a new subdirectory called BIN on the hard disk. If you already have a directory called BIN, type instead the line

MD C:\DOS

Don't forget to use DOS instead of BIN in the following instructions. (Subdirectories are discussed in Chapter 9.)

Now place your copy of the DOS master diskette in drive A and type the following:

COPY A:*.* C:\BIN /V

In less than one minute, you will see this message:

```
23 file(s) copied
```

Again, the number you see here may vary. If you have another DOS diskette containing different programs supplied with your system, put the second diskette into drive A and type:

COPY A:*.* C:\BIN /V

Now all your DOS files should be on the hard disk. Put your DOS diskettes back into their envelopes. Take the diskette you formatted at the beginning of this session and put it into drive A. Then type:

COPY C:\BIN*.* A: /V

This command copies all the DOS files in the BIN subdirectory onto the floppy diskette in drive A. Label this diskette accordingly.

The hard work is over. You have just created two diskettes. One is an exact copy of the DOS master diskette that came with DOS V2, and the other is a copy of all your DOS programs that come with V2. You also used the COPY, DIR, DISKCOPY, and FORMAT commands.

The following chapter continues with the subject of disk drives. Keep at hand the two diskettes you just made. You will need them later. If you copied the DOS programs to your hard disk, leave them there. You will also use that information later.

4

Disks and Diskettes

Disk drives are your computer system's most important peripherals. Keyboards and video screens are useful input and output devices. Printers and modems extend the capability of the system. But disk drives allow the computer to store and retrieve large amounts of information. The first word in "Disk Operating System" says it all.

A computer uses RAM memory to hold temporarily your programs and data. Even DOS is loaded into the RAM memory and run from RAM. Most RAM memory, however, is *volatile*. Whatever is in RAM memory disappears when a computer's power is turned off.

Disk storage, though, is not volatile. When you turn off the power, whatever is on the floppy disk stays. That is why disks are so important.

Consider three popular uses for computers: accounting, spreadsheets, and word processing. For accounting, the disk holds your daily transactions. One stored set of information is used for invoicing, statements, trial balances, and reports. Information does not need to be re-entered or recalculated manually. For spreadsheets, developing a model is time-consuming. Spreadsheets would not be useful if the model could not be stored and recalled. For word processing, visual editing is only half the story. In writing this book, I first typed on the keyboard what I wanted to say. As I typed, the computer captured my keystrokes and stored them on the disk. Then I revised this material until it was correct. Later, an electronic copy of the book was stored on hard disk, and editors worked with this copy.

There are four kinds of disks and disk drives: hard, floppy, minifloppy, and microfloppy. Because floppy and minifloppy disk drives are the most popular, we'll start with them. If you have a spare diskette nearby, get it. The next part of this chapter is a tour of the floppy diskette.

Diskettes

Look at your diskette. Most diskettes come in a flimsy, black cardboard or PCB plastic jacket. The diskette and its jacket are placed inside a white protective envelope. Take the diskette out of the protective envelope. The diskette should slide right out. If it looks as if you need to cut something open to get at the diskette, you have confused the diskette with its envelope.

The floppy diskette got its name from the flexible jacket: the diskette "flops" when you shake it. Because the jacket does not provide much protection for your diskette, you must handle it with care.

A felt-like, plastic material is usually glued to the inside of the jacket. This material traps small particles from the diskette as it whirls around. The felt-like material is usually lubricated with silicone so that the diskettes do not wear while rubbing against the material.

Inside the jacket is the diskette itself. It is usually made of mylar or polyurethane coated with metal oxide. Most diskettes are shiny and dark brown in color, but some new diskettes are red, gold, or even green. The diskette itself is circular with a diameter of 8 or 5 1/4 inches. Most MS-DOS computers use 5 1/4-inch diskettes.

Technically, 8-inch diskettes are called *floppy* diskettes, and the 5 1/4-inch version is a *minifloppy* diskette. Sloppy use has blurred the distinction between these terms. Many times the term "floppy" is used in referring to a 5 1/4-inch diskette, which is technically a minifloppy diskette. (I have used the terms floppy and minifloppy interchangeably in this book, to my chagrin.)

Make sure that the diskette side with the printed label is facing you. This is the front of the diskette. In the center is a large *centering hole*. The disk drive grabs the diskette by this hole. Sometimes a plastic ring is placed on the centering hole to provide extra strength and to help center the diskette when it is in the disk drive.

At the bottom of the diskette jacket on each side is an oblong opening through which the diskette can be seen. These openings are the *access holes,* where the recording heads of the disk drive make contact with the diskette.

Hold the diskette by the cardboard's edge. Have the front side facing you. Hold the diskette so that the access holes are at the bottom, in the 6-o'clock position.

Between the 12-o'clock and 2-o'clock positions on 8-inch diskettes, or the 3:30 position for minifloppies, you will notice a small hole in the cardboard jacket. This hole is the *index* or *timing hole.* Put two fingers in the center hole and gently rotate the diskette until you see a smaller hole in the diskette itself. Keep rotating for a couple of inches to check for other holes.

The disk drive uses the index hole to help determine where things are stored on the diskette. If you can find only one hole, you have a *soft-sectored* diskette. If you rotate the diskette and find more than one timing hole, you have a *hard-sectored* diskette. Hard-sector diskettes can have 11 to 17 holes for a 5 1/4-inch diskette and up to 33 holes for an 8-inch diskette.

Most computers use soft-sectored diskettes. You cannot use hard-sectored diskettes with computers designed for soft-sectored diskettes, nor can you use soft-sectored diskettes with computers designed for hard-sectored diskettes.

If you have an 8-inch diskette, look at the bottom right edge of the cardboard. (On 5 1/4-inch diskettes, look at the upper left-hand side.) You should see a small notch in the cardboard. This is the *write-protect* notch. Eight-inch and 5 1/4-inch disk drives handle the write-protect notch differently.

If you cover the notch on an 8-inch diskette, you can put information on the diskette. If the notch is uncovered, the diskette is write-protected, and no information can be placed on it. For 5 1/4-inch diskettes, you leave the notch uncovered when you want to put information on the diskette. When you cover the notch, the disk is write-protected. Technically, the notch on the 5 1/4-inch diskette is called the *write-enable* notch.

The write-protect notch provides an easy way of protecting diskettes. By covering a 5 1/4-inch diskette's write-protect notch, you stop anyone from putting information on the diskette, as well as from erasing files. Look at the diskettes provided with DOS V2. Most 5 1/4-inch MS-DOS master diskettes do not have a write-protect notch. This permanently write-protects the information on the diskette from being altered or erased by the computer. The 8-inch DOS master diskettes usually have the write-protect notch uncovered, thus protecting the files. You can cover this notch, but I do not advise that. To protect the files on a diskette from accidental erasure or unwelcome changes, keep the write-protect notch uncovered.

Floppy Disk Drives

A floppy disk drive has three major sections: one that holds and spins the floppy diskette, one that moves and controls the recording head (or heads) of the disk drive, and the electronics that communicate to the computer.

The parts that hold and spin the diskette are straightforward. When you close the door, two clutches, one on each side of the disk, grab the center hole of the diskette. The bottom clutch is connected by a belt to a motor that spins the diskette inside its cardboard jacket at 300 rpm. This motor is connected to the rest of the disk drive's electronics.

Inside the disk drive are two connected, mobile arms that hold the recording head (or heads). A disk-drive recording head is smaller than a tape-recorder head and is mainly ceramic, not metal.

Single-sided disk drives have one recording head at the end of the bottom arm. The end of the top arm holds a piece of felt. The felt piece and the recording head face each other.

Double-sided disk drives have a recording head at the end of each arm. As with single-sided disk drives, the ends of the arms face each other.

The arms may be mechanically connected to the door so that they clamp onto the diskette when the door is closed. Some disk drives use a magnetic relay to clamp the arms into place only when the disk drive is reading or writing information to the diskette.

As the arms clamp onto the diskette, it is trapped between the recording heads or the recording head and the felt piece. This clamping keeps the diskette from bouncing away from the recording head(s) and allows information to be written or read reliably.

The coordinated mobile arms move back and forth down the center of the drive. A small "stepper" motor connected to a cam or gear moves the arm. Look at the diskette's access holes and think about how you insert the diskette into the disk drive. Then you can imagine how the recording heads move.

The recording heads, the stepper motor, and the magnetic relay (if used) are also connected to the electronics of the disk drive.

The last part of the disk drive is the electronics for talking to the computer. The write-protect switch is also connected to these circuits. If the write-protect switch senses that the diskette is write-protected, the disk's electronics stop the disk drive from recording information on the diskette.

The small red light on the front of the disk drive comes on whenever the computer is using the disk drive. You should not open the drive door until the light goes out.

The other electronics receive signals from the computer to start the motor that spins the diskette, to clamp the recording arm on the diskette, to move the recording arm, and to get information from or put information on the diskette.

Most of the "intelligence" needed to control the disk drive is on a board inside the computer itself. The floppy disk drive is a fairly "dumb" peripheral. The intelligence needed to control the disk drive is located mainly in the computer on a *disk controller adapter* or *disk controller board*. This means that the BIOS of the operating system coordinates and governs the actions of the floppy disk drive.

Some 8-inch disk drives and most Winchester disks are "intelligent"; they are more electronically sophisticated and can handle a larger workload. In these cases, DOS issues a high-level command, and the disk drive itself figures out what DOS wants. Some intelligent disk drives work faster than their dumb counterparts.

The floppy disk drive is more reliable today than it was several years ago. More information can be packed onto a 5 1/4-inch diskette than could be held on an 8-inch floppy diskette only five years ago.

Care and Maintenance

Diskettes

Floppy diskettes are fragile. It may be hard to believe that a minifloppy diskette can hold between 360,000 and 1,000,000 characters, or more. Eight-inch diskettes can hold over 2,400,000 characters. The cardboard or plastic jacket protects the diskette from about 80 percent of the dust, fingerprints, smoke, and other contaminants that can come in contact with your diskette. A little common sense is necessary to ensure a long life for your diskette. Treat your diskettes like your personal or business records. In some cases, the diskettes *are* your records.

Some diskette manufacturers have instructions on the back of the envelope about caring for your diskettes. You may want to read those instructions after you read this discussion.

Do's for Floppy Diskettes

Put diskettes into the disk drive carefully. "Easy does it" is the best expression. The diskette should slide into the disk drive with very little resistance. You may even hear a soft click as the write-protect switch slides into place. The disk drive door should close with little resistance. In a short time, you will know by touch whether a diskette is properly inserted. If, in inserting the diskette or closing the disk drive door, you sense that there is a problem, take out the diskette and put it back in again. You can damage the diskette, disk drive, or both if you try to "force" a diskette into a disk drive and close the door.

When you're finished with a diskette, put it back in the envelope. The protective envelope's purpose is to protect the diskette when you are not using it. The envelope stops dust and most other contaminants from getting to the diskette's access hole.

Label every diskette. Diskettes multiply like rabbits. Nothing is more frustrating than trying to find one diskette in a group of 50 identical diskettes without labels. This is time-consuming and frustrating. After you format a diskette, put a label on it. You might put down the date you formatted the diskette, the version, or similar information. Write on the label something you will be able to remember later.

A diskette without a label is fair game and also less useful. Treat each diskette with care and protect it with a label.

Once the label is on the diskette, use a felt-tipped pen to write on the label. Don't press down hard or use a pen or pencil. Undue pressure can damage the diskette under the cardboard jacket.

If a label becomes loose, remove it and put on a new one. I learned the importance of this the hard way while writing this book. A diskette that held several chapters of the book had a label that was beginning to peel away. As I removed the diskette from the disk drive, I didn't notice that the label fell off the diskette and became lodged inside the bottom of the drive.

Later that day, I was looking for a diskette to format and grabbed one from the top of a pile of unlabeled diskettes. After several hours, I looked for the diskette that held part of this book. I searched for 20 minutes, then had a sickening thought. I carefully reached inside the disk drive and found the diskette label on the bottom of the drive. I had formatted the wrong diskette and lost my chapters! Fortunately, I had a one-day-old backup copy of the diskette. All I had lost was one day's work. As I said before, "I am an experienced computer user."

To avoid costly loss of information, always check the diskette you're about to format. Make sure that it is blank or has no useful information on it.

Back up diskettes frequently. What saved me from having to re-enter several weeks of work was the fact that I had a backup diskette. Diskettes have a finite life. In the past (1978-1981), they had a *spin life* (the amount of time that a disk drive actually reads or writes information on the diskette) of 40 to 80 hours. The newer diskettes can be used much longer. Exactly how much longer is hard to determine, but a good estimate is well over 1,000 hours of spin life. Diskettes, however, do eventually wear out. Computer malfunctions or inadvertent operations (such as erasing the wrong file) can also destroy information on the diskette.

Very important information should be backed up daily, or every two days when the information is changed, such as with accounting records.

Important information should be backed up every two days, or at least once a week. Backing up diskettes is a very cheap form of insurance.

Keep infrequently used diskettes and backup copies of diskettes away from your computer. Why clutter the place where you work? Why dig through many diskettes to find the one you need? Keep the number of diskettes at your computer to a minimum; have at hand just the ones you constantly need. When you need a different diskette, get it, use it, and put it back. Diskettes are much easier to manage this way.

Keep your diskettes "comfortable." Like phonograph records, diskettes can bend or warp if they are not stored perfectly flat or vertical. It takes several weeks to warp a diskette, but why risk this kind of damage? There are several diskette holders that do a good job of storing diskettes. Some hold 10 diskettes, whereas others hold up to 50. These cases are not too expensive (usually $20 to $40 for the 50-diskette holders) and can also help you organize your diskettes.

Keeping diskettes comfortable also means watching the temperature. Maintain the temperature between 50 and 125 degrees Fahrenheit (10 and 52 degrees Celsius). If your diskettes get cold, let them warm up before you use them. Cold diskettes become rigid and shrink slightly. Information can be misplaced (not recorded at the correct position) on a shrunken diskette. Disk drives do not work reliably with cold diskettes.

Be especially careful about excessive heat. On warm summer days, if you leave your diskettes in your car, keep them out of direct sunlight. The hot summer sun has made roller coaster rides out of diskettes I have left on the back seat of my car. Your car's trunk can also get hot. Needless to say, when diskettes turn into hot frisbees, the information stored on them is lost.

Buy the right diskettes. Diskette prices are very competitive. There are some good buys on quality diskettes. Unfortunately, there are also some "bargain" brands. These are cheap because they are not *certified* (checked to see that the diskette will properly hold information). In addition, there are a few brands I won't touch at all.

You can tell if you have a poor diskette when you format it. DOS will report that a large amount of disk space has been lost to bad sectors. Format your diskettes even if you use the diskette for DISKCOPY

(DISKCOPY will format a diskette "on-the-fly"). Formatting the diskette will show you right away if you have a problem diskette.

If you have a double-sided disk drive, buy double-sided diskettes. Both sides of the diskette are certified. Single-sided diskettes are certified on only one side. Although both sides may be good, why take a chance? You don't trust important personal or business records to scrap paper; so why trust your important information to "scrap" diskettes?

If you use 96-tpi minifloppy disk drives, buy only diskettes that are certified for 96-tpi drive use. Like double-sided diskettes, the diskette meant for a 48-tpi drive may work on a 96-tpi drive, but why take more chances?

When you turn off your computer or move it, take the diskettes out of the drive. In the past, a disk drive might have written garbage on the diskette when the computer was turned on or off. As a result, diskettes were always removed before the computer was turned off, and the computer was turned on before the diskettes were placed into the disk drives.

Today, disk drives are usually manufactured to prevent this problem. However, there is a very small chance, about one in several million, that the disk drive would write garbage on your diskette. If you are in doubt, open the drive door before you turn your computer on or off.

Moving your computer is another story. When the disk drive door is closed, the recording heads are in contact with the diskette's surface. If the disk drive gets bounced around, the heads can scrape the diskette and damage it. When you move your computer, particularly if it is portable, take the diskettes out of the disk drives.

Some Don'ts for Diskettes

Don't touch the diskette's magnetic surface, particularly the area under the access holes. The oil from your fingers can interfere with the recording heads' ability to read and write information. Hold the diskette by the black jacket. If you need to spin the diskette, put your fingers in the centering hole and turn your hand.

Keep your diskettes away from magnetic fields. This one can be tricky. You may not keep a magnet by your diskette, but what about the video monitor, a fan, or even your telephone? Each of these generates a magnetic field that has the potential to "clean" your diskettes and ruin precious information.

Generally, most appliances will not affect your diskettes, unless you keep the diskette near the appliance for a long time. As a rule, keep your diskettes one foot away from the possible offender. However, keep them farther away from appliances with heavy or strong electric motors, such as a pencil sharpener. The heavier the motor, the farther away you should keep your diskettes.

Plastic holders do not stop magnetic fields. Metal boxes do a better job.

Airport security systems are the new problem for the traveling diskette in the 1980s. Generally, the X-ray machines used at airports do not generate a strong enough field to erase diskettes. Also, the distance between the X-ray source and your luggage is more than a foot. However, ask the security people to hand inspect any carry-on diskettes. Don't let them be put on top of the X-ray machine or scanned by a hand scanner. The diskettes would be too close to damaging magnetic sources. I have found that airport security people are usually happy to cooperate with such requests.

If you are mailing diskettes and want extra protection, or just want extra protection when carrying diskettes in the airport, wrap them in aluminum foil. This will reduce the possibility of magnetic fields reaching your diskettes.

Don't let your diskettes take the "Pepsi™ *Challenge" or the "Sanka*™ *Break."* Be careful about having any liquids near diskettes. That also goes for cigarette, cigar, or pipe smoke and ashes, food, and other similar contaminants. If any of these things gets on your diskette and leaves a residue, the recording heads may not be able to retrieve information from the diskette. Also, this residue can lodge on the recording head, making it a menace to other diskettes.

A friend of mine once spilled some sweet dessert wine on a diskette. That diskette gummed up the disk drive's recording head and ruined several other diskettes. The repair bill for the disk drive was minor compared to the loss of information on the diskettes.

Don't bend the diskette. The information on a diskette is tightly packed. If you put a crease in the diskette, the recording head will "jump" over the crease, and you will lose information. Remember the saying for the old punch cards: "Do not fold, spindle, or mutilate."

Don't let your diskette get too full. Some programs generate temporary files for your data. If your diskette gets full, you may lose what you're working on. WordStar, the word-processing program I use, hates full diskettes. If you can't free up some room on the diskette, you will lose the last revision of your work. I don't blame WordStar; I curse myself when I let this happen.

Periodically, run CHKDSK on your diskettes to see how much room is left on a diskette or hard disk. Erase or copy and erase files to make room.

Floppy Disk Drives

Floppy disk drives are fairly rugged pieces of equipment, but they can be damaged. The following general rules about disk drives will help you minimize damage.

When you insert a diskette, close the drive door carefully. As mentioned earlier, if you jam a diskette into the disk drive and try to close the door, you may damage the clutches that clamp down on the diskette, the diskette itself, or both. After a while, you will be able to tell when a diskette is jammed.

Clean the recording heads infrequently. The recording head of a disk drive is ceramic and requires only infrequent cleaning, perhaps once every three months or a year. Overcleaning a disk drive head can cause problems. The cleaning diskettes and solutions can be more abrasive on the recording heads than normal diskettes. Alcohol-based cleaning solutions, if overused, can erode the glue that holds the recording head on the arm. If this happens, the recording head will fall off the arm. Generally, the felt-like material inside the diskette jacket will catch and hold most dust and dirt.

If you get floppy disk errors, run the diagnostics that came with your computer. First, format some blank diskettes on a "known" good disk drive. Then run the diagnostics. If you get disk errors, clean the disk heads with a cleaning diskette and rerun the diagnostics. If there is still a problem, the disk drive may have problems, or the diskette with the errors is bad.

Don't shock your disk drives. In other words, don't give them a strong bump or jar. The arm with the recording heads can get out of place. The belt that makes the diskette spin can fall off. The door to the disk drive can break. A floppy disk drive is made of metal and plastic. The plastic can break if you drop the disk drive or slam something into it.

When moving or shipping your disk drives over long distances, put the cardboard protector in the drive and close the door. With a double-sided disk drive, the recording heads face each other. When the door is closed, the faces of the recording heads are touching each other. If the disk drives receive a lot of bumps or jolts, the recording heads can clap against each other and become damaged. If you put the cardboard protector inside the disk drive and close the door, the cardboard piece will protect the recording heads.

Have your disk drives serviced periodically. Disk drives need a little preventative maintenance about every one to two years. For example, the belt that spins the diskette may stretch. The disk recording heads may move a little out of the track, or the arm mechanism may wear. The write-protect switch may also wear. The timing on the disk drives' motors may be off. Usually, a good service technician can test and shape up your disk drives at a very reasonable cost. This will prevent a small problem from getting bigger.

You can wait for a problem to surface with your disk drives. But at the first sign of problems, run your diagnostics. If the disk drive is malfunctioning, get it repaired before you ruin some information on good diskettes.

Microfloppy Disks

The microfloppy disk drive and diskettes are just beginning to gain popularity in the microcomputer field. One major company that uses the microfloppy disk drive in its machines is Hewlett-Packard, whose MS-DOS computer, the HP-150, comes with two 3 1/2-inch microfloppy disk drives.

The microfloppy is a recent (1980) invention. Like the floppy and minifloppy disk drives, the microfloppy uses a removable diskette. Unlike the floppy and minifloppy drives, the diskette is a rigid platter enclosed in a hard plastic and metal case.

The microfloppy diskette comes in three basic sizes: 3, 3 1/4, and 3 1/2 inches in diameter. The smaller sizes give these diskettes their name.

The microfloppy disk drive is similar to the floppy disk drive, but several differences do exist. One difference stems from the microfloppy diskette itself. A microfloppy diskette has a spring-held cover over the access hole. This mobile cover is closed while the microfloppy is not in the disk drive to protect the microdiskette's surface from dirt and contamination. When the microdiskette is inserted into the drive, the cover opens so that the recording heads can read and write information on the diskette.

The microfloppy diskette uses a two-position switch for write-protection, unlike the traditional floppy and minifloppy diskettes. This switch, usually pushed into the protect or nonprotect position with a finger or pencil point, is sensed by a mechanical switch in the disk drive when the microfloppy is inserted into the disk drive.

Although most microfloppy disk drives record on only one side of the platter, microfloppies typically hold 180K to 512K. More recent microfloppy disk drives can record up to one megabyte (1M) of information.

The microfloppy drive is attractive because it is compact. It is smaller than floppy and minifloppy disk drives and therefore suitable for smaller computers and portables. The microfloppy diskette can be easily carried in a shirt pocket. The microfloppy's hard case protects it better than the thin, flexible envelopes that cover floppy and minifloppy diskettes.

Unlike the early versions of floppy and minifloppy disk drives, the microfloppy disk drive has proved to be very reliable for storing information. In fact, the microfloppy seems to have been designed and built with reliability as a high priority.

Two major disadvantages of the microfloppy diskette, however, are the lack of a clear "winning" size and the slowness of the market to use the disk.

Like the microfloppy diskette, the microfloppy disk drive comes in three sizes: 3, 3 1/4, and 3 1/2 inches. Each disk drive can work only with diskettes of the same size. For example, a 3-inch microfloppy disk drive requires 3-inch diskettes. It cannot use 3 1/4-inch or 3 1/2-inch microfloppy diskettes, just as minifloppy disk drives cannot use 8-inch floppy diskettes.

Many manufacturers, including major U.S. and Japanese disk drive firms, have joined together to support each of the three formats. No one group has captured the market, however. Without a clear winner, it is difficult to predict which microfloppy size will be the dominant format. Computers that use the "losing" formats may find that many software publishers will not write programs for them, so the amount of available software for the less popular disk drives will be limited.

Most software publishers have been slow to bring out their products on microfloppy diskettes because few computers use them. As a result the amount of available software for computers that use this diskette is limited. The most popular format for MS-DOS computers is the 5 1/4-inch minifloppy diskette. Until more computer manufacturers recognize and use microfloppy disk drives, the amount of software available on microfloppy diskettes will continue to be an issue.

The outlook for microfloppy disk drives is not bleak, however. The issues confronting microfloppy disk drives confronted minifloppy disk drives just four years ago. Although many computers that use minifloppy disk drives are incompatible (the information on the diskette cannot be used by other computers), the IBM standard (double density) is becoming popular. Just as a standard is emerging for minifloppy disk drives, one will eventually emerge for microfloppy disk drives.

Hard Disks

Two basic types of hard disks are available: removable cartridge and the Winchester disks. Of the two, the Winchester disk is the most popular hard disk for personal computers. Winchester disks were developed at IBM and have become a practical addition to personal computers. Although we'll look at both types of hard disks, this section devotes more attention to the Winchester disk.

There are several differences between a floppy disk drive and a hard disk. The latter uses a set of rigid platters, similar to those used by the microfloppy diskette. These rigid platters give the "hard" disk drive its name. They are coated with metal oxide and are fixed on a spindle that rotates at a speed of about 3,600 rpm.

A Winchester disk drive has a sealed unit that contains the platters and the recording heads. The cartridge-style drives use a removable platter.

The recording heads reach the disk through an access door in the cartridge. A mobile arm holds the recording heads, one at the top and one at the bottom of each platter. The entire arm moves back and forth like the floppy disk drive's recording heads. The mobile arm moves more precisely and in smaller increments than the floppy disk drive's arm, and the recording heads are smaller than those of a floppy disk drive.

The smaller recording heads and more controlled movement allow more information to be placed on the platter's surface. Because the disk spins faster, the storing and retrieving of information is also faster. Thus, the hard disk can hold more information and store and retrieve it faster than can most floppy disk drives.

Winchester disks for personal computers usually have 5 1/4-inch or 8-inch diameter platters, although some Winchesters use 14-inch platters and 3 1/2-inch drives are just starting to be made. The most common size is the 5 1/4-inch. Usually, the 5 1/4-inch platter holds 2 1/2 megabytes (million bytes) per side. The combination of two sides per platter and two platters in the drive gives you a 10M (megabyte) disk drive.

Cartridge hard disks typically use platters that are 8 to 14 inches in diameter, although less than half of the platter's surface is used for recording. The amount of information held by a cartridge disk varies, but usually each platter can hold between 5 and 20 megabytes. The most popular sizes are the 5- and 10-megabyte platters.

Some problems are unique to hard disk drives. The air pressure generated by the spinning disk lifts the recording heads just thousandths of an inch off the surface. Should the heads hit any contamination (such as a hair, cigarette smoke, or a fingerprint), they will bounce over it and crash into the platters. The Winchester's sealed environment prevents contamination and almost completely eliminates this problem. Removable cartridge disk drives, however, are very susceptible to this problem. To ensure that no particles reach the platter's surfaces, the operator must handle the cartridges carefully; the air in the disk drive must be "purged" through the air filter when the cartridges are inserted or removed.

Severe physical shock can damage a disk's surface. Because the recording heads hover so close to the platter's surface, a strong blow to the disk drive while the unit is operating can cause the recording heads to crash into the disk surface. For this reason, you should not drop or bump a Winchester disk indiscriminately, nor should you strike the table or desk that holds the disk. The risk of damaging a Winchester disk is significantly reduced because the recording heads and platters are mounted into one unit. Cartridge disk drives, however, are very susceptible to this kind of damage.

Winchester disks can take a lot of punishment. When a drive is not in use, it can take a shock of up to 20 Gs (twenty times the force of gravity). When in use, most drives can withstand a shock of only 10 Gs. The maximum allowable shock is lower when the drive is operating because the recording heads can smash into the platter and scrape off the metal coating where the information is stored. Newer Winchester disk drives have an extra coating on the platter to prevent such a loss of information, but the 20G and 10G restrictions remain.

For these reasons, the Winchester disk has gained popularity in the microcomputer market. Its increased reliability and ease of use have made the Winchester the preferred hard disk drive.

The final problem facing hard disk users is backup. Cartridge disks are better at backup than Winchesters because the cartridge is removable, just like a floppy diskette. With two cartridge disk drives, the cartridges can be backed up onto other cartridges. Other hard disks use a fixed disk with the cartridge disk. The fixed disk is backed up, and the contents of the cartridge are moved to the fixed disk, which is then backed up onto another cartridge. This process is clumsier than using two cartridge drives, but it works.

Winchester disks are different. Because you cannot remove the platters, you must transfer information to a separate media for backup. A backup copy of the information on the Winchester is essential because some time between 8,000 to 20,000 hours of use, the Winchester disk drive will fail.

Most personal computers use floppy diskettes for backup. If your minifloppies hold 360K, about 28 diskettes are required to back up a 10-megabyte hard disk. Only nine 1.2M 8-inch floppy diskettes are needed. If you use fewer diskettes to back up the hard disk, the process is more workable. The larger the hard disk, the more time-consuming and less manageable the backup.

Some hard disk drive manufacturers sell cartridge tape units with the hard disk. These 1/4-inch tape units can hold between 13 and 40 megabytes of information. Commonly called *streamers* (the data is sent to the tape as a "stream" of information and is not randomly accessible like a disk), these devices cost between $2,000 and $3,500, but make the backup process easy and manageable.

Tips for Hard Disks

To install the disk drive, follow the manufacturer's directions. Some disk drives, such as those that IBM uses, require no physical setup. Others require that shipping bolts or screws be loosened before use. Usually, some preliminary programs must be run before you can use the drive.

Prepare your disk according to manufacturer's instructions before you move or ship it. The preparation procedure is usually the reverse of installing the disk drive. Remember that, as a rule, hard drives are more fragile than floppy disk drives.

Some manufacturers provide a program that you must run before moving or shipping the disk. This program moves the recording heads to the edge of the disk so that they cannot scrape the platters where information is stored. The program should be run whenever you move the hard disk more than a few feet.

When you use a hard disk drive, avoid bumping the table or the desk that holds the disk.

If you use a cartridge disk drive, avoid bumping or dropping the cartridges and touching the platter's surfaces. Bumping the cartridge or touching the surface can damage the cartridge and ruin the data on the platters, the disk drive, or both. Change the air filters, too, according to your manufacturer's directions. Don't let these filters get too dirty; they remove particles that can cause the recording heads to crash into the platters.

Back up your hard disk frequently. No matter what type of hard disk you use, it will eventually fail. Don't be caught with your only copy of information on a nonworking hard disk.

Finally, you should learn about hierarchical directories because they can help you organize your files. (See Chapter 9.)

How DOS Divides the Diskette

To simplify the handling of a disk or diskette, DOS breaks down the diskette into smaller pieces. First, the diskette is broken down into a series of concentric circles called *tracks*. The number of tracks your diskette has depends on the disk drive and the step size of the stepper motor that moves the recording heads. The smaller the step, the more tracks your diskette will have.

Most minifloppy disk drives have recording heads that record 48 (tpi). This number is the standard for most IBM-compatible minifloppy disk drives. Some minifloppy disk drives record 96 tracks per inch, thus doubling the diskette's capacity. But you cannot use the entire diskette for recording. With 48-tpi drives, you can create only 40 tracks. The 96-tpi disk drives use only 80 tracks. This limitation means that you use a circular band about 5/6-inch wide in the middle of the minifloppy diskette.

Eight-inch disk drives use about 77 tracks per side. The recording band for an 8-inch diskette is also larger.

The tracks are sliced up into *sectors*. The number of sectors per track varies among disks (floppy, minifloppy, microfloppy) and computer systems. The most frequent number of sectors for minifloppy diskettes is 8 or 9. Floppy diskettes may have between 8 and 26 sectors per track; 13 to 16 sectors are the most popular amounts. Tracks and sectors allow the computer to position the disk drive recording head to the correct spot rapidly.

The single index hole of a soft-sectored diskette signals the computer when sector 0 passes under the recording head. DOS determines when the other sectors are below the recording head. *Soft-sector* means that software determines the sector location.

Hard-sectored diskettes use one hole on the diskette as the "master" hole. The hole determines when each sector passes under the recording head. In this case the sectoring is determined by hardware, thus the name hard-sectored diskettes.

How many sectors are on your diskette? IBM PC-compatible double-sided disk drives, using DOS V2, have

40 tracks * 9 sectors * 2 sides = 720 total sectors

These figures can also tell you how much information is stored on a diskette. Each sector on the minifloppy diskette (and hard disk) holds 512 bytes.

The number of bytes stored on a 9-sector, double-sided diskette is

720 sectors * 512 bytes per sector = 368,640 bytes

You can determine the number of Kbytes by dividing this number by 1,024.

368,640 bytes / 1,024 bytes per K = 360K

Most 8-inch diskettes and hard disks also use 512 bytes per sector.

Hard disk drives are divided in a similar manner. The major difference is that the hard disk uses the concept of *cylinders*.

First, let's consider a double-sided diskette. There are 40 tracks recorded on both sides of the diskette. The first track on the top side is directly above the first track on the bottom side, and so on, for each of the other 39 tracks. If you draw a vertical, three-dimemsional figure that passes through the two sides of a diskette at any track, you have a cylinder.

For the hard disk, think about two platters stacked on top of each other on the spindle. The tracks for each side of each platter are in the same vertical plane. If you connect any one track on all four surfaces, you will have a cylinder. Most 5 1/4-inch, 10-megabyte disk drives have 306 cylinders, so each surface on the four platters has 306 tracks. (One of these cylinders is usually used for internal purposes and is not available for storing information.)

Another difference between the minifloppy diskette and the hard disk is that each track on a hard disk platter has 17 sectors instead of 9. The number of cylinders, sides, sectors, and sector size will vary among the different hard disk drives.

DOS starts at the first track (outermost track or track 0) on side one of the diskette. DOS then uses sectors 0 through 8. If the diskette is double sided, DOS uses side two, track 0, sectors 0 through 8. DOS goes back to the first side to use track 1, sectors 0 through 8, then back to side two. This process continues until the entire diskette is full. If the diskette is single sided, DOS does not switch sides. The hard disk works the same way, except that DOS uses each side of the platters (a cylinder) before moving to the next track.

Why does DOS work this way? The answer is speed. Less time is needed to tell the disk drive to use the second side of a diskette than to move the recording heads. The same is true of the hard disk. Using a recording head for a different surface is faster than moving the recording heads.

What DOS Does with the Diskette

Before a new diskette can be used, DOS must first record some dummy information on the diskette. This process is called *formatting*.

When you format a diskette or hard drive, DOS records dummy data in each sector. (Some additional housekeeping information that does not concern us is also recorded.)

Next, DOS sets up three important areas on the disk. The first area is in the first sector of the first track on the diskette's front. This area is called the *boot record*. It contains the bootstrap routine used by DOS to load itself.

FORMAT then sets up two copies of the *File Allocation Table*, also called the *FAT* for short. (FAT is discussed below.) Most 8-sector minifloppy diskettes and most microfloppy diskettes use one sector for each copy of the FAT. On other minifloppy diskettes, each FAT copy is two sectors long. The FAT also tells DOS what type of diskette you are using, floppy or minifloppy, single sided or double sided, and the number of sectors per track.

Next comes the directory, where DOS stores the name of each disk file, the date and time the file was created or last changed, the file attributes (defines the characteristics about the file), the starting cluster entry in the FAT, and the size of the file in bytes. The file attribute can be any combination of:

> *System file*—a file used by the operating system. This file is normally hidden from regular uses of DOS.

> *Hidden file*—another file that is hidden from normal DOS operations.

> *Volume label*—not a disk file, but an 11-character label to help you identify the diskette. The volume label appears when you execute such DOS commands as DIR and CHKDSK.

Subdirectory—not a file, but a different directory that holds similar information about other files.

Archived file—a file that has not been backed up. This attribute is turned on every time DOS creates a file or you put new information into the file.

Every file you create or use has one directory entry 32 bytes long. Directory size can be 4 to 20 (or more) sectors long. Larger-capacity diskettes use more sectors for the directory. The more sectors used, the more files can be held in the directory of the diskettes.

MS-DOS' directory is different from that used by most other operating systems. It does not tell you where the file is located on the diskette. Instead, the entry in the disk's directory for each file points to an entry in the FAT. The FAT tells DOS which sectors on the diskette actually hold the file. In other words, the FAT guides DOS to where information is stored on a diskette. The FAT also indicates what sectors are not being used by a file.

The FAT is very important to DOS, so important that DOS keeps two copies of the FAT for every disk or diskette. DOS uses the directory entry to go to the correct part of the FAT for the file you want to use. Then DOS uses the FAT to find where your file is stored on the diskette. When a file grows, DOS checks the FAT to see what sectors are not being used. When a free sector is found, DOS adds it to the chain for the file and uses the sector.

DOS uses a first-found, first-used routine for this process. In other words, DOS takes the first free sector it finds and puts as much of the file into that sector as possible. DOS then looks for the next free sector and puts more of the file into the new sector. Thus, it is possible for a file to be scattered all over a diskette.

A *cluster* is the smallest unit of disk space that DOS will work with in the FAT. DOS does not actually look for a sector per se, but rather for a cluster.

For most single-sided minifloppy and microfloppy diskettes, a cluster is the same size as a sector. When DOS searches for a free cluster on these diskettes, DOS is looking for a free sector.

Your computer's manufacturer may use a different number of sectors for a cluster, depending on the capacity of the diskette. The more information the disk can hold, the more sectors will be in a cluster. For example, IBM uses two sectors per cluster for double-sided minifloppy diskettes. In this case, when DOS looks for a free cluster on a double-sided diskette, DOS is looking for a free pair of adjacent sectors.

If you use FORMAT with the **/S** switch, FORMAT will also place IO.SYS or MSBIO.SYS, MSDOS.SYS, and COMMAND.COM on your diskette. The use of the **/V** switch varies. Usually, if you don't give the **/V** switch, DOS will create a volume label, a user-definable name for the diskette. The volume label is placed in the directory but has no entry in the FAT. Thus, a volume label does not take up any disk space but does reduce by one the number of files a disk or diskette can hold.

Looking Back

This chapter covered the four different kinds of disks: microfloppy, minifloppy, floppy, and hard. You also learned about the care and handling of your diskettes and how DOS uses a disk. The next chapter will tell you more about DOS and how it works with your disk drives and the rest of your computer system.

5

A Brief Look Inside DOS

DOS has three major components: the I/O system, the Command Processor, and the utilities. The I/O System handles every character that is typed or displayed, printed, and received or sent through the communication adapters. It contains the disk filing system for DOS, which handles the storing and retrieving of programs and information from the disk drives.

The Command Processor has several built-in functions, or subprograms, that handle most common tasks for DOS—copying files, displaying a list of files on the disk, and running your programs.

The utilities are used for housekeeping tasks, such as formatting diskettes, comparing files, finding the free space on a diskette, and doing background printing. All three parts of DOS are used when you execute commands such as FORMAT or CHKDSK.

The I/O System

I/O is the abbreviation for input/output. This term refers to activities related to the computer's central processing unit, or CPU (the "brain" of the computer), and memory. When you type a character on the keyboard, the character moves inwardly, from the keyboard to the CPU and memory. This movement is called *input*. When the computer prints a line on the screen or printer, the line moves outwardly, from the CPU and memory to the screen or printer. This movement is called *output*.

Input and output take place between the computer and the computer's *peripherals*. The screen, keyboard, printer, and disk drives are peripherals. These devices are used by the computer's CPU and memory but are not part of either of them. As you learned in Chapter 2, peripherals are important to the computer because without them, the CPU and memory would have no way to communicate to the outside world.

Each peripheral has a different purpose and method for talking to the computer. Before a computer can use a peripheral, the computer must have a set of instructions telling it how to communicate with the peripheral and control its actions.

The software that performs these function is the *BIOS*, which is short for Basic Input/Output System. The BIOS has fundamental routines that control the keyboard, video display, disk drives, and other peripherals of the computer. Without the BIOS, your computer would not be able to communicate with and control these devices.

Your computer's BIOS is probably located in two places. Part of it may be in read-only memory. The majority of the BIOS is in a disk file called IO.SYS or MSBIO.SYS. Although your computer manufacturer may give this file a slightly different name, the file's purpose is always the same. It holds most of the software routines for controlling and communicating with peripherals.

When you format a disk with the **/S** switch, you copy the I/O system file to the diskette or disk. You may not find this file on the disk because it is a *system file,* used exclusively by the operating system. If you unintentionally erase or alter IO.SYS, you cannot properly use the operating system from this diskette.

The next part of the I/O system is the MSDOS.SYS file, which, like IO.SYS, may have a slightly different name. This file contains the major part of the operating system and holds the routines for controlling the information passed between the computer and its peripherals. MS-

DOS.SYSCOM has two separate filing systems: one for disk drives and one for all nondisk peripherals.

Every peripheral talks to the computer either one character at a time (character-oriented) or in groups of characters called *blocks* (block-oriented). The keyboard, printer, and video screen are three common character-oriented devices; modems also fall into this category. Disk drives are block-oriented.

Because the methods used to control these two sets of devices are so fundamentally different, DOS keeps two separate sets of management routines to handle the two classes of devices.

To receive information from a character-oriented device, DOS checks whether the device has a character to send, then gets the character and puts it in the appropriate spot. To send a character to the screen or printer, DOS checks whether the device is ready to receive another character, then sends it.

DOS tells the disk drive to move its recording head to the appropriate location on the disk and get, or put, a block of information at that location.

The filing system (MSDOS) is the control center. MSDOS communicates its directions to the BIOS, which, in turn, does the actual "talking" to the devices and transmits the filing system's directions.

There is a good reason for the division of tasks between IO.SYS and MSDOS.SYS. All the unique instructions for handling the various devices attached to the computer system are handled in one spot, the BIOS. If additional software routines are needed for new devices, the BIOS will get these new instructions. The filing system portion of DOS remains unchanged. For every computer, the BIOS is changed to handle the equipment that is used by your computer. The MSDOS.SYS file remains unchanged.

The two DOS filing systems—character-oriented and disk—perform different tasks. The character-oriented filing system does the following:

 Gets a character from a device
 Sends a character to a device
 Checks whether a device is ready to get or send a character
 Gets a line of characters from the keyboard
 Sends a line of characters to the screen
 Gets or sets the date and the time

In most cases, the device can be the keyboard, screen, printer, or serial adapters.

The disk filing system performs the following tasks:

> Creates a file
> Opens a file for reading or writing
> Writes information to a file
> Reads information from a file
> Closes a file
> Searches for a file name
> Tells the names of files
> Gives the size of a file
> Changes the name or attributes of a file
> Removes a file
> Resets the disk system
> Indicates the amount of free space on a disk
> Tells which disk drives are being used
> Loads and runs programs
> Sets up (allocates) memory for programs
> Frees allocated memory
> Handles the hierarchical directory system

Although handling memory may not seem to be a block-oriented device function, it does belong here. Because DOS loads and runs programs, it must be able to manage the computer's memory.

Don't worry about new or "foreign" terms in this list. All of these functions are discussed in this book. This list simply gives you a glimpse of all the tasks that DOS handles.

Together, the BIOS and the filing system provide a unified set of routines—the I/O system—for controlling the computer's resources. It, in turn, provides a standard way of controlling and directing the computer.

You may not care how the computer handles information as long as the handling is done correctly. However, you *do* want the programs you buy to work with your computer. If a program uses the standards established by DOS, the program will work with your computer.

For example, BASIC does not have its own routines for controlling the disk drives. It calls on the I/O System to do the hard work. Most programs operate this way. Most word-processing programs do not have the routines to grab information directly from the keyboard. Instead, the programs call on the I/O System to get a character from the keyboard and give the character to the program.

The Command Processor

The second major component of DOS is the Command Processor, COMMAND.COM. It is the program you communicate with, and it, in turn, tells the rest of DOS what to do.

COMMAND.COM prints the A: on the video screen when you start DOS. A:, known as the *system prompt*, indicates that you are talking to COMMAND.COM. When you type a command, COMMAND.COM will interpret it and take the appropriate action.

COMMAND.COM consists of several parts. The first part handles *critical interrupts*. When a hardware device demands attention, COMMAND.COM will divert the computer's attention to the device. Once the device has received the necessary attention and the need for the critical interrupt is over, COMMAND.COM restores the computer's attention to whatever the computer was doing before. If the computer was executing one of your programs, it will continue to do so.

The second part handles *critical errors,* which are usually disk problems or divide-by-zero errors. The computer gives control to COMMAND.COM to handle the error. If you leave a disk drive door open when DOS is trying to read the disk, you may see the message:

```
Disk error reading drive A
Retry, Ignore, Abort
```

COMMAND.COM displays this message and waits for you to take the appropriate action.

The end-of-program housekeeping utilities are the last part of COMMAND.COM. When a program ends, COMMAND.COM tells the filing system to free the RAM memory used by the program so that the space can be used by other programs. COMMAND.COM also checks itself to see that it is intact. If the memory space normally occupied by COMMAND.COM has been used by the program, COMMAND.COM will reload itself from the disk.

COMMAND.COM's contents can be either resident or transient. The *resident* portion always stays in the RAM memory. Most of the COMMAND.COM functions discussed above are resident functions. The *transient* portion also stays in RAM memory but can be freed for use by your programs. If your program uses this part of memory, COMMAND.COM must reload itself from the disk when the program has finished.

The transient portion of COMMAND.COM has several commonly used DOS commands built in. These *internal* commands can be used when you are at the system prompt level, A:. They include:

COPY	Copies files
DATE	Sets or shows the system date
DIR	Shows a list of files (also called CAT)
ERASE or DEL	Erases disk files
RENAME	Changes the name of a disk file
TIME	Sets or shows the system time
TYPE	Displays the contents of a disk file on the screen

COMMAND.COM also handles the following:

The batch files and subcommands ECHO, IF, FOR..IN..DO, GOTO, REM, and PAUSE

The hierarchical directory commands CHDIR, MKDIR, and RMDIR

These commands are covered later in this book. For now, just remember that you can execute any DOS command listed here when you are at system level (A:). You don't have to load a program into memory to use these DOS functions.

The new I/O redirection functions are also built into COM-MAND.COM. (I/O redirection is discussed in Chapter 8.)

Finally, COMMAND.COM directs DOS to load your programs into memory and give them control over the computer. When you type

BASIC, COMMAND.COM goes down the list of internal commands that it knows. BASIC is not one of these commands. COMMAND.COM then tells the filing system to go out to the current disk drive and look for a program called either BASIC.COM or BASIC.EXE. If the filing system finds this program, it is loaded into memory, and COMMAND.COM gives control of the computer to the program. This process invokes the BASIC language.

The process also provides an illustration of how the operating system works. You communicate to COMMAND.COM, which then communicates to the filing systems of DOS. The filing systems communicate to the BIOS, which then talks to the devices. The information constantly passes up and down the line from each major section of the operating system to the devices and to you.

A program that is running fills the place between you and COMMAND.COM. You talk to the program, which talks to portions of COMMAND.COM and the filing system, and the process continues as described.

The operating system, therefore, gives you, the computer user, the power to control the computer's resources. DOS does this job well.

The DOS Utilities

DOS utility programs are housekeeping programs. Housekeeping facilitates your work and keeps it manageable. The housekeeping itself doesn't actually do any "real" work, such as accounting or word processing, but is necessary for effective computer use.

FORMAT is a housekeeping utility. It does not process words, calculate your profits, or keep track of your friends' names and telephone numbers; but you cannot use a new diskette until you FORMAT it.

The DOS utilities help you run and manage your computer system. Among other things, they organize your files, check free space on the disk, copy diskettes, and compare files.

Microsoft, the author of MS-DOS, provides your computer manufacturer with some utilities. Some are complete and ready-to-run; others require customization by the computer manufacturer before they can be used with your computer. The manufacturer may simply adapt the utilities or may add or delete functions. The manufacturer may also write and supply additional utility programs with your copy of MS-DOS.

Unfortunately, it is impossible to list all of the utility programs and features that each manufacturer may supply. The DOS documentation that comes with your computer is the ultimate authority. Check your manuals to be sure that your manufacturer has not changed the names of these utility programs or added or changed their functions and features.

The MS-DOS utility programs include the following commands:

CHKDSK	Displays disk and memory statistics; checks and repairs disks
DISKCOPY	Copies disks; makes a "carbon copy"
EDLIN	Line-oriented text editor
FC	File comparison program
FORMAT	Formats diskettes and hard disks
PRINT	Background printing program
RECOVER	Recovers bad files and disks
SYS	Places the operating system on a diskette

The next three utility programs are programming tools:

DEBUG	Assembly language debugging program
EXE2BIN	Converts .EXE files to .COM or .BIN files
LINK	Program linker

The following three programs are *filters*:

FIND	Finds a string
MORE	Displays a screenful of information and pauses
SORT	Sorting program

(Filters are discussed in Chapter 8.)

You may also see a program called MASM.EXE, which is the Microsoft Macro Assembler (MS-86). Your computer's manufacturer may provide this item with MS-DOS or sell it separately.

Let's skip the list of program tools and filters and look at what the utilities do. Most of the programs assist in the handling of disks or files. These utilities facilitate diskette, disk, and file management.

You may have noticed that I often use the term *utility programs*. The name you give these programs is unimportant. You can call them commands, programs, utilities, tools, or any other name you desire. I call them programs because they reside on your MS-DOS disk; they are not built in to COMMAND.COM. Each utility program in the three previous lists is a disk-resident or *external* command. To use these commands, you must tell DOS where they reside. DOS then loads the command from the disk into RAM memory for execution.

Some of your programs' names may be different. They will all end in either .COM or .EXE, but the first part of the name may differ. FC (file compare) is sometimes called FILCOM. The FIND filter may be called FGREP, which is the name of a similar utility on the UNIX operating system. Eagle Computer calls its formatting program FORMAT48. Check your manual to see what each program is called.

Program features may also differ. FORMAT is the most likely utility to be changed. Your computer manufacturer may have added more functions and features to accommodate different sizes of diskettes or hard disks.

You may have additional programs. If your computer came with a built-in hard disk, the manufacturer has probably provided a set of programs to back up and restore files from your hard disk. Check your documentation to see how these programs are used.

Many of these utility programs are discussed later in this book. Each major command, except the programming tools, will be covered. Most people seldom use the programming tools; any information about them that you may need should be provided by your MS-DOS manuals.

How DOS Starts Up

The process of loading and starting the operating system is called *booting*. It comes from the term "bootstrap," as in pulling oneself up by the bootstraps.

When you do a system reset or turn on the computer, its CPU executes a small program, the bootstrap loader, that resides in the read-only memory (ROM) of your system. This small program reads the first part of the disk and brings in the bootstrap program, which initiates the chain of events that will load and start DOS. The bootstrap loader also starts the primary, or first, disk drive of the computer system. Then the first part of the diskette is read into the RAM memory.

The bootstrap program now takes control. It checks the list of files on the diskette for IO.SYS and MSDOS.SYS (or whatever names your computer manufacturer has given these programs). If the bootstrap program finds the right names, it begins to load IO.SYS. Because of the bootstrap program's limited intelligence, IO.SYS must be the first file on the diskette and must be stored consecutively on the disk. If both conditions are not met, the entire process will fail. Once IO.SYS is loaded, the bootstrap program will bring MSDOS.SYS into memory.

After IO.SYS is in memory, the bootstrap loader gives control to IO.SYS (the BIOS). It checks to see what equipment is attached to the system and sets up the equipment to be used. The term for these activities is *initialization*. If your printer is attached and turned on, you will hear a click as the printing head moves back to the first printing position. The BIOS does this as it initializes the printer adapter.

Once the equipment is initialized (including the keyboard, screen, and serial and parallel adapters), IO.SYS looks for the CONFIG.SYS file in the primary directory of the disk. If CONFIG.SYS is found, IO.SYS loads it and executes its instructions. (CONFIG.SYS is discussed in Chapter 11.)

After IO.SYS has finished its work, it moves MSDOS.SYS to the correct location in memory and gives control to that program. MSDOS.SYS also does setup work. When this is completed, MS-DOS.SYS assigns a portion of memory to hold COMMAND.COM, which is then loaded into memory and receives control of the computer from MSDOS.SYS.

DOS is now fully loaded and functioning. The boot of DOS is complete. The entire process normally takes less than three seconds to complete.

One more thing happens before DOS turns control over to you. It looks for a file called AUTOEXEC.BAT on the boot diskette. If DOS finds the file, DOS will start executing the DOS commands in it. (AUTOEXEC.BAT and batch files are also discussed later in this book.)

If your system uses a hard disk, this process may be slightly different. How different the process is depends on whether your system's ROM searches for a hard disk drive in addition to any floppy disk drives. If the search is made, then the bootstrap loader inside the ROM will first look for a diskette in drive A. If a diskette is not found, the bootstrap loader jumps to the hard disk to look for DOS. If DOS is found on the hard disk, the process is similar to booting DOS from the diskette.

The start-up of DOS is based on one program building on the work of another. This is essentially how your computer system works. Word-processing, accounting, or spreadsheet programs all use the foundation established by DOS.

IBM Compatibility

Now that you know something about the parts of the computer, DOS, and how the two work, this is a good time to turn to the concept of IBM compatibility.

Martin Dean, chairman of Select Information Systems, jokes about the four great new lies of our times: "The Mercedes is paid for, the mortgage is assumable, it's only a cold sore, And it's PC compatible."

IBM has had a tremendous impact on the microcomputer market. The company has created a new market for microcomputers just as it did for mainframes. Many computer manufacturers have sought to profit from the popularity of the IBM Personal Computer by making IBM-compatible computers. For a computer to be IBM compatible, it must meet three conditions.

First, hardware compatibility must exist. The computer must use a member of the Intel 8086 family of CPUs— an 8086, 8088, iAPX 186, or iAPX 286. The peripherals of the IBM-compatible computer must be similar to those used by the IBM PC. They include the video display, keyboard, and disk drives. If any of these peripherals react differently from those used by the IBM PC, programs designed to work with the IBM PC will not work correctly with the other computer.

Second, an IBM-compatible computer must have a BIOS that emulates the ROM BIOS of the IBM PC. This condition is probably the most troublesome. The BIOS does not have to be a "carbon copy" of the PC's BIOS but must work in the same way. Copying the features and functions of the IBM PC's ROM BIOS without copying the actual BIOS program itself is difficult.

Third, an IBM-compatible computer must use the same operating system as the IBM PC. Most programs for the IBM PC operate under PC DOS, which is simply the IBM implementation of MS-DOS.

One final observation should be made about compatibility. A computer can use MS-DOS and the same disk drives used by the IBM Personal Computer, but not be IBM compatible. Using the same disk drives and MS-DOS only ensures that your computer system can read and write the information on the diskette. Programs written especially for the IBM PC are not guaranteed to run on other computer systems.

6
Device and Disk Drive Names

Device is another name for peripheral. The keyboard, video screen, terminal (if you use one), printer, modem, game adapter, and other items you connect to the computer are all devices.

Each device uses a connection, called an *interface*, to talk to the computer. (Interfaces were discussed in Chapter 2.) Most peripherals, with the exception of disk drives, communicate one byte at a time. A complete byte (all eight bits at once) can be transmitted by parallel interface, or the individual bits in a byte can be sent, one at a time, by serial interface. The latter type of device is called *character oriented* because it works with units of one character at a time.

The video display in systems that use memory-mapped video is also character oriented, but in a different way. Characters and their video attributes (inverse video, high and low intensity, etc.) are "sent" to the screen one character at a time. However, the movement of the characters is through RAM memory only, not from the RAM memory to an external device. Don't try to apply the idea of parallel and serial interfaces to memory-mapped video. The concept is inapplicable to memory-mapped video.

What are disk drives? They are serial, character-oriented devices. Bytes are stored on the diskette, or platter, one bit at a time. The electronics of the adapters collect and combine the bits into characters and the characters into blocks. These actions happen so fast that you don't notice the extra work that the interfaces, adapters, and hard disk drives perform. From the standpoint of the computer system, these peripherals are *block-oriented* devices.

In the last chapter, you learned that DOS has two filing systems, one for character-oriented devices and one for block-oriented devices. The software for the basic control of these devices is in the BIOS of the computer system—that is, in the computer's ROM, in the IO.SYS file, or in both.

Every peripheral, or device, has a name. MS-DOS "knows" several device names. For most character-oriented devices, the name is based on the type of interface that connects the peripheral to the computer. Block-oriented devices use different names. (These devices are covered later.)

Device Names

Device names are usually three to four characters long. Every device name, except PRN, ends with a colon, although this is optional with most commands. When a device name is used, DOS will attempt to use the specified interface or device.

Because of the way DOS is constructed, you can use a device name anywhere a file name can be used. You can, therefore, direct DOS to get information from a device (such as a modem) or put information into a device (such as a printer).

Each device name is *reserved* and cannot be used as the root name of a disk file.

The character-oriented device names that DOS recognizes are provided in the following list. Also included are two additional device names used by Microsoft BASIC-86 (Disk BASIC) and GW (Advanced) BASIC, but not recognized by DOS. The colon (optional) is included after each device name.

Table 6.1
Character-Oriented Device Names
MS-DOS

Name	Device
CON:	The computer console, which may be either (1) the terminal or CRT, or (2) the video display and keyboard. Input from CON: comes from the keyboard. Output to CON: goes to the video display.
AUX:	An auxiliary device, usually an asynchronous or RS-232 serial port. If more than one serial port is available, a digit (1-9) is added between the X and the colon to specify which port should be used (for example, AUX1: and AUX2:).
LST:	The printer, usually a parallel printer, such as the Centronics or Epson. This device can be used only for PRN output. As with AUX:, if more than one printer is connected, a number is added after the last letter of the name to specify the printer to which you are referring (for example, LST1:, LST2:, etc.). PRN is assumed to be the first printer. (LST: is an abbreviation for listing device. PRN is an abbreviation for printer.)
NUL:	A null or dummy (nonexistent) device used to test programs. When NUL: is used for input, DOS gives an end-of-file back to the program. When NUL: is used for output, DOS appears to write the information to the device, but nothing is actually output to any device.

Microsoft BASIC-86 and GW BASIC	
Name	Device
KYBD:	The keyboard of the system, an input-only device
SCRN:	The video display, an output-only device

Table 6.2

Rules for Character-Oriented Device Names

1. Valid names for character-oriented devices are CON:, AUX:, LST: or LSTx:, PRN, and NUL:.

2. The colon following these names is usually optional.

3. A character-oriented device name can be used anywhere a file name can be used.

4. If an extension is given with a device name, the extension is ignored. For example, CON.TXT is treated as CON:.

5. The UNIX/XENIX-compatible path name, **\dev***device-name,* may be used for a device. For example, **\DEV\PRN** may be used instead of **PRN** (DOS V2 only).

6. Do not use the name of a device that does not exist. For example, do not use AUX: when you do not have a serial port. (NUL: is the exception to this rule.)

These rules summarize how device names should be used. If the root name of a file is identical to one of these device names, DOS will use the device, not a disk file. (Files and file names are covered in Chapter 7.) Rule 5 will be discussed in more detail later.

Rule 6 is important. Don't .ry to use a device you don't have. At best, DOS will give you an error message. At worst, DOS might act erratically.

Disk Drive Names

Disk drive names tell DOS which file drawer to use. In other words, the disk drive name tells DOS where to find the files you want.

A disk drive name is two characters long. The first character is usually a letter, and the second character must be a colon.

The common name for the starting (or first) disk drive is A:. The name for each additional drive is the next letter of the alphabet. For example, the second disk drive would be B:, the third would be C:, and so on. Notice that the letters used for the disk drive names are in upper case.

MS-DOS V1 allows a maximum of sixteen disk drives; the letters A through P are therefore legal names. In DOS V1, programs do not care if you used an upper- or lower-case letter because DOS always translates the letter to upper case.

DOS V2 allows up to 63 device names. Because the alphabet has only 26 upper-case letters (which can represent only 26 disk drives), DOS V2 starts with A and moves up the ASCII character set for drive names. After Z is used for the 26th disk drive, the disk drive names are very different. The thirtieth disk drive on the system will have the name ^; the fortieth disk drive will use *i*; the fiftieth disk drive will have the name }; and the last possible disk drive will be ~.

Fortunately, most computer systems use only two to four disk drives. Therefore, most users will need only the drive names A:, B:, C:, and D:. DOS automatically translates lower-case letters into upper case if you have less than 27 disk drives on your computer system. Consequently, you can still use either upper- or lower-case characters when you type a disk drive name.

Table 6.3
Rules for Disk Drive Names

1. A disk drive must have a two-character name. The second character must be a colon (:).

2. The first disk drive is A:, the second disk drive is B:, etc.

3. The character for each additional disk drive is one character higher in the ASCII character set.

4. Only the letters A through P are valid for DOS V1. More characters are available for DOS V2.

5. When you use a disk drive name, the letter can be in upper or lower case if you have less than 27 disk drives.

6. When you tell DOS to run a program from disk, the program name may be preceded by a drive name.

7. Almost anytime you give a file name, the disk drive name may precede the file name.

8. Don't use a nonexistent disk drive. DOS will display an error message if you do.

Notice Rules 6 and 7. They explain how you tell DOS where to find your programs and other files.

The system prompt was mentioned earlier. The A in the A: is not a coincidence. The letter indicates the *current disk drive,* which is the drive that DOS will use, *unless* you indicate otherwise. DOS always has only one current disk drive. When you run a program from the disk and don't give a drive name in front of the program name, DOS will get the program from the current disk drive.

Earlier, I also mentioned that your system prompt may be different from mine. Some systems use the greater than sign (>) in place of the colon for the system prompt. Generic MS-DOS uses the colon; so do more than half of the various MS-DOS computers. However, IBM's choice is the greater than sign. Presumably, the > was chosen for those IBM PC owners who previously used CP/M and now would be using both MS-DOS (PC DOS) and CP/M-86 on their systems. CP/M's system prompt uses the >. The computer manufacturers that play "follow the leader" (IBM) will use the >; others attempting to keep their independence will use the colon instead.

To change the current disk drive (sometimes called the default or logged disk drive), type the full name of the new drive at the system prompt level and hit Enter. For example, to make drive C the current disk drive, you type:

```
A:C:
C:
```

The system prompt will then change to C: , indicating that C: is the current disk drive. To change back to A:, type A:.

The colon in the drive name is important. It tells DOS that "this is a disk drive name, not a file name."

To run a program from a different disk drive, enter the drive name before the program name. To run the CHKDSK (check disk) program from a diskette in drive B, you type:

```
A:B:CHKDSK
```

If you have a two-floppy disk system, put a diskette into both disk drives. Make sure that the CHKDSK program is on the diskette in drive B.

If your current disk drive is a hard disk, be certain that CHKDSK is on the hard disk. You should also make sure that a floppy diskette is in drive A, and that the system prompt is A:. Use the letter for the hard disk drive instead of **B:**. For example, use **C:CHKDSK** if your hard disk is drive C.

Now type the command and watch what happens. Did you see what you expected?

Although DOS was directed to get the CHKDSK program from drive B: or C:, DOS analyzed the diskette in A: because you did not tell CHKDSK which disk to analyze. Since CHKDSK did not find a disk drive name, the program used the current disk drive, A:. Unless you tell DOS otherwise, it will always use the current disk drive, not only for running programs, but also as the object of an action. In this case, the action was to analyze the disk (CHKDSK). This concept is important to remember.

To analyze either the diskette in drive B or the hard disk (C:), you have two choices. You can make the disk that holds CHKDSK the current disk drive, then run CHKDSK; or you can tell CHKDSK which disk drive to use. For the first method, you enter:

```
A:B:
B:CHKDSK
```

or

```
A:C:
C:CHKDSK
```

For the second method, you enter:

```
A:B:CHKDSK B:
```

or

```
A:C:CHKDSK C:
```

Volume Labels

DOS V2 allows you to give a volume name to a disk or diskette. The volume name appears when you ask for the directory of a disk, perform a CHKDSK (check disk), or do a variety of other things. This name is convenient for grouping or identifying diskettes. Although the volume label has no significance for DOS, the label is relevant for both disk drives and files.

When you format a disk, DOS will ask you for an 11-character volume name after DOS has formatted the diskette. This procedure is the only way to make a volume label with the provided DOS programs and utilities. Some "outside programs" label or relabel a diskette after it has been formatted, although most have been written for the IBM Personal Computer's version of MS-DOS, not generic MS-DOS.

The volume label of FORMAT is an example of one of DOS V2's "nonstandard" standard programs. FORMAT is supplied with MS-DOS by each computer manufacturer. Each manufacturer is obligated to customize FORMAT for its particular computer system and disk drive(s).

The manufacturer has some leeway in how FORMAT and the other DOS utility programs are implemented. The **/V** switch is one area in which MS-DOS and PC DOS (the IBM implementation), conflict. When the **/V** switch is used with MS-DOS, as supplied by Microsoft, the switch tells FORMAT *not* to write a volume label. If you give the **/V** switch, you will not put a volume label on the diskette.

IBM, on the other hand, chose to use the **/V** switch with PC DOS V2. This switch enables FORMAT to write a volume label. Your manufacturer may follow either Microsoft's or IBM's method for this switch.

This book covers MS-DOS as supplied by Microsoft. Your manufacturer may have implemented special features for your computer or changed the way the MS-DOS utilities work. Keep in mind that this book won't always mention these changes. The MS-DOS reference manual that came with your computer is the final word.

Unfortunately, while I was writing this book, I could run MS-DOS on only ten different computers. Most computer manufacturers followed Microsoft's recommendations in writing their utility programs. However, there were one or two exceptions. Read your MS-DOS book to find any differences between generic MS-DOS and your computer's version.

The rules for volume labels are almost identical to the rules for file names (to be discussed in the next chapter).

There are three important things to remember about volume names. Each diskette or hard disk drive can have only one volume name. You can give a volume name only with a diskette or disk that is formatted for use by DOS V2. DOS V1 knows nothing about volume names and does not handle them correctly; however, this mishandling does not cause any problems. Finally, the rules for volume names are a little less

restrictive than those for file names. A volume name is the only name
that can have a space in it.

Table 6.4
Rules for Volume Labels

1. A volume label can be one to eleven characters long.

2. Valid characters for file names include:
    A. The letters A to Z and a to z
    B. The numbers 0 to 9
    C. The special characters and punctuation symbols $ # &
        @ ! & ( ) - { } ' _ ` ~
    D. The space (which is illegal for file names)

3. These characters cannot be used in a volume label:
    A. Any control character, including escape (27d or 1Bh)
        and delete (127d or 7Fh)
    B. The characters ^ + = / [ ] " : ; , ? * \ < > | .

4. If a character is illegally used or the typed name is too long,
    DOS will ask you to enter the volume label again.

5. A drive name cannot precede the volume label.

6. FORMAT is the only DOS-supplied program that will make
    disk labels. The **/V** switch determines whether you will make
    a volume label.

7

Files and File Names

Files

In the last few chapters, we discussed disk files but never explained what *files* are. A file is a collection of similar items. The analogy that best illustrates how files work with MS-DOS is a file cabinet.

File cabinets usually have several drawers. Inside each drawer are file folders that contain facts about a particular subject: personnel, charge card receipts, bank statements, invoices, the warranty and repair record for a car or appliance, etc. Each folder covers one subject, or topic.

A file folder can be empty or hold one or more papers relating to a particular topic. For example, a folder on a checking account may contain your monthly bank statement and returned checks.

The file folders inside the file cabinet may be sorted alphabetically or according to a coding system. These arrangements help a person find a file about a particular subject. Or files can be organized according to the time of filing, with new folders placed after older ones as new topics are created. Files can also be completely disorganized. The person controlling the file cabinet chooses the filing system.

The information inside each file folder can also be organized or disorganized. The person in control of the file cabinet decides on a particular arrangement.

There's something to be said for filing systems. When a system is used properly, it works well. When new items are not filed in their proper order in the cabinet or in the file folders, straightening up the cabinet is hard work. The same is true if a drawer falls out of the cabinet and the file folders fall out. The worst that can happen is that fire or theft may permanently remove the information from the cabinet. The information is lost unless another copy of the records is stored somewhere else.

This analogy illustrates the concept of disk storage. The file cabinet is the disk drive. The drawers are the diskettes or hard disk platters. The file folder is the disk file.

Programs you use, names and addresses of your customers or friends, or orders for your products can all be placed in a disk file. For example, the electronic version of this chapter is in a disk file.

The computer's ability to handle the information restricts what can be placed in a disk file. The computer must be able to process the information electronically.

The smallest permissible file size is 0—no information at all. The length of the longest disk file depends on the amount of available disk storage. One file cannot exceed the capacity of your diskette or hard disk drive. A file stored on two diskettes is physically two files, not one. Because of the way some programs handle disk storage, they may place further restrictions on file size.

DOS allows files of up to several gigabytes (billions of bytes). The single disk drive that can hold this much information has not yet been created. Disk drives can hold almost one gigabyte. DOS' ability to handle multigigabyte files will be appreciated as video disks are used more and more for storage.

You and your programs have control of the filing system—what you put in each file and the way the data in the file is organized.

Let's complete the filing cabinet analogy. Each sheet of paper in the file folder and each item in the disk file is called a *record*. In DOS, two kinds of records can be defined: physical and logical. A physical record takes up a certain number of bytes, usually 512, whereas a logical record is a related set of items. Each record in the file has the same basic organization. For example, you may have a file containing people's names and addresses, with each name and address occupying one record in the file. Most programs use this logical definition of a record. (For more information on both types of records, look at books on system or assembly language programming, other programming languages, and data management.)

Anything can be in a disk file. How do you know what is in a particular file? There are several ways to find out. First, every disk file has a name, which is stored in the directory. Every file in a directory must have a unique name; otherwise, DOS will be confused. If you can remember the file name, you should be able to remember what is in the file. File names should be memory prompters. For example, this chapter was stored under the name CHP7.TXT.

When you look at the file names in the directory, you may spot a familiar file name. Let us say that this file holds the names and addresses of your friends. How do you display this information? That will depend on what is really in the disk file.

Your computer uses the ASCII character set. *ASCII* is the acronym for American Standard Code for Information Interchange, the standard by which your computer translates its binary ones and zeros into letters, numbers, punctuation, symbols, and special computer characters. Appendix C lists the ASCII character chart.

If the names and addresses are stored on the disk as ASCII text, you can use DOS' TYPE command. "As ASCII text" means that the program you used took each character as you typed it and put it unchanged into the disk file. TYPE assumes that each byte in the file is stored as ASCII characters. This command tells DOS to display on the video screen the information from a file. TYPE provides a quick way to see the contents of a file without having to run another program.

If your program crunches or encrypts information so that it occupies less disk space, then the information is not stored as ASCII text on a character-by-character basis. If you TYPE this file, the information will look like gibberish because TYPE displays only characters that are ASCII text. If your program transforms information when it is stored on the disk, you will need a program that can undo this transformation to show the information on the screen. Generally, the program that stores the information can reverse this encoding.

If you ask for a directory of a disk (the **DIR** command), you may see files that end with .COM or .EXE. Try to type one of these files. At the DOS system prompt (A:), type **TYPE**, a space, and the complete name of the file. Don't be alarmed by what appears on the screen. You may recognize a few words or phrases, but most of what you see will be nonsense because you just asked DOS to type a program file.

To look at a program file, you must use another program. If the program is written in interpretive BASIC (Disk or GW BASIC), you need BASIC to load and list the program. If the program is in machine language (the native language of the computer's CPU), you need a *disassembler,* a program that transforms the binary language of the computer into humanly readable instructions. (This is one of the functions of the DEBUG program provided with DOS, but DEBUG is not covered in this book.)

Remember that DOS stores bytes on the diskette. The bytes can be humanly readable text, manipulated data, or program instructions—DOS does not care which. DOS stores the bytes it is told to store; what these bytes represent is not the system's concern. DOS is like a somewhat mindless file clerk who follows your instructions.

When you want to use a file, give DOS the file name. DOS will go to the drawer (the diskette or hard disk), search for a file with the appropriate name, grab the file, and "open" it. If there is no file by the name you specified, DOS will report that fact. You can tell DOS to create a new file. If a file folder (file) by the specified name exists, the file folder will be emptied before DOS puts any new information in it. Otherwise, DOS types out a new file folder (puts the file name in the directory). You can tell DOS to start at the beginning of the file or to go to a particular location (record) in the file. On your command, DOS will pull information from the file (read) or place information in the file (write).

In all of these cases, DOS does the hard part of the work. DOS handles the mundane problems of expanding a file, creating a file, and retrieving information from or placing information in the file. You and your programs just tell DOS what to do.

The key facts to remember about files are these:

1. A file holds a related set of information.

2. The information in a file may be a program that is humanly readable (ASCII text) or may be usable only by programs.

3. You can display a file's contents on the screen with the TYPE command. If the file holds only ASCII text, you will be able to read it. If the file holds something else, the display will look like nonsense.

4. Every file you use has a name. The name must be unique for the directory that holds the file name.

5. Like a file clerk, DOS handles the storing and retrieving of files. You and your programs are responsible for what is placed in a file and how it is organized.

File Names

Generally, we think in terms of names. A *name* is a word or phrase that we associate with a person, an object, or an action. When a name is understood and accepted, two or more people can use it to identify a particular person, object, or action.

When conversing with computers, we also use names. The last chapter covered two types of names: device and disk drive. You were also introduced to volume labels. Files have names, too. The preceding section of this chapter discussed how DOS knows a disk file by its name. This name becomes the *handle,* or the common phrase that we, our programs, and DOS use when working with a file.

A file name has two parts, a *root name* and a *suffix*. The root name can have one to eight characters. The suffix, or *extension,* can be one to three characters long; it can also be omitted. The root name and suffix, if it is used, are separated by a period (.). Some restrictions apply to the characters you can use in a file name. (These restrictions are discussed later in this chapter.)

For example, the main part of the WordStar program is in a disk file called WS.COM.

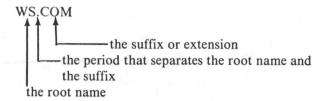

Usually, any name can be used for a file, subject to a few restrictions. Some files don't need an extension (suffix), whereas others do because of program or DOS requirements for a specific root name and/or extension. Whether or not a file needs an extension depends on what the file contains as well as its use.

When you create a file, you give it a name. If you use both a root name and an extension, the complete file name should appear as the root name, followed by a period and an extension. You should use this name whenever you copy, rename, or erase the file. If you do not use an extension, you can omit the period.

Why use an extension? In most instances, DOS or your programs force you to use a certain extension. In other cases, your programs assume that you will use a particular extension unless you indicate otherwise.

Program files use distinct extensions. If you want DOS to run a program stored on the disk, the program must have an extension of .COM or .EXE. COM is the abbreviation for a machine-language *command* file. EXE stands for a DOS-*executable* file. DOS knows from the disk file's extension that it is a program. From the file name, DOS knows what action to take to execute the program.

A batch file must have the extension BAT, or DOS will not recognize it. Batch files are covered in Chapter 10.

If you look at the sample BASIC programs provided with some versions of DOS V2, you will see that each one has the BAS extension. Unless you instruct BASIC to do otherwise, it will store BASIC programs with the BAS extension. This default extension is very convenient. To load and run the menu program called SAMPLES.BAS from BASIC, you type:

RUN"SAMPLES"

instead of

RUN"SAMPLES.BAS"

In the case discussed above, BASIC eliminates some of your work by automatically adding .BAS to the file name. When you load or save the program, BASIC will add the .BAS for you.

Table 7.1 lists some standard extensions. It reflects file name extensions that programs use automatically, extensions that files must have, and some common sense file name extensions that will help you identify files. Usually, the programs you use will determine the extensions you will need.

Table 7.1	
Common File Name Extensions	
Extension	*What It Is*
ASM	Assembler source file
BAK	Backup file
BAS	BASIC program file
BAT	Batch file
BIN	Binary program file
C	C source file
COB	COBOL source file
COM	Command (program) file
DAT	Data file
DOC	Document (text) file
DTA	Data file
EXE	Executable program file
FOR	FORTRAN source file
HLP	Help file
INT	Intermediate program file
LET	Letter
LST	Listing of a program (in a file)
LIB	Program library file
MAP	Linker map file
MSG	Program message file
OBJ	Intermediate object code (program) file
OVL	Program overlay file
OVR	Program overlay file
PAS	Pascal source file
PRN	Listing of a program (in a file)

Table 7.1 *(continued)* Common File Name Extensions	
Extension	*What It is*
SYS	System configuration or device drive file
TMP	Temporary file
TXT	Text file
$$$	Temporary or incorrectly stored file

Note the TMP, BAK, and $$$ extensions. Don't use these extensions. Your programs may create files with these extensions tha could erase useful files you want to keep.

The following notation often appears in this book:

> *d:* **filename**.*ext*

The *d:* is the disk drive name. If the file you are using is not on the current disk drive, substitute the disk drive name for the *d:*. When the d: appears as *d:*, the disk drive name is optional. When it appears as **d:**, you must give the disk drive name. There are also places where only a disk drive name is used. (This convention of showing you when the disk drive name is optional or mandatory is followed throughout this book.)

The **filename** represents the root name of a file. Because the root name is mandatory, it appears **like this** throughout this book.

The .*ext* represents the sometimes optional extension or suffix to the file name. If the extension looks like .*ext,* you should give the file name extension, if the file has one. Otherwise, skip the extension. If the extension appears as **.ext**, you must give the extension if the file has one.

Table 7.2 Rules for File Names

1. A file name includes:
    A. A root name of one to eight characters
    B. An optional extension of one to three characters
    C. A period between the root name and the extension name, if one is used
2. The characters you may use in a file name are these:
    A. The letters A to Z (Lower-case letters are transformed automatically into upper case.)

Table 7.2 *(continued)*

Rules for File Names

    B.   The numbers 0 to 9

    C.   The special characters and punctuation symbols $ # &
        @ ! & ( ) - { } ' _ ` ~

    D.   The symbols | < > \ (for DOS V1 only)

3.   The following characters cannot be used in a file name:

    A.   Any control character, including escape (27d or 1Bh) and delete (127d or 7Fh)

    B.   The four characters mentioned in rule 2-D (for DOS V2)

    C.   A space

    D.   The characters ^ + = / [ ] " : ; , ? *

4.   A device name can be part of a root name but cannot be the entire root name. For example, CONT.TXT is okay, but AUX.TXT is not.

5.   If DOS finds an illegal character in a file name, DOS stops at the preceding character and uses the legal part of the name.

6.   Each file name in a directory must be unique.

7.   A drive name and path name usually precede a file name.

Note: Microsoft BASICs are famous for not translating lower-case letters in file names into upper case. Be careful of this when programming in BASIC.

Look at the following examples of valid file names. Each file name is correctly phrased and has no illegal characters.

```
MYTEST.TXT
COMMAND.COM
PRINTP.EXE
CHRIS
AUXILARY
@12PM
CINDY#2
(CARL)
PUT&GET
GO.COM
```

LETTER.BAK
A_FILE
4-TO-GO
ABCDEFGH.IJK
2WAY.ST
$@#%&()

The file names below are not valid:

ABCDEFGHIJ.KLM	(Too many characters in the root name)
.TXT	(No root name)
TO:GO	(Cannot use a colon)
MY FILE	(Cannot have a space in the name)
PRN.TXT	(PRN is a device name)
THIS,WAY	(Cannot use a comma)
ABCD.EFGH	(Too may letters in the extension)
?ISIT.CAL	(Cannot use ? in a name)

When you use an improper (or illegal) file name, one of two things can happen, depending on what was typed and the program being used. DOS may give you an error message and not perform the operation, or DOS may perform the operation and make a strange file name for it, based on what you typed.

What DOS does will depend on the illegal characters that were used and where they were located in the file name. Generally, DOS will stop forming the root name or extension when the first illegal character is found.

The following shows what DOS will do if it encounters some of the files listed above:

Typed Name	What DOS Would Do
ABCDEFGHIJ.KLM	Use the file called ABCDEFGH.KLM
ABCD.EFGH	Use the file called ABCD.EFG

DOS will ignore any extra characters in a name. This applies to both the root name and the extension; each is treated separately. DOS will recognize the first eight characters of the root name and the first three characters after the period. In the first case, DOS ignores the characters after the eighth letter and before the period (IJ). In the second case, DOS ignores the characters after the letter G.

.TXT   Displays an error message

DOS will give an error message because a file must always have a root name.

TO:GO   Use two names, TO and GO
MY FILE   Use two names, MY and FILE
THIS,WAY   Use two names, THIS and WAY

DOS uses the colon, semicolon, space, comma, quotation mark, and equal sign to separate file names. These separators are called *delimiters*. In each case, DOS sees two names, one before the delimiter and one after it. The delimiter does not become part of the file name. What happens next depends on the program you are using. If you use the COPY command and type

COPY TO:GO MYFILE

COPY will give an error message indicating that you gave too many parameters. In this case, you gave three (the file names TO, GO, and MYFILE) when you should have given two.

A program that is expecting only one name may not check for more names. The program will simply use the file name TO and ignore the file names GO and MYFILE.

PRN.TXT   Use the printer for input or output

PRN is a device name reserved for the printer. If you use this file name, one of three things may happen. First, DOS will try to get information from the "file" (try to input from the printer), then quickly return without getting anything. What happens next depends on the program used. In most cases, the results will not be what you want.

Second, if you are putting information into this "file" and the printer is turned off or not selected, DOS will wait for twenty to thirty seconds, then give an error message telling you that PRN (the printer) is not ready.

Third, if the printer is on and selected, DOS will write the information to the printer and not save it in a disk file.

This example applies any time you use a device name as a root name. DOS will use the device rather than make a disk file. If you use names such as AUX.TXT, PRN.MAC, or NUL.COM, the result will not be what you want.

A word about uniqueness is needed here. Two files in the same directory cannot have identical names. Names must differ by a minimum of one character in the root or extension, for example, LETTER.BAK and LETTERS.BAK. Identical names confuse DOS and prevent it from knowing which file you are talking about.

If you try to change a file name to match a name already in the directory, DOS will give you a Duplicate file name or File not found error message, and will not rename the file. DOS is protecting itself and you from having two files with identical names in the same directory.

COPYing can be dangerous if you are not careful about file names. For example, suppose that the diskette in drive A has a file called MYFILE.DAT, which holds the names and addresses of your clients. The diskette in drive B also has a file called MYFILE.DAT, but it holds the names and addresses of your personal friends. If you copy MYFILE.DAT from drive A to drive B, DOS will first delete the file with your friends' names on drive B, then copy the file holding your clients' names to the diskette in drive B. You have just lost the file that holds the information on your friends.

DOS deleted the original MYFILE.DAT on drive B as a self-defense move. When you tell DOS to copy files, it checks the names. If a file in the directory you are *copying to* has an identical name, DOS will delete that file first. No warning is given and the contents of that file are lost. Then DOS copies the other file. It is wise to check both directories for duplicate file names when you are copying so that you do not inadvertently lose a good file.

The preceding lists of examples included valid and invalid file names. A valid file name is correctly phrased; an invalid name has one or more illegal characters, or too few or too many characters. There are also good and bad file names. A valid file name can be good or bad.

A *good* file name is one that means something to you and the other people who use your files. You can use the name %$!12.XYZ, but how can you tell what is in the file? Will you remember what is in it when you use it several days or weeks later?

Give each file a name that refers to how the file is used or what it contains. For example, it is easy to remember that the file FRIENDS.DAT is a data file that holds your friends' names and addresses, that CHAPT4.TXT is a text file that contains the fourth chapter of a book, and that SMITH3.LET holds the third letter you wrote to Mr. Smith. Grouping and using good file names will help you quickly locate files on your disk.

Some special characters may be used in file names. The question mark (?) and asterisk (*) have special meanings to DOS. They are known as *wild-card* or *global* characters. When you use them in a file name, your file name becomes *ambiguous*. This means that the file name you are using can match more than one file on the disk. Some programs and DOS commands allow wild cards, and others do not.

When these wild-card characters are used, DOS interprets them in the following ways:

   ?   Match any *one* character in the file name
   *   Match any number of characters in the file name

Both ? and * will match places where there are not characters in the file name. In other words, the file name WORDS? will match the files WORDS1, WORDSA, WORDST, and WORDS. In the case of WORDS, the ? matches the nonexistent character after the "S" in the file's root name.

These wild-card characters are very useful with the DIR (directory), ERASE (delete files), CHKDSK (check disk), and RENAME (change file name) commands, as well as with other programs.

The most commonly used ambiguous file name is *.*. It says to "match any number of characters in both the root name and the extension." The longhand form for this name is "????????.???." In other words, *.* matches every file in the directory. This can be the most dangerous ambiguous name when used with ERASE. The command

   ERASE *.*

will delete every file in the current directory of the disk. (DOS V2 will ask you to confirm your intent if you type this command.)

Combinations of ? and * can be used to designate groups of files. **DIR *.BAS** will show all the BASIC files in the directory. **DIR ??FILE.DAT** will display all files that start with any two characters and the word FILE as the root name and with DAT as the extension.

As an exercise, try using the wild-card characters with the directory (DIR) command. Your files will not be harmed. Experimenting with these characters will help you to feel more comfortable with them. For this exercise, use the disk or directory that you created in Chapter 3. The more files on the disk, the better.

Wild-card characters also save you from having to reissue a command several times. When you copied the BASIC files from the DOS diskette, the command with the file name ***.BAS** copied every BASIC file. Using common extensions can therefore be helpful; one command can cover many files.

Remember the caution about COPY. When you use wild-card characters, you can overwrite a good file with a completely different one if the files have the same name. When in doubt, use the DIR command to check the file names.

8

Redirection and Piping

Redirection

If you have a printer attached to your system, turn it on and make sure
that it is ready to print. You should also make sure that your system is
turned on and that DOS is running. Now type the Ctrl-P characters
(hold down the Ctrl key and tap the P key). Then type **DIR**. The
directory of the disk should print on both your screen and the printer.
Type a Ctrl-N.

The Ctrl-P sequence toggles the printer on. The Ctrl-P turns on the
printer. DOS will then print to both the video screen and the printer.
The Ctrl-N turns off this feature.

Now type **DIR >PRN**. What happened? DOS printed a directory of the
disk on the printer, but the directory did not appear on the screen. You
have just used a new DOS V2 feature, known as I/O redirection.

What is I/O redirection? Earlier, you saw that I/O stands for input and
output. *Redirection* allows you to tell DOS to change the source or
destination that DOS normally uses for input and output.

To explain this, let's look at the standards that DOS uses. *Standard
input* is the keyboard, where your programs and DOS normally expect

characters to be typed. The keyboard may be a separate unit or part of the terminal, if you use one. *Standard output* is the video screen, where programs and DOS usually display information. This may be the video screen of your terminal or a video monitor. *Standard error* is the same video screen, where your programs and DOS report any errors that occur.

When you redirect I/O, you tell DOS to get characters from or put characters to some device other than the video screen. You can tell DOS to get characters from a disk file or any other device, rather than from the keyboard. You can also tell DOS to display characters into a disk file, printer, or other device. That's what happened when you typed **DIR >PRN**. When you run a program, DOS tricks the program into thinking that it is getting or putting information on the standard devices: standard input (the keyboard), and standard output (the screen).

The following three new characters are involved in this process:

    <   Redirects the input of a program
    >   Redirects the output of a program
    >> Redirects the output of a program, but also adds to an established file

You can use these symbols only at the DOS system prompt level. You add them, along with the file or device name, to the command you type. The syntax is

    symbol devicename

or

    symbol *d:***filename.***ext*

(Although the concept of a path name has not been covered yet, you can place one behind the disk drive name and in front of the file name.)

Look at these examples:

    1. `DIR >DISKDIR`

        Redirects the output of the directory command to a disk file called DISKDIR

    2. `CHKDSK >AUX`

        Redirects the output of the CHKDSK program to the serial port

3. MYPROG <ANSWERS

    Redirects the input of MYPROG to the disk file
    ANSWERS

In the last example, MYPROG is not expecting you to type anything from the keyboard. Instead, MYPROG will get its input from the disk file ANSWERS.

When you use the > to redirect output and the output is a disk file, DOS will erase any disk file named ANSWERS in the directory, then create a new file to hold the output. In the first example, if a file in the current directory has the name DISKDIR, the file is erased first. Don't give a file name that you don't want erased with the > output redirection command.

To add the redirected output to an established file, use >>. This symbol appends the output to the file (adds to the end of the existing file), but does not erase its original contents. To change the first example and to add this additional copy of the directory to DISKDIR, you would type **DIR >>DISKDIR.**

The direction in which the symbol points will help you remember how it works. The < sign points *away* from the device or file and says to "get the input from here." The > and >> point *towards* the device or file and say to "put the output here."

The SORT.EXE. program on your DOS disk sorts the lines in a file. I created a file called WORDS that has one word on each line. To sort this file and put the sorted words in a file called SWORDS (sorted words), I type:

SORT <WORDS >SWORDS

This command tells DOS to run the SORT program, get the lines for SORT from the file called WORDS, and put the output of SORT into a file called SWORDS.

For system programmers reading this book, DOS grabs the redirection command. It never appears on the command line passed to the program.

Redirection is most commonly used to print what is normally displayed on the video screen. Redirection is also frequently used to put what would be displayed on the video screen into a disk file and to debug programs. Programmers debug programs by establishing a file of "answers" for the program, then running the program and redirecting the input to the disk file. These steps save time.

What happens to error messages when you redirect the output, say, to a printer or a disk file? If you have asked this question, you have already noted the need for standard error. If your program uses the new concept of *standard error,* the message will appear on your video screen, not at the redirected file or device. If the program does not use standard error, then the error messages will be redirected. You may not see the error messages displayed by the program because they are sent to a file, not to the video display. Fortunately, all DOS V2 commands and programs use standard error. (Microsoft BASIC V2 has provisions for standard input, output, and error.)

As an exercise, experiment first with the redirection of output. Use the > and >> symbols to redirect the output of the DIR and CHKDSK commands. Put the output to the printer and into a disk file.

Once you are comfortable with the redirection of output, make a text file that answers a program's questions. See what "responses" can come from a disk file.

Be careful. There is a bug in DOS V2.00. If you don't place enough answers in the text file to answer all of the program's questions, DOS will wait forever for the rest of the answers. The computer will actually "lock up," and the only way to free it will be to reset it. This bug exists only in V2.00. If you have a later version of DOS, such as DEC's DOS V2.05, you won't have to worry about this problem.

Piping

The concept of piping is linked to I/O redirection. A *pipe* is a computer-made line that connects two programs. The output of the first program becomes the input for the second program. A simple example is the program MORE. It displays one screen of information that it gets from the standard input, then displays the message -- More --. When you tap a key, MORE will display the next screenful of information and repeat this process until the entire input has been displayed.

MORE is a *filter,* a program that performs some manipulation on the stream of characters that come, one after the other, from the standard input and go to the standard output. A filter gets data from the standard input, modifies the data, then writes it to the standard output (screen). This modification is called "filtering" the data. MORE waits for you to press a key after a screenful of information is displayed. Filtering is the manipulation that MORE performs.

If you are confused, try the example below. It will show you the advantage of a filter like MORE.

Use the diskette containing all your DOS and sample BASIC programs. Put the diskette in drive A:, then type:

```
A:DIR | MORE
```

and hit the space bar when you see -- More --at the bottom of your screen. The character between the words DIR and MORE is the vertical bar—the pipe character.

Here's what happens when you issue the preceding command:

1. DOS executes the DIR command.

2. Instead of printing the information on the video screen, DOS places the information in a file called %PIPE1.$$$

3. DOS executes the MORE filter.

4. DOS tricks MORE into using the file %PIPE1.$$$ for input.

5. MORE performs its work and displays its information on the screen.

6. DOS deletes the file %PIPE1.$$$

You can do the same thing by issuing these three commands:

```
A:DIR > %PIPE1.$$$
A:MORE < %PIPE1.$$$
A:ERASE %PIPE1.$$$
```

Technically, *piping* is the chaining together of two or more programs with automatic redirection. Temporary files are created in the root directory of the disk for this redirection. (Don't worry about root directories yet. They are the subject of the next chapter.) The names of the files are %PIPEx.$$$ where DOS assigns a number to *x*.

I/O redirection and piping are UNIX features. Although DOS shares these functions with UNIX, DOS does not perform them in the same way. DOS uses temporary disk files; UNIX does not. When you use piping, make sure that your disk has enough room to hold the temporary file or files; otherwise, the piping will not work.

You are not restricted to using just one pipe at a time. However, only one program name may be on each side of the pipe. You can redirect the input of the first program and the output of the final program in the pipe.

Piping, like redirection, works only at the DOS command level. You cannot use piping after you have run a program. You must pipe things when you type the line to run the program.

Earlier, we saw that MORE is a filter. The following three standard filters are provided with DOS V2:

> FIND   Finds a string
> MORE Displays a screenful, then waits for a keystroke
> SORT   Is a sorting utility

Sometimes, the FIND filter is called FGREP, the name of a similar program on the UNIX operating system.

After you have finished reading this chapter, you may want to skip to the Command Summary at the back of the book to find out how each filter is used.

The following example uses two filters: SORT and MORE. As before, I have a text file called WORDS that has several words in it. Each word is on a separate line. This example sorts the WORDS file and uses MORE to display one screenful of words.

SORT < WORDS | MORE

SORT tells DOS to take the words from the file called WORDS, sort the lines (remember that I put one word to a line), and run the results through MORE to display one screenful of lines at a time. The command line also shows that the first program can have its input redirected.

The following example shows the redirection of the final program and how piping can be used with several filters:

DIR | FIND "1-01-80" | SORT > DIRS

This command tells DOS to find in the DIR command any line that has the characters "1-01-80." The result is passed to SORT, which sorts the lines and places the output into the file called DIRS. This example shows you the files created on "1-01-80," the default starting date for DOS. Try this with your diskettes or hard disk. If you have always answered the date and time questions when DOS started up, you should not have any files like this one.

The best way to learn about redirection, piping, and filters is to experiment with them. Read about FIND, SORT, and MORE. Don't forget the caution about redirection. If you redirect a program's output to a disk file with the > symbol, anything in that disk file will be erased before DOS uses it. Be careful about the file names you use.

This chapter introduced two UNIX features—redirection and piping—used by MS-DOS. The next chapter introduces a third feature, the hierarchical directory system.

9

Hierarchical Directories

If you have used DOS V1.x, or other operating systems, you know that each diskette has its own directory. Every diskette has one, and only one, directory. This system works well. If, by chance, you store the maximum number of files that a diskette or hard disk can hold (the directory is the restricting factor), you can still "wade" through the directory to find a file.

When you have a large number of files in a directory, however, the DIR command is clumsy to use. You must often pause the listing of the files so that the file you are looking for does not scroll off the top of the screen.

DOS V2 adds some new options to the directory command to aid in searching for a file. The **/W** switch gives a short, wide listing of just the file names. The **/P** switch pauses the display after a screenful of files. When you tap a key, the next screenful of files is listed. These switches allow DOS to address the problems associated with long directories.

The **/W** and **/P** options to the DIR command address only the displaying of the directory. They do not address DOS' limitations in handling the disk's directory.

The hard disk can store hundreds or thousands of files. Somehow, the hard disk's directory had to be expanded to accommodate these files. Expanding the single directory of the diskette would slow DOS down; it would have to wade internally through the directory to find a particular file. From the standpoint of performance, this simple solution does not work.

Another solution was to subdivide the hard disk into smaller disks. Many manufacturers used this approach under DOS 1.x for their hard disk systems. The physical hard disk was "logically" (apparently) divided into two or more disks. DOS saw each "logical" hard disk as a separate disk drive, each with its own name. Smaller directories and somewhat faster searches for information were therefore possible. The drawback was that the largest file a disk could hold was restricted to the size of the "logical" disk drives. In a 10M hard disk divided into two 5M hard disks, the largest single file could be 5M.

To solve the directory problem, Microsoft borrowed a concept from the UNIX operating system: hierarchical directories.

Why Hierarchical Directories?

With hierarchical directories, files can be grouped and organized on the hard disk in a manner similar to the way most people organize floppy diskettes. These diskettes are usually organized by purpose. Each diskette contains the programs and data files needed for a certain task. I have one floppy diskette for my word-processing program; another for infrequently used DOS utilities; and some diskettes for programming in BASIC, C, and machine language. I have other diskettes for my spreadsheets, and still others for creating models.

This arrangement logically groups programs and data files across many diskettes. It therefore works well for floppy diskettes.

Can files be organized the same way on the hard disk? They can if you place almost every diskette into a subdirectory on the hard disk. To find out what a subdirectory is, let's look at the directory system as a whole.

Every disk or diskette starts with one directory. It is stored on the disk and holds the names of your files as well as other information. The directory itself is really a file. Although you cannot store programs or data in the directory, DOS stores its own data in the directory file. You will understand directories better if you can visualize the directory as a file.

The starting directory of every disk is the *root* or *system* directory. It holds program or data files, but now can also hold the names of other directories. These additional directories are called *subdirectories*.

Subdirectories are also files. A subdirectory is set up just like the main or root directory and can hold the names of your files and other information. Like the root directory, subdirectories can contain the names of other subdirectories.

The amount of free space on the disk is all that restricts subdirectories. Otherwise, subdirectories can hold an unlimited number of files. As you add more files, DOS will automatically make the subdirectory bigger. This is the major difference between subdirectories and the root directory of a disk. The latter is fixed both in size and in the number of files it can hold. The subdirectory can be extended as needed, subject only to free disk space.

To understand how directories work, imagine a family tree with the founding parents as the base of the tree. Their children are branches on the tree. When the children grow up, marry, and have children, the tree grows more branches. The process continues for each generation as children marry and have children.

The root directory is like the founding parents. Just as the founding parents have children, the root directory can have subdirectories. Each subdirectory (child) of the root (parent) directory can in turn become a parent of another generation of subdirectories. As you create each new subdirectory, you create a new branch on the tree.

The terms *parent* and *child* are often used in discussing the directory system. The parent directory "owns" its child subdirectories. In turn, each child can trace itself back to its parent. A subtle fact to remember is that although a parent directory can have many child subdirectories, a child subdirectory is owned by only one parent directory. You can, therefore, trace any subdirectory back to the root directory of the disk.

Look at Appendix B. You will see a sample directory setup that illustrates how hierarchical directories work. This illustration will be used only to demonstrate how the directory system works and is not intended to show the best way to organize your files.

The root directory is at the top and contains several normal (non-directory) files: IO.SYS, MSDOS.SYS, AUTOEXEC.BAT, CONFIG.SYS, and VDISK.SYS. You may recognize some of these file names. The root directory also has two subdirectories: DOS and WORDS. The DOS side contains DOS programs and programming files. The WORDS side holds word-processing files. In this case, the parent directory owns two children: the DOS and WORDS subdirectories.

Note that there is no directory called "root." The topmost root directory uses a special symbol, the backslash (\), for its name. A backslash for the directory name signifies the root directory. Call for a directory of any DOS diskette in drive A. You will see the line

```
Directory of A:\
```

The single backslash tells you that you are getting a directory listing of the diskette's root directory.

Let's descend one level on the word-processing side. You have moved down to the WORDS subdirectory. If you are familiar with WordStar, you will recognize the names of the three WordStar program files. In addition to these files, WORDS also owns two children: the subdirectories LETTERS and CONTRACTS. The LETTERS subdirectory holds the letters that I write—in this case, letters to DEC, JACK, and DOUG. LETTERS also holds the previous revisions of the letters to DEC and JACK (the files that end in .BAK). The CONTRACTS subdirectory holds the drafts of my contracts with MEYERS and ANDRESON.

In this case, the hierarchical directories were used to organize word-processing files by purpose, such as letters and contracts.

(This example is not completely accurate. When this book was written, WordStar would not allow the use of files that were not in the same directory as the WordStar program.)

Let's move back up through WORDS to return to the root directory. Now we will move down one level to the DOS directory, which holds a copy of the Microsoft Macro Assembler (MASM1.EXE) and an assembly language file called VDISK.ASM. (This is the RAM disk program that is in the IBM DOS V2 manual on pages 14-27 through 14-34. With very minor changes, the program works with any MS-DOS system.)

DOS owns three children: BASIC, UTIL, and HARDDISK. The BASIC directory holds two versions of the BASIC language. Some DOS utility programs are in the UTIL directory, and programs for the hard disk are in the HARDDISK directory.

Did you notice that I used the term directories for subdirectories? The two terms are interchangeable if you are referring to any directory other than the root directory of a disk. The root directory cannot be a subdirectory, but any subdirectory is a directory in its own right. From this point on, the term subdirectory is used only when needed for clarity.

Let's step down one more level into the BASIC directory. BASIC owns two directories: a SAMPLES directory, which contains the sample programs provided with IBM DOS V2; and a TEST directory with some BASIC programs I created to test the disk speed (DSK-SPED.BAS) and the screen (SCRNTST.BAS) in the TEST directory.

Before we start using the new directory system, let's look at one new term, path. A *path* is a chain of directory names that tells DOS how to maneuver through the directories to find the directory or file you want. Each directory name is separated by the path character, the backslash (\).

Don't let this dual use of the backslash confuse you. Remember that if the backslash is the first character of the path, it means, "start at the root directory of the disk." Otherwise, the backslash just separates directory names. Also remember that if you need to use a file name with a path, one more path character must precede the file name.

In the chapter about file names, you learned that no two files can have the same file name in the same directory. You cannot substitute disk for directory in this rule. Because a diskette or hard disk can have several directories, the same file name can exist in several directories on the same disk or diskette. This does not confuse DOS at all.

A word of warning: Never put a program or batch file with the same name as a subdirectory in the subdirectory's parent directory. When executing a program or batch file, you use only the root name of the file. If a subdirectory's file name is identical to the root name of a program or batch in the parent directory (where the subdirectory is held), DOS may not be sure whether you are talking about the program or the directory when you execute a file or attempt to give a path name.

Look at the following rules about directories and path names. You may notice some similarities between directory names and file names. They are closely related.

Table 9.1

Rules for Directory Names

1. A directory name has the following:
    A. A root name that is one to eight characters long
    B. An optional one-to-three-character extension
    C. Aperiod separating the root name from the extension

2. Valid characters for a directory name include:
    A. The letters A to Z (Lower-case a to z letters are transformed to upper-case A to Z.)
    B. The numbers 0 to 9
    C. The special characters and punctuation symbols $ # & @ ! & ( ) - { } ' _ ` ~

3. The following characters cannot be used in a directory name:
    A. Any control character, including escape (27d or 1Bh) and delete (127d or 7Fh)
    B. A space
    C. The characters ^ + = / [ ] " : ; , ? * \ < > | .

4. You cannot create a directory called . (single period) or .. (double period). The single period (.) is shorthand for the current directory, and the double period (..) is shorthand for the parent directory.

5. A device name may be part of a directory name but may not be the entire directory name. For example, CONT is okay, but CON is not.

Table 9.2

Rules for Path Names

1. A path name can be from 1 to 63 characters long.

2. The path is composed of directory names separated by the backslash (\).

3. A drive name may precede a path name.

4. Generally, a file name may follow a path name. When this happens, separate the path name from the file name by a backslash.

5. Each drive has its own path, which DOS keeps in memory.

6. The symbols . (current directory) and .. (parent directory) are valid in a path name.

7. To start with the root (uppermost) directory, precede the path name with a backslash. (A drive name before the path does not contradict this rule.)

8. If you don't start with the root directory, DOS will start with the disk's current directory.

You will recall the notation used for a disk drive and filename earlier in this book. The new (and correct) notation is

*d:path***filename**.*ext*

This full-file specification starts with the optional disk drive name, followed by an optional path name, the mandatory root file name, and finally the optional extension. This file specification is called *filespec* in the DOS manual.

In Chapter 6, device names in the format *dev**dev* were discussed. An invisible subdirectory called **dev** is in every disk's root directory. You don't see **dev** on any diskette or disk because DOS keeps this subdirectory internally. The designation **dev** refers to the device directory and is used to specify devices. For example, **dev****prn** refers to the printer, and **dev****con** specifies the system console. Both UNIX and XENIX use device directories to handle their devices. Now DOS V2 also has this capability. To use this feature, type **dev**\\ and the device name in upper- or lower-case letters. Because the standard for UNIX is lower-case letters, they are used in this discussion.

Moving through Directories

For these examples, look at the sample disk directory in Appendix B.

We'll start at the root directory. The objective is to get to the LETTERS directory to see what I wrote to Doug (DOUG.LET), then to run CHKDSK to see how much space is left on the disk.

There are two ways to accomplish this task: the hard way and the easy way. The hard way is to move down to the WORDS directory, then to the LETTERS directory. At this point you can use the TYPE command to ask DOS to show you what is in the DOUG.LET file. TYPE displays the contents of a disk file on the video screen.

To move down to the WORDS directory, we would use the DOS V2 command CHDIR (change directories) and type:

> A:**CHDIR WORDS**

DOS checks the root directory to find a subdirectory called WORDS. If DOS finds the subdirectory, DOS will go there. Now we can move down another level to the LETTERS directory by typing the line

> A:**CHDIR LETTERS**

When you are in the correct directory, typing

> A:**TYPE DOUG.LET**

will display the characters in this file. (Because WordStar does some funny things to a file, the display will have some strange characters in it. If you type a WordStar document file, you will see what I mean.)

Now we must return to the root directory. To do this, we would type:

A:**CHDIR** \

The path given to DOS was just the backslash character, which tells DOS to move back to the root directory. Remember that when the path starts with a backslash, it tells DOS to start with the root directory. In the case of **CHDIR LETTERS**, DOS assumed that I meant to start with the directory I was in, because I did not start the path with a \ character.

The easy way to type this file would be to enter the following:

TYPE WORDS\LETTERS\DOUG.LET

The TYPE command will take a path name before the file name. DOS interprets this command to mean: look in the current directory for a subdirectory called WORDS; move into this directory and find the subdirectory called LETTERS; move into this directory and find the file called DOUG.LET; display on the video screen the characters in this file; and, finally, move back to the directory where you began.

Notice that the path character was used between each directory name. The path character was also used between the last directory name and the name of the file to be typed. You must phrase your command to DOS this way when you use a path name and a file name.

Notice the last thing DOS did when executing the TYPE command. DOS returned to the directory where the TYPE command was issued. DOS remembers the current directory for every disk that you use. If you give DOS a command to go into a different directory to get a file, DOS will get the file and then bounce back to the starting directory. The only way you can change the current directory on a disk is to use the CHDIR command.

The second objective in this example is to run the CHKDSK (check disk) program on this diskette. To do this, we would first move from the root directory to the UTIL directory by typing:

```
A:CD DOS\UTIL
```

CD is the abbreviation for the CHDIR command. Both CD and CHDIR are recognized as the same command. Here, DOS was told to move down from the root directory through the DOS subdirectory to the UTIL subdirectory. Once UTIL is the current directory, we would type:

```
A:CHKDSK
```

DOS will then load and execute the check disk program.

(Why we moved into the UTIL directory and then executed the CHKDSK program is explained in the next section.)

Some Hands-on Experience

In this session, we will use the hierarchical directory commands CHDIR (change directory), MKDIR (make a new directory), and RMDIR (remove a directory). The abbreviations for these commands are CD, MD, and RD, respectively. Because DOS recognizes both forms, the abbreviations are used here.

For this session, you will need the following:

1. A computer with two or more disk drives. One drive must be the floppy disk drive; the other can be either a floppy disk drive or a hard disk.

2.   A copy of your DOS diskette with the sample BASIC programs

3.   If you are using two floppy disk drives, you will also need one formatted diskette with the DOS operating system on it. Label this diskette "Practice Directory Diskette," or something similar.

Drives A and B are floppy disk drives. If you use a hard disk, make one important change in the directions. Whenever drive B is mentioned, change that reference to the letter of your hard disk drive. If drive A is your hard disk, you should also change the A: in the example to the name of your floppy disk drive.

For example, suppose that your hard disk is drive C. Whenever drive B is mentioned, substitute the letter C.

In the command

```
A:COPY A:*.BAS B:
```

you should change the B: to C: This will change the directions to:

```
A:COPY A:*.BAS C:
```

Keep this requirement in mind as you read the directions. If you make a mistake and have already hit Enter, type the panic button (Ctrl-C) and try the command again. Otherwise, use your backspace or Esc key and retype the command.

Step 1

Put your copy of the DOS diskette into drive A.

Step 2 (For those with two floppy disk drives)

Put the practice diskette into drive B.

Step 2 (For hard disk owners)

Make sure that you are at the root directory of the hard disk by typing **CD C:**. If your hard disk is not drive C:, substitute the appropriate letter of the hard disk drive for the letter C.

Step 3

Type **MD B:COMS**

If you have a hard disk, don't forget to change the B: to C:, or whatever is appropriate for your system.

This command makes a new subdirectory called COMS on the disk.

Step 4

Type **MD B:COMS\BDEMOS**

This command makes a new subdirectory called BDEMOS in the subdirectory COMS. At this point, the root directory owns a directory called COMS, which, in turn, owns a directory called BDEMOS. Notice that you have used a path name in this command. DOS moves down through the path name and knows that when it reaches the last name in the path (BDEMOS), it should create a new directory called BDEMOS rather than try to move again.

This path sequence can be a source of confusion for beginners. To keep the order of implementation clear in your mind, think of the path as instructions that tell DOS where to do things, and regard the last name in the path (**BDEMOS**) as the object of your action.

Step 5

Type **DIR B:**

What you see is the listing of root directory files on the disk. You may see several files if you are using the hard disk. Look for a listing that starts like this in the directory:

```
COMS <DIR>
```

The <DIR> in the directory tells you that this "file" is a directory, not a normal file. The date and time when you created the directory should also appear on this line. Make a note of the time you see on the screen. Look at the rest of the screen. Notice the line that tells you what disk drive you are using and the directory you are viewing. Study the screen for a few seconds, then move to the next step.

Step 6

Type **DIR B:COMS**

Now you will see a directory of the COMS directory. You should see just three files listed as

```
    .           <DIR>
    ..          <DIR>
   BDEMOS       <DIR>
```

The BDEMOS directory should be no surprise, but what are the period and double-period directories?

The period represents the subdirectory you are viewing. You can think of it as the subdirectory's "I exist to myself" symbol. The double period represents the parent directory of the COMS subdirectory.

Notice that the root directory does not contain these directory symbols. Only subdirectories have the period (.) and double-period (..) symbols.

If you want to tell DOS specifically to start with the directory you are using, use the period as the first character in the path. To tell DOS to move up one level of subdirectories, use the double period.

Take a look at the dates and times on the lines with the period and double-period symbols. These dates and times should be the same as those for the entries for COMS <DIR> in the root directory. When DOS creates subdirectories, it not only makes an entry in the parent directory, but also establishes the . and .. files, giving all three items the same date and time.

This command copies from drive A to the subdirectory COMS on drive B (**B:\COMS**) all the files that end with .COM (**A:*.COM**). As before, the **/V** tells DOS to verify that the copies are correct.

Notice that when a disk drive name must be specified, it appears first. The path comes next, then the file name. With **A:*.COM**, a path was not needed because we were using the directory containing all of the DOS programs we wanted. For **B:\COMS**, a disk drive (drive B) and a path (**\COMS**) were specified. Because we did not want to give the files a new name when they were copied, we did not need to use a file name.

The usual order is a drive name, followed by a path and finally a file name. If you don't need one part, such as the path or drive name, leave it out.

Step 8

Type **CD B:\COMS**

This command makes COMS the current directory on drive B.

Step 9

In this step, you will copy two files to the COMS directory. Type:

    COPY A:SORT.EXE B: /V

After SORT.EXE is copied, type:

    COPY A:FIND.EXE B: /V

Because COMS is the current directory for drive B, which is where we want to move the new programs, we do not need to specify a path name.

Step 10

Display a list of the files for the root, COMS, and BDEMOS directories on drive B. Briefly look at each directory before doing the next one. The required commands are

    DIR B:..
    DIR B:
    DIR B:BDEMOS

The first command tells DOS to step up one level of directories and show the list of files. The second tells DOS to list the files in the current directory. The final command tells DOS to list the files in the BDEMOS subdirectory.

Step 11

At this point, you will copy the BASIC programs from the DOS diskette. If they are on a different diskette, put the diskette holding the BASIC programs into drive A. To copy the BASIC program files from drive A to the BDEMOS directory, type:

COPY A:*.BAS B:BDEMOS /V

Step 12

To move to the BDEMOS directory, type:

CD B:BDEMOS

Step 13

If your system has two floppy disk drives, exchange the diskettes in drives A and B. Then call for a directory of drive A and a directory of drive B. What happened?

In both cases, you got a listing of the files in the root directory. If you change diskettes, DOS will reset the current directory back to the root directory. This way DOS does not get confused when you change diskettes.

If you have a two-floppy disk system, move back to the BDEMOS directory by typing **CD COMS\BDEMOS**.

If you are using a hard disk, make it the current disk drive. Type the letter of the disk drive, a colon, and hit Enter. In my case, the hard disk drive is C: and I would type **C:◄┘**.

Step 14

Create a new directory called TEST in BDEMOS. The command is

MK TEST

Now call for a directory of TEST. (Use the command **DIR TEST**.) You should see only the . and .. entries.

Step 15

Now copy the BASIC language into the test directory.

If the diskette in drive A does not have BASIC.COM on it, put a diskette that does have BASIC.COM into the B: drive, and copy BASIC.COM (**COPY B:BASIC.COM A:\COMS /V**). Now type:

COPY ..\BASIC.COM TEST /V

This command tells DOS to step up one directory to COMS to get BASIC.COM (Disk BASIC) and copy it into the TEST subdirectory.

(Some computers, such as the Compaq, also have a file called BASIC.EXE or BASICA.EXE on the same diskette. You do not need to copy this file now. It will be copied in a later step.)

Step 16

Type **RD TEST**

You should see an error message. RD, or RMDIR, is the remove directory command. You just told DOS to erase the TEST directory. The message you see on your screen tells you that you cannot remove a directory which is not empty. You can remove a subdirectory if the only files in it are the . or .. directory symbols. No other files or subdirectories are allowed. This is for their safety. DOS assumes that if you want to remove a subdirectory, you will empty it first.

You cannot use RD on the current directory, nor can you remove the diskette's root directory. If you try to do either, you will get a different error message.

Move to the TEST directory and try to remove it. Move back to the BDEMOS directory before going on to step 17.

Step 17

To remove the TEST directory successfully, type the following command. Make sure that you type it correctly before you hit Enter.

ERASE TEST*.*

DOS will now ask, Are you sure (Y/N)? _ This is another safety precaution. You have just told DOS to erase all files in the TEST subdirectory. Whenever you tell DOS to erase all files, DOS will ask you to confirm your request.

Because we do want to erase all of the files, answer **Y**. Otherwise, you would answer **N**, and the system prompt would return.

Next, call for a directory of TEST (**DIR TEST**). You will see that BASIC.COM was erased, but the . and .. entries remain. You cannot erase a subdirectory with the ERASE command. The only way to remove a directory is to use the RMDIR (or RD) command.

You can remove the directory by typing:

RD TEST

Now call for a DIR. You will see that the TEST directory has been removed.

Step 18

In this step, you will try to run the BASIC sample programs. To do this, load the GW (Advanced) BASIC language, then run the sample programs. I presume the name of the BASIC menu program is DEMO, but this name may be different. You might want to check your BASIC manual to be sure and substitute the correct name.

First, we'll try to invoke GW BASIC, which is in the UTIL directory. Type:

..\BASICA DEMO

Nothing happened. Why? Let's try telling DOS to start at the top, move down to COMS, and get BASIC. Type:

\COMS\BASICA DEMO

The same thing happened. The disk whirled, and the system prompt reappeared. Why?

You did not do anything wrong. You have just seen one of DOS' limitations. The system will not let you execute a program that is not in your current directory. Unlike UNIX and XENIX, which allow a path name in front of a command or program name, DOS currently does not.

You are now faced with two choices. You can copy BASICA.COM into the BDEMOS directory. This will work well, but you will have to keep a copy of BASICA.COM or Disk BASIC (BASIC.COM) in each subdirectory. This is not a very efficient way of conserving disk space.

Using the PATH command is the other choice. It allows you to tell DOS to search in other subdirectories for the programs you want to run. If DOS does not find the program in the current directory, DOS will search the directories you named in the PATH command.

Try typing:

PATH \COMS

This command tells DOS to look in the COMS subdirectory if DOS cannot find in the current directory the program you want to run. As with many other DOS commands, the last directory named in the path (COMS) is searched and no other (in this case, the disk's root directory). If you want DOS to search both, you must use the PATH command and type in the directories to be searched, separating them with semicolons. If you want DOS to search both the root directory and the COMS directory, you type **PATH \;\COMS**.

Now that the PATH command has been properly set, type:

BASICA DEMO

This should load and run GW BASIC from the COMS directory. BASIC will then load and execute the BASIC menu program.

Three Notes about the PATH Command

The PATH command can accept a disk drive name in front of the path name. Give the PATH command the name for your hard disk (such as C:, then the path) if you have one. DOS will automatically return to the hard disk drive to find a program in the specified path.

When you use the PATH command, always start paths with the root directory. This way you can be in any subdirectory on the disk and DOS will always start at the root directory. If you don't specify the root directory as the beginning of these paths, DOS will try to move down the path(s) you specified, starting with the current directory. This means that you must give a new PATH command every time you change subdirectories. The easy way is to start your paths with the PATH command and a backslash.

Unfortunately, the PATH command works only when you are running programs or batch files from the DOS system prompt. (Batch files are discussed later). Your programs must know where to get any additional program or data files. You cannot change this with the PATH command.

Some Final Thoughts

Hierarchical directories are a powerful tool for organizing your files. This system allows you to group files by purpose, which is a major benefit for hard disk owners.

Unfortunately, at the time of this writing, most programs do not take advantage of the hierarchical directories. You may have to keep your programs and data files together in a directory instead of having programs in one directory and data files in separate subdirectories. Program publishers should catch on to the hierarchical directory feature and you will soon be able to tell the program which subdirectory holds program or data files.

The biggest problem is programs with additional program files that are constantly used while the program is running. WordStar is one example. The WordStar program uses the two overlay files, WSOVLY1.OVR and WSMSGS.OVR, while it is running. Although you can put the main WordStar program file in the subdirectory used by the PATH command, you must keep a copy of the two overlay files in each subdirectory you use with WordStar.

I keep all my common programs (the DOS utilities, other disk utilities, text editors, etc.) on my hard disk in a subdirectory called BIN. The PATH command I use is **C:\BIN**. I can be anywhere and run programs or batch files that are in the BIN subdirectory. This includes the times when the floppy disk drive is the current drive.

After you use the new directory system for a while, you will probably have many subdirectories. One command will help you find all the subdirectories on a disk: CHKDSK with the **/V** (verbose) switch. Occasionally, use I/O redirection to print a copy. Keep this copy on hand; a newcomer who uses your computer will appreciate this directory road map.

If you'd like to try the *dev* subdirectory, type **DIR >\DEV\PRN** while your printer is on and selected. Typing **PRN** is easier than typing **\dev\prn**, but the latter will help you use UNIX later.

Experiment with the new directory system. Make some directories, copy files, and erase files and subdirectories while you are in a different directory. Practicing with the hierarchical directories is the best way to learn the new system.

10
Batch Commands

Up to this point, you've learned most of the facts about using DOS, but how do you make DOS use itself? Batch files are the convenient and time-saving DOS feature that makes DOS do work for you.

What Is a Batch File?

A *batch file* is a series of DOS commands that are placed in a disk file. When instructed, DOS executes the commands in the file, one line at a time. DOS treats these commands as if they were individually typed from the keyboard.

Batch files have several advantages. After the correctly phrased commands have been placed in the file, you can direct DOS to execute them by typing the batch file's root name. Once the file's commands have worked correctly, you don't have to worry about misspelling them; nor do they have to be reentered each time you execute them. You can direct DOS to perform one or hundreds of commands just by typing the batch file's root name.

137

After a batch file has been invoked, DOS will execute each command in a batch file without your intervention. You are free to do other tasks or simply to relax while the computer does the hard work. DOS does not need your attention until it has finished running the batch file. Some programs may take a long time to run. In the past, if you needed to run several long programs back to back, you started each program and waited until it was finished before starting the next one. Waiting can be tedious. Why should you wait for the computer if you don't have to?

If a program needs your input to answer a question or change diskettes, the batch file cannot do it for you. In this case, your attention will be required. You can use a batch file, however, to execute programs or commands without having to type the program or command name each time. By redirecting the program's input to a file, you can avoid having to answer manually a program's questions. (Redirection and batch files are discussed later.)

Batch File Rules

Table 10.1

Rules for Creating Batch Files

1. A batch file contains ASCII text. You may use the DOS command COPY; EDLIN, the DOS line editor; or another text editor to create a batch file. If you use a word processor, make sure that it is in the programming, or nondocument, mode.

2. The root name of a batch file can be one to eight characters long and must conform to the rules for file names.

3. The file name extension must be .BAT.

4. The batch file's root name should not be the same root name as that of a program file (a file ending with .COM or .EXE) in the current directory. Nor should the root name be the same as the name of an internal DOS command, such as COPY or DATE. If you use one of these root names, DOS will not know whether you want to execute the batch file, the program, or the command.

5. You may enter any valid DOS commands that you type at the keyboard. You may also use the parameter markers (%0-%9) and the batch subcommands.

6. To use the percent sign (%) in a command, enter the percent symbol twice. For example, to use a file called A100%.TXT, you enter A100%%.TXT. This does not apply to the parameter markers (%0-%9.)

To run batch files, the syntax is

d:filename *parameters*

where *d:* is the optional name of the disk drive holding the batch file; **filename** is the root name of the batch file; and *parameters* are the additional information to be used by the batch file.

Table 10.2

Rules for Running Batch Files

1. If you do not give a disk drive name, the current disk drive will be used.

2. To invoke a batch file, simply type its root name. For example, to invoke a batch file called OFTEN.BAT, you type **OFTEN**.

3. If the batch file is not in the disk drive's current directory, DOS will search the directory(ies) specified by the PATH command to find the batch file.

4. DOS will execute each command, one line at a time. The specified parameters will be substituted for the markers when the command is used.

5. DOS recognizes a maximum of ten parameters. You may use the SHIFT subcommand to get around this limitation.

6. If DOS encounters an incorrectly phrased batch subcommand when running a batch file, a Syntax error message will be displayed. DOS will ignore the rest of the commands in the batch file, and the system prompt will reappear.

7. You can stop a running batch file by typing Ctrl-C. DOS will display the message:

    Terminate batch job (Y/N)? _

    If you answer **Y** , the rest of the commands will be ignored, and the system prompt will appear.

    If you answer **N** , DOS will skip the current command but will continue processing the other commands in the file.

8. DOS remembers which disk holds the batch file. If you remove the diskette that holds the batch file, DOS will prompt you to place that diskette into the original drive to get the next command.

9. DOS remembers which directory holds the batch file. Your batch file may change directories at any time.

10. You can make DOS execute a second batch file, immediately after DOS finishes the first one, by entering the name of the second batch file as the last command in the first file.

AUTOEXEC.BAT

Table 10.3
Rules for AUTOEXEC.BAT

1. The file must be called AUTOEXEC.BAT and reside in the root directory of the boot disk.

2. The contents of the AUTOEXEC.BAT file must conform to the rules for creating batch files.

3. When DOS is booted, it automatically executes the AUTO-EXEC.BAT file.

4. When AUTOEXEC.BAT is executed after DOS is booted, the date and time are not requested automatically. To get the current date and time, you must put the DATE and TIME commands into the AUTOEXEC.BAT file.

To understand batch files, let's look at an example. We'll use the AUTOEXEC.BAT file on the IBM VisiCalc® diskette. When you TYPE this file, you will see:

```
VC80
```

When you boot the computer, DOS loads itself into the computer's memory. Next, DOS scans the diskette's root directory for the AUTOEXEC.BAT file. After finding the file, DOS executes the commands in the file. In this case, the only command is VC80, which loads and executes the 80-column version of VisiCalc, VC80.COM.

AUTOEXEC.BAT is a useful feature. It allows the computer operator to insert a diskette into drive A, turn on the computer, and have the computer automatically load VisiCalc. This process is called *turnkey capability*.

Another advantage is that the contents of the AUTOEXEC.BAT file can easily be modified to perform different or additional functions. If you use a 40-column video screen—a television set, for example—you will want to run the 40-column version of VisiCalc, VC40. To do this, you simply edit the AUTOEXEC.BAT file on the VisiCalc diskette by changing the VC80 to **VC40**. DOS then executes the 40-column version instead of the 80-column version.

This batch file has one slight disadvantage. No provision is made to get the current date and time. DOS date stamps each VisiCalc data file with "1-1-80," the default DOS date. When you do a directory of the disk, it is difficult to tell when a VisiCalc data file was created or changed.

Lotus Development Corporation, author of 1-2-3™, uses a slightly different AUTOEXEC.BAT file for MS-DOS computers. When you type this file, you see:

```
DATE
TIME
LOTUS
```

When DOS is booted from this diskette, DOS executes the DATE command to get the current date, and the TIME command to get the current time. DOS then loads and executes the 1-2-3 menu program, LOTUS.EXE.

You can make your own AUTOEXEC.BAT files by creating a file that contains all the commands you need to start your program. To make a batch file that automatically runs the BASIC sample program called DEMO, you put the following command in the AUTOEXEC.BAT file on a copy of the DOS diskette:

BASICA DEMO

This command loads GW (Advanced) BASIC, which then loads and executes the DEMO.BAS program. If you want to try this, format a diskette and place the operating system on it (**FORMAT /S**). Copy BASICA.COM from your DOS master diskette to the new diskette. If you have a program called BASIC.EXE, copy this file also. Then copy all the .BAS (BASIC) programs that come with the DOS diskette. Make your AUTOEXEC.BAT file and reboot the computer with the new diskette in drive A.

The concept of batch files is simple. The computer executes the commands from the file as if you typed them at the keyboard. The AUTOEXEC.BAT file is slightly different. DOS automatically executes this file when you start the computer. You can also execute this batch file at any time by typing **AUTOEXEC** while the diskette is in the current disk drive.

Batch files allow you to execute a long series of commands without having to type them in. Let's look at 1-2-3's installation batch file, INSTALL.BAT. The instructions in this file are to place a DOS system diskette in drive A, place the 1-2-3 Utility disk in drive B, then type **B:INSTALL**. The contents of the INSTALL.BAT file are listed below.

```
REM Please check that you have placed a DOS disk in Drive A.
REM Also check that the LOTUS Utility disk is in drive B.
REM If this is not the case, press [Ctrl] and C and start over.
REM If the disks are correct, press any other key.
PAUSE
A:SYS B:
COPY A:COMMAND.COM B:
COPY A:DISKCOPY.COM B:
COPY A:DISKCOMP.COM B:
COPY A:FORMAT.COM B:
COPY A:CHKDSK.COM B:
```

The first four lines of the file are displayed when the batch file is run. *REM* is short for remark, a batch command that displays whatever follows it on the video screen. The message tells you to make sure that the correct diskettes are in the right drives and to hit any key to continue or a Ctrl-C to stop the batch file.

PAUSE, another special batch file subcommand, puts a message on the screen, Press any key to continue, and then waits. When you press a key, the batch file will continue. The PAUSE subcommand is used when you want the operator to read a lengthy message or change diskettes. After the appropriate action has been taken, pressing any key on the keyboard will allow DOS to continue with the batch file.

The next command, A:SYS B:, tells DOS to place a copy of the operating system on the diskette in drive B, the 1-2-3 Utilities diskette. This will make the Utilities diskette *bootable* (able to be used to start DOS).

The command in line 7 copies the DOS command processor, COM-MAND.COM, to the 1-2-3 diskette. The rest of the commands copy some DOS utility programs to the 1-2-3 Utilities diskette.

You could execute each command separately by typing it at the keyboard. However, it is much simpler just to type **B:INSTALL** than to type the last six lines in the batch file.

Parameters

What is a batch file parameter? In DOS, many commands accept information that you type in when you run the program. COPY is one example. The name of the file you want to copy, the destination of the copy, and the additional switches you enter are all parameters. *Parameters* are the additional information that is typed on the command line after the program name. Programs can use whatever information is in the parameters.

For example, in the line

COPY FORMAT.COM B: /V

FORMAT.COM, **B:**, and **/V** are parameters. Each parameter tells COPY what to do. In this case, they tell COPY to copy the program FORMAT.COM from the default disk to the diskette in drive B and verify that the copy was made correctly.

Batch files also use parameters, but in a different way. When you type the name of the batch file, you can type additional information on the same line before you press Enter. *Markers* tell DOS where to use the parameters that you typed when you invoked the batch file. A marker starts with a percent sign (%), followed by a number from 0 to 9. These ten markers tell DOS to substitute whatever is typed on the command line for the markers.

On the command line, every word that is separated by a space, comma, semicolon, or other valid delimiter is a parameter, including the name of the program or batch file you are going to run.

The first parameter on the command line is the program or batch file name. This is the 0 parameter. Computers usually start numbering with 0. For them, 0 is a true number, not a placeholder as you may have been taught in arithmetic.

The second word on the command line is parameter 1. The third word is parameter 2, and so forth. This works well because the name of the program or batch file is often ignored when parameters are counted. The first item placed on the command line after the program or batch file name is usually considered the first parameter.

With a text editor or COPY, place the following line into a file called TEST.BAT.

echo Hello, %1

Now type **TEST**, a space, your first name, and press <Enter>. In my case, I saw:

```
A:TEST CHRIS
A:echo Hello, CHRIS
Hello, CHRIS
A:
```

The ECHO subcommand is a new batch command. It shows the text on the line following the word "ECHO" on the video display. However, the "%1" is the real object of this discussion. Why didn't DOS print "Hello, %1"?

DOS substituted your name for the "%1." Your name, the second word on the line, became the first parameter.

Now create another batch file called TEST1.BAT. This is also a one-line file.

ECHO %0 %1 %2 %3 %4

After you have created this file, type **TEST1**, a space, your name, another space, and your address. Here's how my file looked.

```
A:TEST1 CHRIS 1234 THUNDERBIRD AVENUE
A:ECHO TEST1 CHRIS 1234 THUNDERBIRD AVENUE
TEST1 CHRIS 1234 THUNDERBIRD AVENUE
A:
```

We have requested that DOS show parameters 0 through 4 on the video display. This worked out to be:

WORD: TEST1 CHRIS 1234 THUNDERBIRD AVENUE
PARAMETER: %0   %1   %2   %3   %4

What happens if you don't give enough information on the command line to fill each parameter? Let's run TEST1 again, but this time give only your first name. I saw:

```
A:TEST1 CHRIS
A:ECHO TEST1 CHRIS
TEST1 CHRIS
A:
```

DOS displayed the batch file name and my name. No other information was "echoed" on the video display. If you do not give enough parameters on the command line, DOS will ignore the unfilled markers and replace them with nothing. In this case, only parameters 0 and 1 were printed. Parameters 2, 3, and 4 were ignored.

One last comment about the 0 parameter should be made. If you give a drive name with the name of the batch command, the drive name will appear with the batch file name. If I had typed **A:TEST1 CHRIS**, I would have seen:

```
A:ECHO A:TEST1 CHRIS
A:TEST1 CHRIS
A:
```

Let's construct a batch file that takes advantage of blank parameters. Because I have a hard disk system, I use floppy diskettes for moving information between computers or for backing up information on the hard disk. Sometimes I edit a file on another computer, then move the information back to the hard disk on my computer. I don't need the copy of the file on the floppy disk after the file has been copied to the hard disk, which is drive C. Many times, I remove the file from the floppy diskette. To do this, you must:

1. Copy the file from the floppy diskette to the hard disk

2. Erase the file from the floppy diskette

You can do this with a batch file by typing just the batch file name. Suppose that you constructed a batch file called C&E.BAT (copy and erase).

```
COPY A:%1 C:%2
ERASE A:%1
```

To use this file, you type:

```
C&E oldfilename newfilename
```

where the **oldfilename** is the name of the file you want to copy to the hard disk, and **newfilename** is the new name for the file you copied (if you want to change the file name as it is being copied). Now suppose that you put a diskette containing the file NOTES.TXT into drive A and wanted to copy it to the hard disk. To do this, you type:

```
A:C&E NOTES.TXT
A:COPY A:NOTES.TXT C:
1 file(s) copied
A:ERASE A:NOTES.TXT
A:
```

In this example, ignoring empty markers worked well. Because we did not want to change the file name, we did not give a second parameter. DOS copied NOTES.TXT from drive A to drive C, then deleted the file. The "%2" parameter was "dropped" in the batch file so that the file did not get a new name when it was copied.

One of the benefits of constructing a batch file in this way is that you can also use a path name as the second parameter and copy the file from the floppy disk into a different directory on the hard disk. For example, to copy NOTES.TXT to a second-level directory called WORDS, you type:

C&E NOTES.TXT /WORDS

Line 2 from the batch file then becomes the following:

COPY A:NOTES.TXT C:/WORDS

Because WORDS is a directory name, DOS knows to copy the file NOTES.TXT into the directory WORDS, not copy the file into the current directory and name the file WORDS.

Batch Subcommands

The following is a list of the batch subcommands for DOS V2:

ECHO	Turns on or off the display of batch commands and can display a message on the screen
FOR..IN..DO	Allows you to use the same batch command for several files
GOTO	Jumps to the line after a label in the batch file
IF	Allows you to execute conditionally a command
SHIFT	Shifts the command line parameters one parameter to the left
PAUSE	Halts processing until a key is struck and optionally displays a message
REM	Displays a message on the display

ECHO

The ECHO command performs two tasks. It turns on or off the display of commands or remarks from the batch file. Turning ECHO off is useful when you don't want to display these commands or remarks. The screen stays uncluttered and does not confuse the operator.

The second part of the ECHO command displays a message on the screen. REM (remark) also does this. However, if ECHO is OFF, no REM statement will appear on the video screen. When you ECHO a message, it always appears on the video display, regardless of whether ECHO is ON or OFF. If you always want to display a message in your batch file, use ECHO rather than REM.

PAUSE

The PAUSE command stops the processing of the batch file, shows any message on the rest of the line (just like the REM subcommand), displays the message Strike a key when ready . . ., and waits for you to press a key. After you do this, DOS continues processing the batch file. The PAUSE command allows you to change diskettes while in the middle of a batch file. (The other use for PAUSE is discussed in the GOTO section.)

As mentioned above, PAUSE can also display a message. As with REM, if ECHO is OFF, the message is not displayed. The message Strike a key when ready is always displayed, whether ECHO is ON or OFF.

GOTO

GOTO is a new DOS V2 command. It allows you to jump to a part of your batch file, for example, the GOTO command of the BASIC language. The major difference is that you use a label rather than a line number with DOS' GOTO. A *label* is a line that starts with a colon (:), followed by a one-to eight-character name. The name can be longer, but only the first eight characters are significant to DOS; it ignores any additional characters.

When you enter **GOTO label**, DOS jumps to the line after the one holding the label. The batch file TEST2.BAT is shown below. It is very similar to TEST.BAT, but also contains the GOTO and PAUSE subcommands.

```
:START
ECHO Hello, %1
PAUSE
GOTO START
```

When I type **TEST2 CHRIS**, the following is displayed:

```
A:TEST2 CHRIS
A:ECHO Hello, CHRIS
A:PAUSE
Strike a key when ready . . .<space>
A:GOTO START
A:ECHO Hello, CHRIS
A:PAUSE
Strike a key when ready . . .Ctrl-C

Terminate batch job (Y/N)? Y
A:
```

The batch file starts by echoing the message with my name in it. Before continuing, the file then pauses for me to hit a key. After I do this, DOS executes the GOTO START command, then jumps to the line after **:START** and continues processing. When DOS pauses a second time, I type a Ctrl-C to stop the batch file. DOS then asks if I want to stop the batch file. I answer **Y** for yes, and DOS stops processing the batch file. With this type of batch file, the only way to stop DOS from looping continuously is to type the Ctrl-Break sequence.

This "endless looping" batch file can be used to repeat the contents of a batch file several times, but the number of times varies with each repetition. For instance, suppose that, initially, I want to put CHKDSK.COM, FORMAT.COM, DISKCOMP.COM, and DISK-COPY.COM on four diskettes, but that the next time I run this batch file, I want to copy these programs onto one, two, or as many as ten diskettes. I can write a batch file to make DOS do the hard work. For this example, we'll assume that the computer has two disk drives. The disk with CHKDSK.COM, FORMAT.COM, DISKCOMP.COM, DISKCOPY.COM, and my new batch file will be in drive A. The diskette to receive the programs will go into drive B.

First, I'll create a file called FLOPPY.BAT.

```
1    ECHO OFF
2    :START
3    ECHO Place the diskette to receive CHKDSK.COM, FORMAT.COM,
4    ECHO DISKCOMP.COM, and DISKCOPY.COM in drive B or ...
5    ECHO
6    ECHO To stop, type Ctrl-C Y instead
7    PAUSE
8    COPY A:CHKDSK.COM B: /V
9    COPY A:FORMAT.COM B: /V
10   COPY A:DISKCOMP.COM B: /V
11   COPY A:DISKCOPY.COM B: /V
12   ECHO Files are copied.
13   GOTO START
```

The GOTO subcommand in this file causes an endless loop. It can be used to copy these four programs to one diskette or to 100 or more diskettes. This file also illustrates several batch commands.

Line 1 turns off ECHO to avoid confusing the operator. When ECHO is turned off, the commands are not displayed.

Lines 2 through 6 tell the operator either to put a diskette into drive B or to type Ctrl-C to stop.

Line 7 is the PAUSE command that displays the message telling you to strike a key to continue. At this point, if you have finished copying these files, typing a **Ctrl-C** and a **Y** (to answer the question about terminating the batch job) will take you out of the batch file. I could not place a message on the line with the PAUSE command because ECHO had been turned off, and any message on the same line with the PAUSE subcommand would not be displayed.

Lines 8 through 11 transfer the four programs to the diskette in drive B.

Line 12 is the reassurance line. It tells the operator that the files have been transferred. This line performs no work whatsoever, only assures the operator that all has gone well. A reassurance line also make the computer less intimidating.

Line 13 is the GOTO line that starts the process over again.

The only batch commands we have not covered are IF and FOR..IN..DO. Both are simple when you understand how they work.

IF

The IF command is a "test and do" command. Perform the test; if it is true, carry out the instructions on the rest of the line. If the test is false, ignore the line. The command can be used to test these three conditions:

1. The ERRORLEVEL of a program
2. Whether a string is equal to another string
3. Whether a file exists

You can also test for the opposite of these conditions (test whether a condition is false) by adding the word "NOT" after "IF." Let's look at each condition and how it can be used.

The first condition is ERRORLEVEL. A better name for this would have been "exit level." ERRORLEVEL is a number that your program leaves for DOS when it is finished executing. You will notice in the Command Summary that no current DOS commands have an exit code. A 0 exit code means that everything went smoothly. Anything above 0 indicates that a problem occurred, such as no files were found to back up or restore, the operator aborted the program, or the program encountered an error. ERRORLEVEL lets you test to see if the program worked properly.

ERRORLEVEL is true if your program's exit code is equal to or greater than the number you specify in the batch file. You can think of this condition as a BASIC-like statement:

IF ERRORLEVEL >= number THEN do this

For example, if your batch file invoked PROGRAM.COM, you could test to see if the PROGRAM worked successfully by inserting the lines:

PROGRAM
IF ERRORLEVEL 1 ECHO PROGRAM DID NOT WORK!!

These lines would test the exit code of PROGRAM. If the exit code was 1 or greater, PROGRAM DID NOT WORK! would be displayed on the screen. Otherwise, nothing would be displayed. If the condition (ERRORLEVEL 1) is false (the exit code was 0 or less), the line is skipped. This example supposes that PROGRAM.COM actually gave DOS an error code, something that is not true for most programs (including most current DOS utilities).

The best way to test the ERRORLEVEL with a batch file is to use the IF statement to move around in the rest of the batch file:

PROGRAM
IF ERRORLEVEL 1 GOTO OPPS

.
.
.

GOTO END
OPPS:
ECHO PROGRAM DID NOT WORK!
END:

This batch file invokes PROGRAM. If the exit code is 1 or greater, the batch file jumps to the line after the OPPS label. If the exit code is 0 or less, the rest of the batch file is processed. Notice that the GOTO END statement is placed before the OPPS. You don't want the batch file to say PROGRAM DID NOT WORK when the program did work. If the batch file does the rest of the work correctly, DOS jumps to the end of the batch file, the END label. When DOS reaches this label, no more lines are left to execute and DOS will stop processing the batch file.

The *IF string1 == string2* is normally used with command line parameters and markers. One simple example is the batch file ISMSDOS.BAT, shown below.

IF %1 == MSDOS ECHO This computer uses MS DOS.

If you type

ISMSDOS MSDOS

you will see

This computer uses MS DOS.

If you type anything other than **MSDOS** as the first parameter, including MS DOS (a space between the MS and the DOS), you won't see anything on the screen. A better example is the batch file I have for the Computer Innovations C86 C compiler.

The C86 compiler takes four steps to compile a C program. First, you must run CC1.EXE, CC2.EXE, and CC3.EXE. Each time you run one of these programs, you must give the root name of your C program. In the final step, you "link" (bring together) your C program with the compiler's library of subroutines. A separate library of subroutines for using the 8087 numeric coprocessor is also provided.

To compile and produce a program called TEST.C, I normally type:

```
A:CC1 TEST
A:CC2 TEST
A:CC3 TEST
A:CL TEST CLIB
```

The last line runs the C86 linker and joins my program with the library of subroutines (CLIB). To eliminate having to type all of these commands each time, I created the following batch file, called CC.BAT:

```
CC1 %1
CC2 %1
CC3 %1
CL %1 CLIB
```

When I type **CC TEST**, the batch file does all the work of the previous example. However, there are two hitches. First, to use the subroutines for the 8087 coprocessor, I must tell the CL program to link the subroutines for the 8087—a file called 8087. The last line must be changed to:

```
CL %1 8087 CLIB
```

The second hitch is that sometimes I don't want to run the CL program. In this case, the last line, with the CL command on it, must be removed. The IF command allows me to do all these things with one batch file, CCS.BAT, which is shown below.

```
1   CC1 %1
2   CC2 %1
3   CC3 %1
4   IF %2 == 8087 GOTO 8087
5   GOTO END
5   :8087
6   CL %1 8087 CLIB
7   :END
```

This file is two batch files in one. As before, lines 1 through 3 compile the C program. Line 4 tests if the second parameter given on the command line is "8087." If it is, DOS jumps to the line after the 8087 label. Line 6 runs the CL program with the correct subroutine libraries. For any other second parameter, DOS jumps to the end of the batch file.

To compile the TEST program, I type **CC TEST**. To compile the program *and* use the 8087 coprocessor routines, I type **CCS TEST 8087**. If I want to compile my C program but not run the CL program, I type **CCS TEST NOLINK**. I could actually type anything but 8087 for the second parameter and have the same result.

Two important facts should be noted about this part of the IF command. DOS will give you a Syntax error and abort the batch file if you don't give enough parameters for use with the IF subcommand. For example, if I type **CCS TEST**, the "%2" in the fourth line will be changed to nothing, a null parameter. DOS does not like to compare null parameters and returns a syntax error if you try it. That's why a second parameter must be given when you use CCS.BAT; otherwise, DOS will abort the batch file when DOS encounters line 4.

DOS compares the strings literally. This means that upper-case characters are different from lower-case characters. If I invoke the earlier batch file, ISMSDOS.BAT, with the line

ISMSDOS msdos

DOS will compare the lower-case "msdos" with the upper-case "MSDOS" and decide that the two strings are not the same. The IF test would fail, and the ECHO This computer uses MS DOS. would not be performed. The same would happen if you typed:

ISMSDOS MS DOS

DOS will see two parameters, MS and DOS. The IF comparison becomes **IF MS=MSDOS** and fails the IF test.

The last part of the IF subcommand is *IF EXIST filename* . This IF tests whether the file *filename* is on the disk. If you are testing for a file on a disk other than the disk in the current drive, put the disk drive name in front of the file name (for example, B:CHKDSK.COM). IF NOT EXIST filename can also be used to check if a file is not on the disk. As with the other IF commands, the file name to check is placed after IF NOT EXIST.

FOR..IN..DO

FOR..IN..DO is an unusual and extremely powerful batch command. Its syntax is

> **FOR %%variable IN (file set) DO command**

In this example, **variable** is a one-letter name. The **%%** in front of the *variable* is important. If you use a single **%**, DOS may confuse the symbol with the parameter markers. The **command** is the command you want performed.

file set is the name or names of the disk files you want to use. Wild cards in the file names can be used. However, path names are not allowed with the file name (an exception to most DOS commands). If you have more than one file name in the **file set**, use a space between each name.

An interesting example is a simple batch file that compares file names on a copy of the DOS master diskette with those on any other diskette. Find a working DOS diskette and put the batch file CHECKIT.BAT on it.

> **ECHO OFF**
> **FOR %%a IN (*.*) DO IF EXIST B:%%a ECHO %%a is on this disk also.**

Now put the diskette with the CHECKIT.BAT file in drive A and a copy of your DOS master diskette in drive B. Type CHECKIT and watch the results.

The FOR..IN..DO command means: For every file that is specified, do the command. In this case, every specified file corresponds to all the files on drive A because we gave the wild-card file name *.*, which matches every file on the disk. This command says: If the file exists on drive B, then display the message that the file is on the DOS disk.

I wrote a simple program in C, called PR.EXE, that produces a line-numbered printout of a text file. To print all my C text files and my macro assembler files, I wrote a very simple batch file. All C text files end with a .C extension, and all macro assembler files end with an .ASM extension. The batch file created to print all of these files contained only one line:

FOR %%a IN (*.C *.ASM) DO PR %%a

The FOR..IN..DO command finds every C and assembler text file and invokes the PR command for every matching file name. With one batch file command, I was able to get a numbered listing of 35 C and assembler programs.

This last example of FOR..IN..DO developed out of necessity. I was faced with updating more than 40 DOS V1.1 diskettes to DOS V2. In the process of updating each diskette, I had to do the following:

1. Place the DOS V2 operating system on any diskette that had a copy of DOS V1.x on it

2. Remove any old versions of the DOS utility program

3. Put the V2 versions of the DOS utility programs on the diskettes

I made one assumption about the diskettes. When you do a **FORMAT /S** command, DOS places both the operating system and a copy of COMMAND.COM on the diskette. I assumed that if a diskette did not have the COMMAND.COM file on it, it didn't hold a copy of DOS either.

(This may or may not be true for your diskettes. To find out if DOS is on an old diskette, do a CHKDSK of the diskette. If CHKDSK reports two or more hidden files on the diskette, then it probably has DOS on it. Make sure that you use Version 2 of DOS with CHKDSK!)

To complicate the matter, some diskettes did not have all of the DOS utility programs. Some had FORMAT.COM; others did not. Some had CHKDSK.COM; other diskettes did not. This was true for all of the DOS utilities on all of the old diskettes. Because some of the diskettes were almost full, I did not want to copy all the DOS utilities, just replace the utilities that were already there.

One way to accomplish this task is to do a directory of each old diskette, decide whether to put DOS on the diskette, then replace the old version of the DOS utility programs with the new version. However, there is a better way.

I created a copy of my DOS V2 master diskette that held all of the utility programs (all .COM and .EXE files) and DOS itself. Then I created the following batch file, called UPDATE2.BAT:

```
 1    ECHO OFF
 2    :START
 3    ECHO Place the diskette to be updated in drive B and press a key
 4    ECHO or type Ctrl-C to quit updating diskettes
 5    PAUSE
 6    IF EXIST B:COMMAND.COM SYS B:
 7    B:
 8    FOR %%a IN (*.*) DO IF EXIST A:%%a COPY A:%%a B:
 9    A:
10    ECHO Done!
11    GOTO START
```

This batch file is powerful, yet simple. Line 1 turns off the display of batch file commands. Line 2 is the label for the endless loop. Because I had to update many diskettes, I decided to use the GOTO command and type a Ctrl-C when I was finished. Lines 3 and 4 tell the operator to put the diskette to be updated in drive B or type a Ctrl-C to exit. Line 5 pauses the batch file while the operator changes diskettes or exits the batch file.

Line 6 holds the IF EXIST filename construction. DOS checks to see if the file COMMAND.COM is on the diskette in drive B. If it is, DOS performs the SYS command that places a copy of DOS V2 on the diskette. (This is the assumption that I made. If COMMAND.COM is on a diskette, the DOS V1.1 operating system should also be on the diskette and must be replaced by DOS V2.)

Line 7 makes B: the current disk drive. Because DOS will remember where the batch file is, I can change the current disk drive (and current directory) without confusing DOS.

Line 8 does the major work. This line means: For every file on the current disk (drive B), check to see if the file also exists on drive A. If the file exists on drive A, copy the file from drive A to drive B.

Only the DOS V2 programs and this batch file can be on the diskette in drive A. DOS checks every file on the diskette in drive B. Then it checks to see if a file by the same name exists on drive A, the copy of DOS V2. If the file is on drive A, DOS copies the new V2 version of the program to the diskette in drive B. If a file on drive B is not a DOS utility, then it doesn't exist on drive A and, in this case, no file is copied.

Line 9 switches the current disk drive back to A. Line 10 is my reassurance line. Line 11 goes back and repeats the process. There is a good reason for switching the current drive from A: to B:. The first version I tried of this program used the line

FOR %%a IN (B:*.*) IF EXIST %%A COPY A:%%A B:

instead of line 8 in the batch file above. This version failed miserably. Remember that the variable **%%a** becomes each matching file name that appears in parentheses. This includes any disk drive names you have added to the file name. When I tried the program the first time, the disk file on drive B was COMMAND.COM. DOS translated line 8 into:

```
IF EXIST B:COMMAND.COM COPY A:B:COMMAND.COM B:
```

DOS correctly added the B: in front of each file name. Because A: was specified as the drive for the copy, DOS found this syntax objectionable. The batch file line didn't accomplish what I wanted, which was to test if the file was on drive A, not drive B. A little more testing produced the correct results.

This example works with any two-floppy or minifloppy diskette drive system. With some changes, you can make this file work on a computer that has a hard disk, if DOS is already on the hard disk. First, create a new subdirectory on the hard disk. Copy all the DOS utility programs, including COMMAND.COM, to this subdirectory. Edit the UP-DATE2 batch file by replacing all occurrences of A: with C: (lines 8 and 9), and all references to B: with A: (lines 3, 6, 7, and 8). Move into the new subdirectory and run the batch file. Use drive A for the floppy diskettes.

SHIFT

SHIFT is the last batch command. It moves the command line parameters one parameter to the left. SHIFT is used to trick DOS into using more than 10 parameters. The diagram of SHIFT is

$$\%0 \leftarrow \%1 \leftarrow \%2 \leftarrow \%3 \leftarrow \%4 \leftarrow \%5 \ ...$$

bit bucket

The 0 parameter is dropped. The old parameter 1 becomes parameter 0. Old parameter 2 becomes parameter 1, 3 becomes 2, 4 becomes 3, etc.

SHIFTIT.BAT is a simple example.

```
:START
ECHO %0 %1 %2 %3 %4 %5 %6 %7 %8 %9
SHIFT
PAUSE
GOTO START
```

When you type

```
SHIFTIT A B C D E F G H I J K L M N O P Q R S T U V W X Y Z
```

the first time, ECHO shows:

```
SHIFTIT A B C D E F G H I
```

After you strike a key to continue, ECHO will show:

```
A B C D E F G H I J
```

Strike any key to keep moving down the line, or hit a Ctrl-C when you want to stop.

I have yet to find a good use for SHIFT. However, don't let that stop you from experimenting with the SHIFT command.

Summary

Batch files are a helpful feature of DOS V2. You may never need to use them; on the other hand, you may find them very handy. They make your computer do the hard work for you—tedious typing, for example. Additional commands, such as IF, FOR..IN..DO, and GOTO, can make your batch files very powerful. Experimenting with batch files will show you how useful they can be.

11

Configuring DOS with CONFIG.SYS

To configure means to set up for proper operation. Configuring your system is setting up your computer for operation. There are many levels of configuration.

Your system must be physically installed. You plug your printer or modem into the computer, turn switches on and off, and construct and use various cables and adapters. This is the *physical configuration* of your system.

An *operating configuration* takes place when you set up your files in the various directories on diskettes.

Configuring the operating system usually means changing the Basic Input/Output System to meet your needs. In the past, the only way to do this was by writing assembly language routines and adding them to the BIOS. Newcomers did not find these to be easy tasks.

DOS V2 has a major feature that assists in the configuration process: CONFIG.SYS. This special text file lies in your boot disk's root directory and contains commands that can improve or alter your computer's performance and flexibility. If you don't yet have this file on your disk, don't worry. By the end of this chapter, you will have made your own CONFIG.SYS file.

In earlier chapters, you learned how DOS starts up, or boots. After DOS starts, but before the AUTOEXEC.BAT file is searched, DOS looks for the CONFIG.SYS file. What can CONFIG.SYS do for you?

The CONFIG.SYS file name really tells the story. It is a *system configuration* file, which contains commands that DOS uses to alter some of its functions and features. Certain functions can be used immediately. Others are advanced features that you should not use until you are comfortable with your computer and very experienced at using DOS.

Configuration File Commands

The following commands can be in the configuration file: BREAK, BUFFERS, DEVICE, FILES, SHELL, and SWITCHAR. When the commands are assembled alphabetically, they are arranged almost in order of least to most complex.

If you are a beginner, the command you will be most interested in is BUFFERS. DEVICE will probably be next in importance, and BREAK will follow.

BUFFERS

This command tells DOS how many disk buffers to use. Of all the commands, BUFFERS can have the greatest impact on disk performance. I strongly recommend that you take advantage of this feature.

The syntax for this command is

BUFFERS = nn

where **nn** is the number of disk buffers you want. The number can be between 1 and 99. DOS will start with two buffers, unless you indicate otherwise, but this number may vary among computer manufacturers.

A *disk buffer* is a reserved area of RAM memory that DOS sets up. The disk buffer is just a little larger than a disk sector, which is usually 512 bytes. DOS uses the extra bytes in the disk buffer to keep track of what disk sector the disk buffer is holding. When DOS is asked to get or put information on a disk that isn't the same size as a disk sector, DOS will put the information into the disk buffer. When the buffer is full, DOS writes the information to the disk. This is called *flushing* the buffer. When reading in information from the disk, DOS will go to the disk when the information inside the disk buffer is exhausted. The buffers are also flushed when you "close" a disk file in a program.

When a disk buffer becomes full or empty, DOS marks the buffer to indicate that it has been used recently. Then DOS goes through the list of disk buffers to find the one that hasn't been used for the longest time. The technical term for this buffer is *least recently used*. This process is repeated for any disk activity.

In some ways, this procedure is similar to a RAM disk, except only parts of the disk (rather than the entire disk) are kept in RAM memory. When your program reads part of a data file, DOS brings this portion of the file into the RAM memory, the disk buffer. As your program writes information to the disk, the program goes into the disk buffer first. This method also applies to program overlays like those of WordStar. DOS will load an overlay into memory and give it to WordStar as needed. DOS handles all of this activity for you.

If you don't give a BUFFERS command in the CONFIG.SYS file, DOS will start with two disk buffers. This means that DOS will hold two sections of approximately 512 bytes of memory each, for transferring information to and from the disk drives. When your program wants a piece of information from the disk, DOS will check its disk buffers first. If that information is already in one of the two disk buffers, DOS will perform a high-speed, memory-to-memory transfer. If the information is not in memory, DOS goes to the disk and transfers the sector holding the information into the disk buffer. Then DOS hands the information to your program.

If your program does a lot of *random disk work* (reading and writing information in different parts of a file), you will want more disk buffers. The more you have, the better the chance that the information DOS wants is already hidden away in memory (the disk buffer). Using disk buffers will make your programs read and write disks faster. Data base programs, which jump around a lot in a file, run much faster if you use more disk buffers.

Some programs do not benefit as much from using disk buffers. If your program does *sequential reading and writing* (reads and/or writes information from the start of the file straight through to the end), disk buffers won't help much. Because of the way you move through the file, one disk sector at a time, having many disk buffers doesn't give you any advantage. DOS still has to read each sector and then write it out.

Disk buffers are a real advantage if your program does a lot of random reading or writing of disk sectors, especially with data base or accounting programs. Some word-processing programs can benefit from many disk buffers, but many other programs will not.

How many disk buffers should you have? The answer depends on what programs you run on your computer, whether you have a hard disk, and how much memory you have.

If your day-to-day use of the computer does not involve accounting or data base work, two disk buffers may be sufficient. Otherwise, you may need to increase the number to between ten and twenty.

If you use a hard disk, start with at least three disk buffers. In most cases, the more disk buffers your computer has, the better.

The memory issue is important. Each disk buffer takes 528 bytes of memory. This means that every two disk buffers you use cost you just over 1K of RAM memory that your programs could use instead. If you have a 64K system, you don't have much space for disk buffers. If you have a 128K system, or larger, balance the number of disk buffers against the memory space your programs need. If you have over 192K, you can use as many disk buffers as you like. Otherwise, there is little sense in robbing Peter (your programs) to pay Paul (DOS' disk buffers).

DOS can have 99 disk buffers, but try to avoid having more than 20. There is a point at which DOS bogs down and becomes sluggish because it is spending so much time searching and handling the disk buffers rather than simply reading the information from the disk.

Find the number of disk buffers that is best for your system. I would advise you to start with ten disk buffers, then increase or decrease that number by one or two every day or every couple of hours. Reboot DOS and get the general "feel" of the computer's performance. Continue this process until you think the system is functioning at its optimum level. (I run twenty disk buffers on a 256K IBM Personal Computer XT and find that this number is "just right" for what I do. For my floppy-disk-based 128K Victor and 512K Compaq, ten buffers work well.)

DEVICE

The DEVICE command is the "flexibility" command for DOS V2. With this command and the proper software, you can make better use of your current computer hardware and use other hardware that your computer could not easily use before.

The syntax for the DEVICE command is

DEVICE = *d:path***filename.ext**

where *d:* is the disk drive holding the device driver file, *path* is the directory path to the device driver file, and **filename.ext** is the name of the file holding the device driver.

What is a device driver? A device is any peripheral: a disk drive, keyboard, video display, terminal, printer, etc. A *device driver* is the software that links itself to the operating system so that the computer can use the particular device. DOS itself has the software necessary to control the peripherals provided with your computer.

However, what if you want to use a device that the operating system knows nothing about? The most common example of such a device is a letter-quality printer that uses a set of special characters (*software protocols*) to regulate information coming from and going to the computer. To use such a device, DOS needs to know what type of device it is, and how to talk and listen to it. If there are two or more letter-quality printers, DOS simply will not know how to handle them.

A piece of software tells the operating system how to control the letter-quality printer. This software is the device driver. Earlier versions of DOS had few easy ways to tell DOS how to handle a new or different device. Users needed a simple method of installing into DOS the software necessary for handling different devices.

The DEVICE command in CONFIG.SYS solves this problem. Device-driver software is written according to the specifications in the DOS manual. (This software may be written by the manufacturer of the device, by you, or by a third party.) Then the device driver is placed on the boot diskette. The CONFIG.SYS file can be edited (or created) with the line

DEVICE = device driver filename

where you substitute the name of the file that holds the device driver software for **device driver filename**. When DOS boots, it loads and installs the appropriate device driver software. Then the computer system can use the device.

Most computer manufacturers provide a device driver file called ANSI.SYS. This software alters the way DOS handles the video screen and keyboard (or terminal). The ANSI.SYS file allows you to control the video screen's color and graphics from any program and to reprogram the entire keyboard if you desire.

To use the ANSI.SYS file, add the following line to your CONFIG.SYS file:

DEVICE=ANSI.SYS

Make sure that the ANSI.SYS file is in your boot diskette's root directory. When DOS boots, it will automatically load and use the new device driver.

You can load as many device drivers as you like. To date, not many device drivers have been written. If you look in the IBM DOS V2 manual, you will see an example of a device driver on pages 14-27 through 14-34. This is the device driver for a 180K RAM disk. You will need a text editor, Macro Assembler, and EXE2BIN.EXE to type in and use this driver. You may need to change the driver slightly for it to work properly with your system. The DOS V2 market is just beginning to catch on to the concept of installing device drivers through the CONFIG.SYS file.

If you use floppy diskettes, you will probably want to put the device drivers in the root directory. Hard disk users should make a special subdirectory called SYS and put the device drivers in it, out of the way of daily files. If you do this, be sure to add the directory path name in front of the device driver file name, as in **DEVICE=\SYS\ANSI.SYS**.

BREAK

CONFIG.SYS' BREAK command is identical to the normal DOS command. If BREAK is ON, DOS will check to see whether you have typed a Ctrl-C every time a program requests some activity from DOS (performs a DOS function call). If BREAK is OFF, DOS will check for a Ctrl-C only when DOS is working with the video display, keyboard (or terminal), printer, or serial interface.

For long disk-bound programs that do a lot of disk access but very little keyboard or screen work, you might want to set BREAK ON. This would allow you to break out of a long program if it goes awry.

The syntax for this command is

BREAK ON   (to turn on BREAK)

or

BREAK OFF (to turn off BREAK)

Because DOS starts with BREAK off, you do not have to give the command at all if you want to leave BREAK off.

FILES

The FILES command is new to DOS V2. The syntax is

FILES=nn

where **nn** is the number of XENIX-type files you want open at any time. The maximum number is 99, and the minimum is 5. If you give a FILES= command with a number less than 5, DOS will bump the number up to 5. DOS starts with 8 files, which are usually sufficient. Each additional file over 8 increases the size of DOS by 39 bytes.

With the introduction of DOS V2, new operating system calls were added. These new calls closely resemble those of XENIX, Microsoft's version of UNIX. Most programs use the old CP/M-like system calls to handle files. The FILES command does not affect these older programs, only newer programs that use the XENIX-like operating system calls for DOS V2. Because few programs use the new calls at this time, the default value of 8 is sufficient. As more programs begin to use the new features of DOS V2, you may have to increase this number.

The difference between the old and new ways of referencing and using files involves *handles*. With the old method, a special area of memory called *FCB*, file control block, was created. When you told DOS to get or put information in a file, you used the FCB to tell DOS what file you were working with. The FCB contained much more information than just the file name. The new method uses a *handle*, which is a two-byte number. You give DOS the name of the file or device you want to use; DOS gives you back a two-byte handle. From this point on, you use the handle, rather than the FCB, to tell DOS what file you are going to use.

If you use BASIC or don't program at all, don't worry about handles. You may need to remember them only when a program gives you an error message about not having enough handles. Then you will want to add the FILES= command to the CONFIG.SYS file.

If you write assembly language programs, read the information about handles in the DOS manual. Handles and the new DOS system calls are powerful and very useful.

SHELL

The SHELL command is an advanced CONFIG.SYS command. Don't try using it until you are very comfortable with DOS.

The syntax for SHELL is

SHELL = **filename.ext** *d:path* */P* */C string*

where **filename.ext** is the name of the new command processor, *d:* is the drive containing the command processor, and *path* is the directory path to the command processor.

The switches are

/P	Stay *permanent*
/C	Give the new command processor this *command string*
string	The command you'd like the command processor to execute immediately

The normal command processor for DOS is COMMAND.COM. You can write your own command processor if you prefer. (I am not very good at assembly language programming and would not even attempt such a task.)

There is one possible everyday use for this command. SHELL allows you to move COMMAND.COM out of your root directory and into a subdirectory. This command may help some hard disk system owners. I put COMMAND.COM in the SYS subdirectory on my hard disk and used the following in CONFIG.SYS:

SHELL=COMMAND.COM C:\SYS /P /C AUTOEXEC

It worked. I also found that when I typed the SET command, I saw the line

```
COMSPEC=C:\SYS\COMMAND.COM
```

telling me that DOS remembers where COMMAND.COM is located.

Don't try this with a floppy diskette system. Floppy diskettes can be changed, and the new floppy diskette might not have a subdirectory called SYS with the file COMMAND.COM. DOS will give you a message to put a DOS diskette into the floppy disk drive when the operating system needs to reload COMMAND.COM. Unless you insert the diskette that has the SYS subdirectory with COM-MAND.COM in it, DOS will keep insisting that you place the "right" diskette in the disk drive.

SWITCHAR

The last CONFIG.SYS command is SWITCHAR. A word of warning about this command: SWITCHAR is an undocumented function of DOS. Several DOS V2 commands do not use the SWITCHAR function and will not work properly if you reset SWITCHAR. The author of DOS, Microsoft, is not bound to support this function in any update or new release of DOS. You use this function at your own risk.

To paraphrase, SWITCHAR is here now, but may not be here later. If you use it, several programs may not function correctly. RESTORE V2.00, the IBM utility that restores files which have been backed up from the hard disk, is one program that did not work properly with SWITCHAR. I spent a very painful day learning this fact. If SWITCHAR does not exist in the next version of DOS, the user will be responsible for "fixing" any problems that the command may have caused.

SWITCHAR is actually an innocuous character. It is the switch character for the DOS commands. DOS uses the slash (/) for the switch character. With SWITCHAR, you may use a different character.

The syntax for SWITCHAR is

SWITCHAR=newcharacter

where **newcharacter** is the new switch character. Because UNIX uses the minus sign (-) as its switch character, I tried the command

SWITCHAR = -

with the CONFIG.SYS file. When you change the switch character from the slash to the minus sign, DOS changes the path separator from the backslash (\) to the slash (/). The slash is also the UNIX path separator. This change allowed me to type such lines as

COPY A:*.COM C:/BIN/BASIC -V

whose style is similar to that used on UNIX/XENIX systems. All the DOS commands seemed to work correctly. Resetting the switch character was no problem, but resetting the path separator was. Some programs were constructed to use only the normal path character, the backslash.

For example, one day I wanted to "clean up" my hard disk. First I backed up the entire hard disk with BACKUP. Then I reformatted the hard disk, erasing everything on it. When I tried to RESTORE all of the files from backup diskettes to the hard disk, I discovered that RESTORE would accept only the backslash as the path character.

I had more than six megabytes of files on backup floppy diskettes that I suddenly could not use. Every program was correctly backed up, but RESTORE would not recover the files.

If you are wondering how I got out of this predicament, I wrote a program in the C language that changed the slashes to backslashes on the backup diskettes. Then I ran RESTORE again. This time, it worked properly.

Now you know why I don't recommend that you use this undocumented function. If you do, you may have to fix any problems that occur.

Making a CONFIG.SYS File

You may want to use two major commands with DOS V2: BUFFERS and DEVICE. You can use any text editor, including EDLIN, or the COPY command to make this file. Remember that the file must be called CONFIG.SYS.

BUFFERS=10
DEVICE=ANSI.SYS

If you don't have a file called ANSI.SYS, drop this line from your CONFIG.SYS file. You may need to add other DEVICE= lines to your file. Your DOS manual will tell you how to do this.

Put this file in your DOS boot diskette's root directory. If your computer automatically boots from the hard disk, put the file in the hard disk's root directory. If you have included the second line, DEVICE=ANSI.SYS, or any other DEVICE= lines, copy the ANSI.SYS and other device driver files to the root directory of the disk you will use for booting.

After you have saved the file, use your new disk to reboot the system. DOS will read the CONFIG.SYS file and alter itself to accommodate any commands in the file.

Any changes you make in the CONFIG.SYS file will be implemented the next time you boot the system from the disk. Remember that CONFIG.SYS is used only when DOS starts up.

12

Other DOS Commands

Now that you've learned and tried many of DOS V2's commands, functions, and features, let's look at one of the system's more interesting features and some of the more general commands.

Two Disk Drives in One

Did you know that if you have a computer system with one floppy disk drive and one or more hard disks, you have two floppy disk drives? The second floppy disk drive is hidden in the first one.

It is up to computer manufacturers to implement this feature in DOS. One-floppy-disk/one-hard-disk computer systems have become very popular, and most MS-DOS computer manufacturers have implemented the "two-drives-in-one" feature.

MS-DOS knows how many disk drives you physically have. If you have only one physical floppy disk drive, DOS will treat it as two *logical* (apparent) disk drives. The A: drive is also the B: drive.

If you have a computer with one floppy disk drive, put a floppy diskette into the disk drive and type:

DIR B:

The following message should appear:

```
Insert diskette for drive B: and strike
any key when ready
```

Press a key. You will see the directory of the diskette. Now type:

DIR A:

The message

```
Insert diskette for drive A: and strike
any key when ready
```

will appear. If you press a key, the same directory will appear. There is one difference. The first line of the directory states that it is the directory of A:\ rather than B:\.

If you could perform the preceding example, you have two logical floppy disk drives, even though you have only one physical disk drive. This stretching of the one disk drive can be used with FC/FILCOM (compare files), COPY, FORMAT, and other floppy disk commands. When you specify the A: and the B:, DOS will prompt you to change diskettes at the appropriate time.

This "two-drives-in-one" system works best with FORMAT, the disk formatting program. You get one more message to change diskettes before you format. If you **DISKCOPY A: B:** or **DISKCOMP A: B:**, you will also get these messages. If you use DISKCOPY, remember to write-protect the original diskette in case you don't have the correct diskette in the disk drive at the right time.

Using the COPY program with the "two-drives-in-one" system is bothersome. You must change diskettes for each file that is copied between drive A and pseudodrive B. To copy ten files between the floppy diskettes, you must make twenty diskette changes.

The best way to copy many files between floppy diskettes and a hard disk is to create a new subdirectory on the hard disk. COPY the files to this new subdirectory from the first floppy diskette. Then change diskettes and COPY from the subdirectory back to the floppy diskette. Erase these files from the hard disk but keep the subdirectory for the next time you need to copy floppy diskette-based files between diskettes.

DIR

You have already used the DIR command several times. This command allows you to get a listing of the files in the current or specified directory. If you give a file name, with or without a wild-card character, you can get a partial listing.

DIR has two switches. **/P** pauses the listing after 23 lines of files are displayed. When you hit a key, the next set of files is displayed. This is helpful when a directory is long and you don't want the listing to scroll off the screen. The disadvantage is that the top few lines containing the volume label, disk drive name, and path leave the screen before DIR pauses. On long displays, you must use the pause-display sequence (Ctrl-S) to see these lines.

/W gives a *wide* display of the screen. Five file names are displayed per line. This switch is good for tight displays of long directories. The disadvantage is that the file size, <DIR> symbol for directories, and file date and time are not displayed.

The following examples illustrate how both switches can be used.

A>**DIR C:\BIN\UTIL**

```
 Volume in drive C is QUE DISK
 Directory of   C:\BIN\UTIL

.    <DIR>       8-06-83   5:03p
..   <DIR>       8-06-83   5:03p
SYS      COM      1408    7-23-83   5:31p
DISKCOPY COM      2444    7-23-83   5:31p
DISKCOMP COM      2074    7-23-83   5:31p
EDLIN    COM      4608    7-23-83   5:31p
RECOVER  COM      2304    7-23-83   5:31p
COMP     COM      2523    7-23-83   5:31p
DEBUG    COM     11904    7-23-83   5:31p
EXE2BIN  EXE      1664    7-23-83   5:32p
LINK     EXE     39936    7-23-83   5:32p
BASIC    COM     16256    1-01-80  11:40p
BASICA   COM     25984    7-23-83   5:31p
BATHIDE  COM      7477    7-23-83   5:39p
BEEP     COM       151    7-23-83   5:39p
BLOAD    COM     17685    7-23-83   5:39p
SM       COM     19168    7-23-83   5:39p
DISKOPT  COM      6245    7-23-83   5:39p
DL       COM     32712    7-23-83   5:39p
FH       COM     14036    7-23-83   5:39p
FILEFIX  COM      7287    7-23-83   5:39p
FILESORT COM      6924    7-23-83   5:39p
HL       COM     35607    7-23-83   5:39p
HM       COM     21590    7-23-83   5:40p
HU       COM     27490    7-23-83   5:40p
LABEL    COM      8063    7-23-83   5:40p
LPRINT   COM     24125    7-23-83   5:40p
REVERSE  COM      1298    7-23-83   5:40p
SCRATR   COM      3426    7-23-83   5:40p
SSAR     COM     23768    7-23-83   5:40p
TIMEMARK COM      7045    7-23-83   5:40p
UE       COM     26026    7-23-83   5:40p
FDISK    COM      6177    7-23-83   5:31p
BACKUP   COM      3687    7-23-83   5:31p
RESTORE  COM      4003    7-23-83   5:31p
ASCOM    COM     20096    8-04-83   9:12a
DSORTE   BAT        46    8-08-83  12:50p
        37 File(s)    3809280 bytes free
```

A>**DIR C:\BIN\UTIL /P**

Volume in drive C is QUE DISK
Directory of   C:\BIN\UTIL

```
.        <DIR>      8-06-83    5:03p
..       <DIR>      8-06-83    5:03p
SYS       COM       1408     7-23-83    5:31p
DISKCOPY  COM       2444     7-23-83    5:31p
DISKCOMP  COM       2074     7-23-83    5:31p
EDLIN     COM       4608     7-23-83    5:31p
RECOVER   COM       2304     7-23-83    5:31p
COMP      COM       2523     7-23-83    5:31p
DEBUG     COM      11904     7-23-83    5:31p
EXE2BIN   EXE       1664     7-23-83    5:32p
LINK      EXE      39936     7-23-83    5:32p
BASIC     COM      16256     1-01-80   11:40p
BASICA    COM      25984     7-23-83    5:31p
BATHIDE   COM       7477     7-23-83    5:39p
BEEP      COM        151     7-23-83    5:39p
BLOAD     COM      17685     7-23-83    5:39p
SM        COM      19168     7-23-83    5:39p
DISKOPT   COM       6245     7-23-83    5:39p
DL        COM      32712     7-23-83    5:39p
FH        COM      14036     7-23-83    5:39p
FILEFIX   COM       7287     7-23-83    5:39p
FILESORT  COM       6924     7-23-83    5:39p
HL        COM      35607     7-23-83    5:39p
Strike a key when ready . . .
```

```
BLOAD      COM    17685    7-23-83    5:39p
SM         COM    19168    7-23-83    5:39p
DISKOPT    COM     6245    7-23-83    5:39p
DL         COM    32712    7-23-83    5:39p
FH         COM    14036    7-23-83    5:39p
FILEFIX    COM     7287    7-23-83    5:39p
FILESORT   COM     6924    7-23-83    5:39p
HL         COM    35607    7-23-83    5:39p
Strike a key when ready . . .
HM         COM    21590    7-23-83    5:40p
HU         COM    27490    7-23-83    5:40p
LABEL      COM     8063    7-23-83    5:40p
LPRINT     COM    24125    7-23-83    5:40p
REVERSE    COM     1298    7-23-83    5:40p
SCRATR     COM     3426    7-23-83    5:40p
SSAR       COM    23768    7-23-83    5:40p
TIMEMARK   COM     7045    7-23-83    5:40p
UE         COM    26026    7-23-83    5:40p
FDISK      COM     6177    7-23-83    5:31p
BACKUP     COM     3687    7-23-83    5:31p
RESTORE    COM     4003    7-23-83    5:31p
ASCOM      COM    20096    8-04-83    9:12a
DSORTE     BAT       46    8-08-83   12:50p
        37 File(s)    3809280 bytes free
```

```
A>DIR C:\BIN\UTIL /W

  Volume in drive C is QUE DISK
  Directory of   C:\BIN\UTIL

.                ..              SYS     COM   DISKCOPY COM   DISKCOMP COM
EDLIN    COM   RECOVER  COM   COMP    COM   DEBUG    COM   EXE2BIN  EXE
LINK     EXE   BASIC    COM   BASICA  COM   BATHIDE  COM   BEEP     COM
BLOAD    COM   SM       COM   DISKOPT COM   DL       COM   FH       COM
FILEFIX  COM   FILESORT COM   HL      COM   HM       COM   HU       COM
LABEL    COM   LPRINT   COM   REVERSE COM   SCRATR   COM   SSAR     COM
TIMEMARK COM   UE       COM   FDISK   COM   BACKUP   COM   RESTORE  COM
ASCOM    COM   DSORTE   BAT
       37 File(s)    3809280 bytes free
```

RENAME

The RENAME command, or REN for short, allows you to change the name of a file. DOS will accept either version of this command. RENAME is fairly straightforward.

Old file name --▶ new file name

(If you have used CP/M, you will notice a big difference between CP/M and DOS. All CP/M commands put the new file name before the old file name. In DOS commands, the old file name precedes the new one. This is not necessarily good or bad. However, it is easier to use commands that change "what it is now" to "what it will be.")

The syntax for RENAME is

RENAME *d:path***oldfilename**.*ext* **newfilename**.*ext*

The *d:* for the disk drive name and *path*\ for the directory path to the file name are optional. You can skip them if the file you are renaming is on the current disk drive or in the current directory.

The **oldfilename** is the root name of the file whose name will be changed. If the file has an extension (*.ext*), you must give it.

The **newfilename** is the file's new root name. You can use the same file extension, change the extension, or drop it if you like.

Wild-card characters are allowed in the root file names and extensions. Obviously, wild cards are not allowed for disk drive names or path names. (I have not yet found a DOS command that uses wild cards for disk drive or path names.)

Notice that you give a disk drive or path name only with the original file, not with the new file name. Once DOS knows the old file name and where it is (drive and path), DOS changes the name but does not move the file. That's why you do not need to give (nor does DOS allow) a disk drive or path name with the new name.

DOS protects itself from having two files with the same name. RENAME issues an error message if you try to do this. For example, wild cards in the name could produce two files with identical names; DOS will then stop and give a Duplicate file name error message. Files before the potential duplicate name are changed, but those after the duplicate name are left unchanged. You must use RENAME again to change the names of the rest of the files.

Remember that RENAME does not touch what is in the file. RENAME changes only the file's name in the appropriate directory. DOS perceives a file whose name has been changed as a different file. You can't use the old file name with the new file, unless you change the name again.

Your programs may look for a file with a specific name. If you change that name, your programs will not be able to find the file. *You* may know that it's the same file, but your programs will not. Be careful when changing file names; you don't want to confuse your programs.

COPY

COPY copies files. You have frequently used this command in the preceding chapters of this book.

Part I

COPY can copy files between disk drives, between devices, or between a disk drive and a device. COPY demonstrates how a file can actually be a device. Instead of copying merely from a disk file to another disk file, we can copy from a disk file to a device, from a device to a disk file, or from one device to another.

Because COPY can work between disks and nondisk devices, two additional switches may be used. They are not part of the normal MS-DOS COPY program, but have been added by IBM and several other manufacturers. You should check your DOS manual to see if this discussion applies to your computer system.

These special switches are

/A   An ASCII file
/B   A binary file

ASCII files use a special character called the end-of-file marker to signal the end of a file. This character is represented as Ctrl-Z, CHR$(26), or 1A in the hexadecimal numbering system. You hit the Ctrl key and the Z key at the same time to produce a ^Z. Every program recognizes that this character marks the end of an ASCII text or data file. Anything beyond the end-of-file marker in an ASCII text file is considered invalid and is not used.

This system works well for text files because all programs respect it. However, a program or non-ASCII data file may actually use 1A. A program can use this character as an instruction or a memory location; a compressed data file (or BASIC random-access file) may use 1A for data.

COPY makes one assumption about the files it copies: a file that does not come from a character-oriented device must be a binary file. When DOS copies binary files, it uses the file size from the directory to determine how much information to copy. This means that DOS will copy everything in a disk file.

This also works for ASCII files. The end-of-file marker, which is reflected in the directory size, is copied with the rest of the file's information. Therefore, any programs that use text files will see the end-of-file marker.

Nondisk devices function differently. DOS has no way of knowing how many characters will be involved with nondisk devices. The indicator is the Ctrl-Z, the end-of-file character. When DOS receives a Ctrl-Z from the console, serial port, or other nondisk device, DOS knows that all information has been received or sent. If this convention were not followed, DOS would "wait forever" for the end of the file when copying from a device.

When copying files with COPY, you can use switches to force conditions. The **/A** switch makes DOS handle the transfer as ASCII text. For source files, DOS copies all information up to, but not including, the first Ctrl-Z. For a destination file, DOS adds a Ctrl-Z to the end. This ensures that a good end-of-file marker is placed in the file. When you copy from a device other than a disk drive, the **/A** switch is assumed.

/B is the opposite of **/A**. It tells DOS to copy binary (program) files. For source files, the file, based on its directory size, is copied. For destination files, no Ctrl-Z is added. When you copy from one disk to another, the **/B** switch is assumed.

You cannot force DOS to copy a binary file from a device. DOS will have no way of knowing when the information has ended. If you enter the **/B** with the source device name, DOS will give you an error message and halt the command.

The placement of the switch is also important. A COPY switch affects the file or device name that precedes the switch and all file/device names after it until contradicted by another switch. For example, using an **/A** after the first file/device name will affect the entire line. If, however, you use the **/A** after the second file name, the switch will affect the second file and any other files that follow.

If you are copying files between a disk drive and a device or between disk drives, you can put the switch after the word COPY, after the first file or device name, or after the second file or device name. When you put the switch after the word COPY (before the first file name) or between the first and second file/device names, the switch will affect all files (the file before the switch and all files after it). If you put the switch after the second file/device name, then only the second file/device is affected. (The only file or device name before the switch is the destination file). The first source file does not change.

There is a third switch used with COPY: **/V**, which verifies that the copies are correctly made on the diskettes. We've used this switch several times. It is standard for all MS-DOS computers. When you use the **/V** switch, you must place it after the last file name. **/V** does not affect the **/A** or **/B** switches.

Part II

COPY does more than copy files. Starting with DOS V2, COPY can also join (*concatenate*) files together on all MS-DOS computers. The syntax is

COPY */A/B d1:path1***filename1**.*ext1/A/B*
*+ d2:path2***filename2**.*ext2/A/B + ...*
d0:path0**filename0**.*ext0 /A/B/V*

where *d1:, d2:,* and *d0:* are valid disk drive names; *path1\\,* path2\\, and *path0* are valid path names; and **filename1**.*ext1,* **filename2**.*ext2,* and **filename0**.*ext0* are valid file names. Wild cards are acceptable.

The ... represent additional files in the form of *dx:pathx***filenamex**.*extx*.

Numbers also have a special notation. The file names above marked *1* and *2* are the source files. Names marked with a *0* usually represent *destination* files. The *source* files are those you want to join. The destination files (there can be more than one) will hold the product of this concatenation.

Can there be more than one destination? Yes, COPY can produce several destination files. This tricky and potentially dangerous process involves wild-card characters (which are discussed later).

Source files can be binary files (program or non-ASCII data files) or ASCII files. When you concatenate, COPY assumes ASCII files and issues an invisible **/A** switch.(Disk-based files are copied in the opposite way; they are assumed to be binary, and COPY issues an invisible **/B** switch.) Because non-ASCII files are rarely concatenated, this assumption is helpful.

The syntax of this command is

A:**COPY FILE1.TXT + FILE2.TXT + FILE3.TXT FILE.ALL /V**

The contents of FILE1.TXT are moved to a file called FILE.ALL. The contents of FILE2.TXT are added to the end of FILE.ALL, and the contents of FILE3.TXT are also appended to the end of FILE.ALL. The **/V** verifies the concatenation. Because no disk drive name or path names are given, the entire activity will take place on drive A in the current directory.

Each source file name can have a disk drive name and a path name. The normal rules about current disk drives and current directory file names apply.

Wild-card characters are allowed. They force COPY to join any file that matches the given wild-card name. With one file name, you can join several files.

If you must give additional file names, separate each one with a plus sign (+). This tells DOS that you are joining files. When necessary, give disk drive names and path names for these additional files.

The destination file, the last file name on the command line, does not have a plus sign in front of its name. If you look at the previous example, you will see that there is only a space, not a plus sign, between FILE.ALL and the last file to be concatenated (FILE3.TXT).

If you don't give an explicit destination file name (using plus signs between each file and the next file name), the same rule applies. The last file name without a + in front of it is the destination file. The first source file name becomes the destination file. DOS will add the second and subsequent files to the end of the first file.

This can be confusing. Just remember that the last file without a plus sign in front of its name is the destination file.

If you use matching wild cards for the root names of both the source and the destination names, you can create multiple destination files. For example, this line from the Microsoft DOS manual

    COPY *.PRN + *.REF *.LST

takes each root name with a .PRN extension, joins the root name with a file that has the same root name but an .REF extension, and places the joined result into a file with the same root name but with an .LST extension. This process allows you to produce multiple destination files. If you use a wild card in the destination name, you will get destination files with the same source root-file name.

Look at the following three sets of files:

```
MYFILE.PRN  APROG.PRN    FILE3.PRN
MYFILE.REF  APROG.REF    FILE3.REF
```

The previous command would combine these files this way:

```
MYFILE.PRN  + MYFILE.REF  → MYFILE.LST
APROG.PRN   + APROG.REF   → APROG.LST
FILE3.PRN   + FILE3.REF   → FILE3.LST
```

Each set of files with matching root names and the extensions .PRN and .REF is combined and placed into an .LST file.

The next example involves wild cards with a destination file that is also a source file. The following sample list shows the files in the order as they appear in the directory:

```
COUNT.C
PREP.C
DSKTIME.C
VERTEST.C
ALL.C
SWITCHAR.C
```

To combine these source program files into one destination file called ALL.C., I used the command

COPY *.C ALL.C

This will give me an error message, but the message comes too late. COUNT.C has already been placed in the file called ALL.C, followed by PREP.C, then DSKTIME.C and VERTEST.C. Now the error occurs. Why? Because the destination file is ALL.C. However, ALL.C is also a source file. Here's the sequence of events.

Because the destination file does not have the same name as the first source file, DOS copies the first source file to the destination file. This is a destructive copy because the contents of the destination file are lost before the copy is made. Each additional source file is appended to the end of the destination file.

DOS now encounters a source file name that is identical to the destination file name. DOS has already destroyed the old contents of the original destination file. There is little sense in copying this file. DOS displays the `Contents of destination lost before copy` message and proceeds to handle the rest of the source files.

When you use wild-card names, DOS scans the directory from beginning to end. When DOS encounters a file that matches the wild-card name, DOS operates on the matching file. ALL.C was not the first file in the directory. The first file was COUNT.C. DOS saw that this file name was not the same as ALL.C, the destination file, so DOS created a new ALL.C. Four files later, DOS discovered that ALL.C was also a source file. DOS has already altered this file—hence, the error message and the problem. The command used above was not correctly phrased. Unfortunately, the error message comes too late.

The correct way to copy all the .C files into ALL.C is

COPY ALL.C + *.C

The last file without a + in front of it is ALL.C. It becomes the destination file. ALL.C is also the first source file. DOS skips copying ALL.C and begins to append all other .C files to ALL.C. The second time DOS finds ALL.C in the directory, DOS will simply skip this file.

You can also change the date and time of a file when you copy it to a different disk. When you copy a file, DOS preserves the date and time. To change B:ALL.C's date and time, you type:

```
A:COPY B:ALL.C+
```

DOS will then join all the files named ALL.C (only one, in this instance) on drive B and place the results on drive A, the default disk drive in this case. The date and time are changed because the file on drive A is a "new" file, the product of all the files called ALL.C on drive B. In reality, the contents of the file are unchanged. This is a useful DOS quirk.

To "copy" the file B:ALL.C without moving it and to change the date and time, you type:

```
A: COPY B:ALL.C+,, B:
```

Two commas follow the **+**. You must specify **B:** to keep the file on drive B. **B:** is thus the destination file name. However, there is no source file to join with ALL.C. Using two commas tells DOS that there is no other file name after the plus sign.

To do the same with a program or binary data file, you must add the **/B** switch after either the word COPY or the file name. To redate COMMAND.COM, type:

COPY COMMAND.COM /B +,,

or

COPY /B COMMAND.COM+,,

Either command will work. The **/B** (binary file) switch is important. The program or binary data file may contain an end-of-file marker (Ctrl-Z). If you don't use the **/B** switch, COPY will not copy the entire file. The redated version will not run at all, run erratically, or lose data. To redate a program or data file, use the **/B** switch.

The two commas in the two examples tell DOS that it has reached the end of the source file names. DOS expects a file name after the **+** sign. The two commas ensure that DOS does not confuse the destination file name with the nonexistent additional source file name.

The COPY command above appends B:ALL.C or COMMAND.COM on the current disk drive to a file by the same name on the same drive. When no file name and extension are used for the destination, DOS will use the same file name as the source. What really happens is that DOS leaves the file in place and just changes the date and time.

Watch out for wild-card names with the previous example. If you typed

COPY B:*.* + ,, B:

DOS would combine all of the files on drive B into the first file found on B:! You probably do not want to do this.

The second part of COPY, concatenating files, may seem difficult to comprehend at first. After you have learned all the quirks and rules, however, COPY will be easier to work with.

PRINT

The PRINT command is DOS V2's *background* printing facility. It allows you to print a disk file while another program is running. In essence, PRINT is a very primitive form of *multitasking,* which is having your computer do two or more different things at the same time.

Microsoft provides PRINT, a utility program, for your computer manufacturer. It is then up to the manufacturer to furnish additional features and functions of PRINT. Thus, the command may act slightly different or have varying features, depending on the computer.

Only disk files can be background printed. Make sure, however, that you print only ASCII text files. Program or non-ASCII data files usually have control characters in them. PRINTing these files is like TYPEing them: the characters appear as nonsense. They can drive your printer crazy. Don't try to PRINT files that contain these characters.

The first time you use PRINT, DOS loads part of the PRINT program into memory and hooks the program into DOS. As a result, PRINT will steal about 3,200 bytes of memory. When you reboot DOS or turn your computer off, then on again, this memory will be freed.

PRINT works by stealing idle time from the CPU. When your programs are running, there are times when the computer is waiting for you. When a program is waiting for your response, the CPU runs in a loop. At this time, you can easily divert the CPU's attention into doing something else while it is waiting.

PRINT prints during these waiting periods. While the CPU is looping (waiting for something to happen), DOS sends the file's characters to the printer. As soon as the CPU finds something to do, DOS stops printing and continues with the program that was running before. This means that PRINT can be slow. If the CPU has little free time, not much will be printed.

One related term that you should know is queue. A *queue* is a line in which one waits for a turn. When you PRINT a file, you place it in a queue to await printing. DOS handles the queue in order. The first file in PRINT is at the front of the queue and is the first file printed. Any files that follow are printed in the order in which they were placed in the line.

The standard syntax of the PRINT command is

PRINT *d:filename.ext* */ T / C / P ...*

where *d:filename.ext* is the name of the file and the optional disk drive that holds the file. You can use wild-card characters in the file name to queue up several files to be printed with only one file name. Notice that path names are not allowed in the Microsoft version of PRINT. The file you are going to print must be in the current directory of the disk.

The three switches for PRINT are

>/T   *Terminate,* stop printing
>/C   *Cancel* the printing of the file
>/P   *Print* this file

If you don't give a switch, DOS will assume that you are going to type the **/P** switch, and will print the files on the line.

The ... in the command represent other files and switches on the command line. Several files and switches can be on the same line.

PRINT's switches work like COPY's. A switch affects the file name given before the switch and all files after it, until DOS finds another switch. For this example, assume that each file is an ASCII file on the current disk drive and in the current directory.

The following line

PRINT MYFILE.TXT /P NEXTFILE.TXT

tells DOS to background print MYFILE.TXT and NEXTFILE.TXT. The **/P** switch affects the file immediately preceding the switch (MYFILE.TXT) and the file after the switch (NEXTFILE.TXT).

The command

PRINT MYFILE.TXT /C NEXTFILE.TXT FILE3.TXT /P

cancels the printing of MYFILE.TXT and NEXTFILE.TXT and puts FILE3.TXT in the queue. The **/C** works on the file names before and after the switch. The **/P** works on the file name before the switch

(FILE3.TXT). If additional files were typed after the **/P** switch, they would also be printed.

You should familiarize yourself with the way these switches are used. The COPY command also has switches that work this way.

There is little sense in giving a file name when you use the **/T** switch. **/T** is the "stop everything you're printing and forget it" switch.

The first time you PRINT a file, DOS will ask:

```
    Name of list device [PRN]: _
```

DOS is asking you where to print its files. You can give any valid and connected device name, such as AUX, LST, etc. If you hit Enter without typing in a name, the usual list device (PRN) will be used. Don't give a device name that is not on your system, or DOS will act erratically.

This printing-destination assignment remains in effect until the queue is empty—when all the files have been either printed or canceled. When the queue empties, PRINT will ask you where you want the files printed the next time you use the command.

Changing directories does not affect PRINT. You can queue up additional files or cancel them even if you change directories. Remember, you can queue up only files that are in your current directory, but you can cancel files from anywhere.

Note some warnings about PRINT: it can handle a maximum of ten files. Don't exceed this number or PRINT will act erratically! You may lose the ability to cancel files when you change directories. The easiest way to overload PRINT is by using wild-card characters. If more than ten files match the wild-card name, you will have problems.

If you are printing a file on a floppy diskette, don't remove the diskette until PRINT has printed the file. If you remove the diskette prematurely, PRINT will print an error message on the printer and skip the file. Generally, PRINT is more gracious about handling this error than it is about the more-than-ten-file overload problem.

Don't try to use the printer again until PRINT is finished. Microsoft BASIC will give you a `Device not ready` or similar error message. If your computer has a print-screen feature (which prints on the printer the contents of the screen), screen printing should, but not always, produce a similar error message. If DOS gives you this message, type **A** to abort, and DOS will continue.

This "lockout" of the printer while PRINT is working does not always work. I have sometimes found that what you are screen printing can end up in the middle of the printing job that PRINT is currently handling. If you have exceeded the ten-file limitation of PRINT, DOS may be even more erratic.

PRINT is not a sophisticated function. It is not designed to take a file and do the underscoring, bold facing, nice margins, and page numbering that a word processor can do. PRINT prints only what is in a disk file, exactly as it is, although PRINT does expand tabs out to every ninth column. (For more information on PRINT, see the Command Summary.)

RECOVER

RECOVER works with either a complete disk or with one file at a time. The part that works with a complete disk is *dangerous* and should not be run unless you have read and heeded the precautions. This form of RECOVER works with your diskette's root directory. Don't run this part of RECOVER unless you have no alternative. Once DOS has "fixed" the root directory, you may spend hours trying to recover from RECOVER. The other part of RECOVER is not risky.

In previous versions of DOS, a disk that developed a bad sector where a file was recorded was a major problem. To bypass the bad sector, you had to copy the file to another diskette and answer "I" (for ignore) when DOS encountered the bad sector and gave an error message. The alternative was to copy the other files to a new diskette and reformat or retire the old diskette. You would then copy the file you needed from your backup diskette. This method was inconvenient, but it worked.

Hard disks and hierarchical directories are a new problem. There is no backup copy, in the physical sense, of a hard disk. You don't have a second set of hard disk platters that you can install. (However, you presumably have a backup copy of the files.)

How do you recover a file that has a defective sector on the hard disk? Subdirectories are also files. What happens if the sectors holding the subdirectories become defective? This can be a disaster. You may not be able to access any files in this subdirectory or in any subdirectory beneath it.

RECOVER is the program to use. It can make a new copy of a file, minus the data held in the bad sectors. A bonus is that the bad sectors are marked as "in use" so that they will not be used again.

The syntax for using this form of RECOVER is

RECOVER *d:path***filename**.*ext*

where *d:* is the optional disk drive name if the file is not on the current disk drive. The *path* is the optional path name to the file if it is not in the current directory. The **filename** is the root name of the file to RECOVER, and *.ext* is the extension name if the file has an extension. You may use wild cards in the file name, but only one file can be recovered at a time. If you use a wild card, DOS will use the first file in the directory that matches the wild-card name.

After RECOVER has finished, the file you were recovering will have the same name as before. The diskette's bad sectors have been "removed" from use, but the material in them is still lost. This means that the total capacity of the disk is decreased by the number of bad sectors.

The only files that you should recover are text and data files. Don't bother recovering program files. Because information has been lost from these files, a program may not run at all, or worse, run erratically when you recover it. Use a backup copy of the program instead.

Text or data files will need some editing. For text or ASCII-stored data files, use a text editor to get rid of any garbage or to add any lost information. For non-ASCII data files, you may need to write special programs to restore the file to its original state.

There is little reason for using RECOVER to recover a file. If you make daily backup copies of your diskettes and hard disk, you can usually restore your files easily from the backup copies and add or reedit them. However, you should run RECOVER to "remove" the bad sectors from the disk.

The only way to remove bad sectors is to reformat the disk. If the disk is damaged (a physical problem with the disk's magnetic coating), formatting will not help. If the disk is a floppy diskette, retire it. Hard disks, however, are difficult to retire; you'll just have to live with any flaws.

Bad sectors are a bad sign. Either the magnetic coating on the disk is damaged, or an electronics problem exists. The most likely reasons—in order—are mishandling of the diskette or hard disk; physical wear from normal use of the diskette (seldom applicable to hard disks because the recording heads do not touch the surface when the drive is in use); mechanical or electronic failure of the disk drive; electronic failure of the disk interface or controller card (the board inside your computer); a damaged disk drive cable; or bad RAM memory in the computer.

Bad RAM memory is an infrequent problem for most personal computers. If the memory holding DOS were to go bad, the machine-language instructions that the CPU executes would change. This change could cause erratic or disastrous disk performance. The best you could hope for is that nothing would happen, that DOS would just go "dead in the water." The worst that could happen is that DOS would reformat the disk or garbage directories. To prevent this, most computers use memory parity checking. When a parity error is detected, the computer "locks up." Only the work in progress is destroyed, rather than some or all of the previous work and programs stored on the disks.

A diskette that is physically worn should be retired. Look at the diskette's surface through the access holes. Dark grooves indicate wear. Dark or dull splotches can indicate spots where the diskette has been mishandled or contaminated. If you see a fold or crease, retire the diskette.

Mechanical or electronic problems are more difficult to analyze. Run the diagnostics that come with your computer. For floppy disk drives, use a diskette that has been formatted on a disk drive that you know is good. If the problem is the hard disk, back it up now!

If problems show up when you run the diagnostics, get your computer or disk drive repaired immediately, before other diskettes are harmed. If a disk drive problem shows up in the diagnostics, the entire computer should be suspected. The problem may be caused by the disk drive, the interface board inside the computer, the cable that connects the board and the disk drive, the disk drive's power supply, or possibly something else in the computer's main circuitry. Whatever the problem, have it repaired immediately.

You seldom damage electronically a diskette or hard disk when you read information from it. If the problem is not in the diskette itself and you have not written information to it, the diskette and its file are probably still intact. There is always a small chance that the disk drive wrote some garbage instead of reading information. Inspect all the diskettes that you used since you first detected a problem. Make sure that the information is intact.

Bad sectors that develop in directories are a major concern. Bad sectors in the root directory are a very serious problem. The root directory is located on a fixed part of the diskette or hard disk. DOS cannot relocate the root directory so the problem can be fatal for diskettes or hard disks. The second part of RECOVER is used to recover damaged root directories.

If the bad sector is in a subdirectory, the problem is serious but not fatal. CHKDSK can cope with this. (For more information about CHKDSK, read the Command Summary.) Before you run CHKDSK, carry out the following steps for copying your disk or diskette. If CHKDSK does not work, RECOVER is your final choice.

First, COPY and/or back up all the files you can. Use a different set of diskettes from your last backup copies. Keep your last backup diskette or diskettes intact. You may need to use them if all else fails.

If the defect is in the directory on a floppy diskette, use a different floppy from the last backup copy of the floppy diskette. Use COPY to copy each file to a second separate diskette. Then use your diskette copying program (usually called DISKCOPY) to make an exact copy of the bad diskette on a third diskette.

If the offender is the hard disk, run your backup program using a different set of media. Keep the master and last daily backup of your hard disk intact.

Because the cause of the bad sectors is unknown at this point, you should suspect any copy of the files that you have just made. Whatever caused the directory to develop bad sectors may have damaged other areas on the disk or diskette. Make sure that the files you just copied or backed up are correct before you fully trust them.

(If the problem is a subdirectory, stop and use CHKDSK now. If this does not work, use RECOVER. Either way, read the rest of the section.)

The next step is RECOVER. The syntax for this form of RECOVER is

RECOVER *d:*

The *d:* is the optional disk drive name. If the current disk drive is *not* the disk or diskette to recover, give the appropriate disk drive name.

DOS will now run through the File Allocation Table. Remember that the FAT knows the disk clusters (sectors) where the files are stored; but it does not know the previous file name, its characteristics (system, hidden, etc.), or the file's date and time.

First, DOS creates a new root directory. Then DOS begins to create files called *FILEnnnn.REC* in the root directory. The *nnnn* is a number from 0000 to 9999. Each file created by DOS represents one of the recovered files from the disk. Every file on the disk becomes a FILEnnnn.REC file, including program files, data files, and sub-directories.

Now the detective work begins. Each FILEnnnn.REC can be anything, a normal file or a subdirectory. You must now find which FILEnnnn.REC holds the information you need to keep and which FILEnnnn.REC holds information you can discard (such as sub-directories). The previous names of the files are lost. Their dates and times are also lost. The major clue to what is in a file is the file itself.

You will need several tools to help you. TYPE can type the characters in a file. This command will help you locate ASCII text files. Program files and subdirectories are different. Most of their information is displayed as gibberish. You will need DEBUG, or a similar program, to display the contents of these files.

Using these tools, locate the files you were not able to COPY or back up. COPY these files to another diskette and change their names back to what they were. Make sure that the files are intact. There is a small chance that whatever caused the directory to develop bad sectors may have affected other areas of the disk or diskette and also made these files bad.

The task of identifying each file is difficult. For practice, I took a backup copy of a good diskette and ran RESTORE on the diskette. (I had another backup copy.) I then tried to locate the files. TYPEing and using DEBUG to identify the files was a tedious process that took several hours, even though I wrote a utility or two to help.

RECOVERing a diskette or disk is very, very difficult and should be a last-resort measure. Unless your backup copies are extremely out of date, re-creating or reediting files is better than trying to RECOVER a disk or diskette.

Before you use RECOVER on a disk, practice on a copy of a diskette. This will help you gain the knowledge you will need to RECOVER the real thing, a damaged directory. If you botch up the copy, nothing is really lost.

When you try to recover a diskette that has a flawed directory, use a copy. If you make a mistake with the copy, you can make another copy of the original, flawed diskette. If you work with the flawed diskette and don't have a copy, a mistake can be costly.

Remember that this discussion does not apply to RECOVER *filename,* where RECOVER is used on a single file. Because this process works on one file at a time, the worst that can happen is that you will lose part of the file.

When you have re-created your files, reformat your diskette or hard disk. FORMAT gives a message when it cannot properly format any system area, including the areas for the boot record, the root directory, and the FAT. If you format with the **/S** switch, the areas for IO.SYS and MSDOS.SYS are also checked, and error messages are given if these areas are bad. The error messages indicate that the diskette or hard disk is currently unusable. You can retire a diskette, but hard disks must be repaired.

Remember to back up frequently. You will have less work, frustration, and anxiety if you back up your diskettes and hard disk rather than try to re-create them, using RECOVER.

File Compare

I have a great deal of respect for the way IBM and Microsoft have implemented MS-DOS on personal computers. The IBM utilities are generally easy-to-use, comprehensive, and valuable aids in managing your computer. The "IBM-only" utilities include BACKUP (for hard disk backup), RESTORE (hard disk restore), DISKCOMP (compares two diskettes), GRAPHICS (allows graphics print screening), and several others.

IBM's COMP program, however, does not win the award for the most useful program. COMP compares two files and tells you if the files are the same or different. After COMP finds ten mismatches between files, it stops the comparison.

The Microsoft program, FC or file compare, is far more useful. This is one case where generic MS-DOS is better than PC DOS.

You invoke FC by typing

> **FC** /# /B /W /C d1:path1**filename1**.ext1
> d2:path2**filename2**.ext2

where *d1:* and *d2:* are the optional names of disk drives holding the files to be compared; *path1* and *path2* are the optional directory paths to the files to be compared; **filename1** and **filename2** are the root names of the files to be compared; and *.ext1* and *ext2* are the optional file name extensions.

FC compares both text files and binary files. When it compares binary files (programs, non-ASCII data files, etc.), each file is taken on a literal, byte-for-byte basis. This method lets you know if there are any differences between the two files.

Comparing text files (for example, documents or *source code,* the humanly readable instructions for a programming language) is different. Here you want a line-by-line comparison to see if any changes have been made within a line. If a difference is found, you want to skip to where the lines match up again and then continue the comparison for further differences. You may also want to ignore multiple spaces between words; if you don't, lines that are identical (except for an additional space or two) will not match up.

The */B* switch tells FC to do a *B*inary comparison of the two files. Without this switch, FC will assume that you want a text comparison.

FC will load as much of the two files as possible into RAM memory, then begin the comparison. When FC finds a discrepancy, it is reported in the following format:

```
--ADDRS----F1----F2-
00019A0    AB    07
00019A1    45    CA
00020AB    CD    04
```

The ADDRS is the relative address of the start of each file. The address numbers start at 0000000 and can go to FFFFFFF. As you probably noticed, all numbers in a binary comparison are given in hexadecimal, base 16. F1 lists the contents of the bytes in the first file, and F2 lists what was found in the second file. In a binary comparison, FC will not give the names of the files you are comparing. You have to remember which files you asked FC to compare.

If the two files are larger than your computer's RAM memory, FC will compare as much of the files as possible, then load the next part of the two files and continue the comparison. This process is repeated until the comparison has been completed.

If FC reaches the end of one file and finds that the other file still has information, FC reports:

```
***Data left in Fx****
```

where x is the number of the file with information left over.

When FC compares text files, it tries to load as much of the two files as possible into RAM memory. If FC cannot find any matches between the sections of the two files in RAM, FC gives up and says:

```
Files are different
```

The other File Compare switches should be used only if you have not given the /B switch.

The /# tells FC how many lines to check after a discrepancy is found. The # is a number between 1 and 9. You type this number, not the "#". After FC finds a difference, it will look at # number of lines to see if the files match up again. If the files match within the specified number of lines, FC resychronizes the comparison. FC then reports the different lines, finds where the lines match up, and starts looking for more differences from the point of the matchup. If you don't give a number of lines for this, FC will look for match-ups within 3 lines of a discrepancy.

The /W switch tells FC to ignore *white spaces* (extra spaces or tab characters) in the two files. Remember, computers are very literal in making comparisons. For the two lines

    This is a line of text.
    This is a   line of   text.

FC checks the lines on a character-by-character basis. Normally, FC says that these two lines are different, even through they contain the same characters but have extra spaces between the words. If you use the /W switch, FC ignores the extra spaces or tab characters between the words and says that the two lines are the same. This switch is helpful in comparing WordStar files because when WordStar is in document mode, extra spaces are put into a line to right-justify text.

The /C switch tells FC to ignore the difference between upper- and lower-case letters. As you recall, computers know that a capital C is not the same as a small "c." We may not care about the difference between upper- and lower-case letters, but computers do. To tell FC that it should treat all letters the same way and ignore this difference, use the /C switch.

With FC, discrepancies between two text files are reported in a manner that is different from that for binary files. FC gives the names of the files you are comparing, the lines that are different, then the lines where rematching was started. The following example comes from two earlier versions of this chapter:

```
A:FC /W /C /9 MSDCHP12.TXT MSDCHP12.BAK
----------a:msdchp12.txt
/W gives a wide display of the screen. Five file names are
displayed per line. This switch is good for tight
----------a:msdchp12.bak
The /W switch gives a wide display of the screen. Five file names
are displayed per line. This switch is good for tight
------------------------------------------------
----------a:msdchp12.txt
ASCII files use a special character called the end-of-file marker
to signal the end of a file. This character is represented as
----------a:msdchp12.bak
ASCII files use a special character (the end-of-file marker)
to signal the end of a file. This character is represented as
------------------------------------------------
```

Experiment with FC. Try creating a short text file. Put some extra spaces or tabs between some of the words. Then make a copy of the file and give it a new name. Edit the new file by adding a new line or two of text and change one or two words on a line. Also change the word spacing slightly on one or two lines. Then run FC several times, using different switches to see the effect of each. Remember that the switches must come between the word FC and the file names. After a short time, you will find that FC is a useful utility for file comparison.

You should not need to run FC often. To find the most current revision of a file, the date and time stamp in the disk's directory should give you most of the information you will need. If the date and time stamp does not help, however, FC can.

13
Final Thoughts

This book covered most DOS commands, features, and functions. You learned how to use DOS effectively, had some hands-on experience, and should now feel comfortable with your system.

No book on DOS can cover everything about it. This book is no exception. For example, we did not examine:

- Special commands for your hard disk

- How to use the ANSI terminal code for DOS

- LINK, the DOS linker; CREF, the cross-reference program; EDLIN, the line editor; or other programming tools for DOS

- The DOS system calls

- Some technical details of DOS

- Every switch (option) available for all DOS programs

The ANSI terminal codes were mentioned briefly in this book. These codes are for programmers and are listed in the DOS manual. The codes do not work with Microsoft Disk or GW BASIC. The following is a hint for those planning to use the codes in programs: when you give a number, give the ASCII, not the binary. If you want to print 42, print "42," not the equivalent of CHR$(42).

DOS system calls and the more technical information are inappropriate for a user's guide. Programmers (but usually not BASIC programmers) use these calls to control DOS. You can find additional information on DOS system calls in your DOS technical manual.

Some additional switches are covered in the Command Summary at the end of this book. Read this section and return to it when you are stuck on a command. Many helpful hints are listed in this section.

Dangerous Commands

Several times in this book, commands were labeled as "dangerous." These commands are not dangerous to you personally, but to the data recorded on your disk. If not properly used, the commands can erase or destroy files.

It takes time and work to record anything on a disk. The data may take only seconds to copy or change, but it could represent the heart of your business or personal livelihood. Common sense should tell you that this data must be protected. By applying that common sense to the operation of your computer, you should have few problems.

FORMAT and DISKCOPY are the two most "dangerous" commands. If you FORMAT or DISKCOPY the wrong diskette, you can destroy many files in just a few seconds. ERASE is also dangerous because it deletes files. Although these three commands appear to do the same thing, there are differences among them.

When you ERASE a file, you don't remove it from the disk. DOS simply marks the directory entry holding this file name as "erased" and frees the sectors that held this file in the FAT. With the proper programs, you can unERASE a file if you have not added anything else to the disk. Once you add or extend a file, it can take the directory entry for your erased file or use the sectors that held your file. If you inadvertently erase a file, you can use program tools to recover it. Just don't put anything else on this diskette until you run the unERASE program.

FORMAT and DISKCOPY record new information on the entire diskette. When you format a diskette, dummy information is recorded. When you DISKCOPY, every bit of information from the first diskette is copied to the second one. If you use either FORMAT or DISKCOPY on a diskette that has useful information, the information will no longer be usable; it is lost.

If you run FORMAT while the hard disk is the current disk drive and don't give a disk drive name to FORMAT, you will have problems. For instance, my hard disk is drive C. If I run FORMAT while drive C is the current disk drive, the following message will appear:

```
Strike any key to begin formatting drive C:
```

If I hit a key, I will format the hard disk and lose up to 10 megabytes of information. If you see this message on your screen and want to lose the information, hit any key. If this is not what you want, carefully press Ctrl-C to stop the command.

COPY can be troublesome. If you COPY an old version of a file to the diskette holding a newer version and don't change the file name, you will be in trouble. You have just destroyed the new version of your file. Be cautious when you COPY.

The RECOVER command can also be troublesome. For a single file, RECOVER is easy and simple to use. When RECOVER is used to recover a complete disk, however, you may need hours or days to recover. Practice before using RECOVER on "live" disks.

Hard Disks

To those of you who own a hard disk computer system, I apologize. You have had to do things slightly differently throughout most of this book. I would have liked to have given you examples of how to back up and restore your hard disk, but generic MS-DOS does not include a hard disk backup and restore program. Because the biggest problem with hard disks is backup and because there are no standard programs for handling backup, I cannot provide you with an illustrated, step-by-step description for backing up your hard disk.

I can, however, give you some advice.

Backing Up a Hard Disk

Back up your hard disk frequently. If you can back up files using the disk's directory date option, what follows is a procedure for efficiently backing up your disk.

First, you will need three sets of backup media: diskettes, tapes, or whatever your system uses. Each set should be able to hold the entire hard disk and should be kept in a separate box, or organized so that you know which disk or tape is from a particular set.

Don't forget that when I talk about backing up your hard disk, you will need to back up all the files in all the subdirectories. Presumably, your backup program can handle this.

Once every month or so, back up the entire hard disk, using the first set of media. Try to do this on the same date each month.

Each day, or every couple of days, back up the hard disk, using the date option. The second and third sets of media should be used for this procedure, rotating the sets each time. When you back up by date, the date you give should be the day you backed up the entire hard disk. That way you will back up each file that has changed since the "master" backup of the hard disk.

The monthly backup takes the most time, although the daily backup takes longer each time you do it. Once you have completed the backup process, the entire hard disk and every file that has changed will be on two sets of media. The third set is for safety. If you have a problem with a "daily" diskette or tape, you can go to the other set. You will lose some work on this file, but that is better than losing a month's work.

To restore the entire hard disk, run your restoration program twice. First restore the monthly set of backup media, then the daily set. You have now restored the entire hard disk.

Running a backup like this requires a little more work each day, but a lot less work when a crisis comes. A crisis will come some day; all disk drives fail eventually.

When I first used hard disks in 1979, my disk failed after a couple of months. The last good backup copy I had was several weeks old. It took me more than a week to restore most of the files. Some files were lost permanently. Experienced? Yes, I am.

One final note about backing up and VERIFY. Most programs that use floppy diskettes for backup follow the status of VERIFY. If VERIFY is OFF, your backup files will not be checked to see if they have been recorded properly. If VERIFY is ON, the files will be checked. Turn VERIFY on before doing a monthly backup. This will ensure that your backup files are good. Be sure to turn VERIFY off afterward. VERIFY slows DOS down more than 90 percent on the floppy disk. That's why you should turn on VERIFY only when necessary. You may occasionally chance it on daily backups because it is usually safe. You will be the best judge of whether you should have VERIFY on or off while you are backing up the hard disk.

When to Back Up

The suggestion that you back up your hard disk frequently also applies to floppy diskettes. There are two other times that you should back up your complete hard disk: when you reorganize your hard disk, and when you have heavy fragmentation of the hard disk.

Reorganizing a hard disk involves copying many files to different directories. It may also involve creating new directories, deleting unused directories, and deleting old copies of files. After you have reorganized the hard disk, you will want to *snapshot* (capture an image of, in this case, a binary image) the hard disk, or back it up. By backing up your hard disk, you will not have to repeat the work you did to reorganize the hard disk if a disk "crash" occurs.

Fragmentation means that a file is not stored continuously on the surface of the hard disk. After you have deleted and added several files, a new file can be scattered across the entire hard disk. This hurts neither DOS nor your file, but DOS must work longer to retrieve the file. The hard disk's recording heads must move across the disk several times to read your file. As a result, the performance of the hard disk decreases. This can also occur after a major reorganization of the hard disk.

The solution to the fragmentation problem is to back up your entire hard disk, reformat it, then restore your files. Formatting will erase all the files and directories from the hard disk. As you restore each file and subdirectory, the information will be stored on consecutive sectors, which will increase the performance of the hard disk.

If you are a newcomer, don't bother with this process! The chance of losing information if you make a mistake is great. If you are experienced and have found that the programs for backing up and restoring your hard disk are adequate for this task, then proceed very carefully. Taking the time to make two complete backup copies of the hard disk is better than losing files.

If in doubt about this process, contact a computer-knowledgeable friend or co-worker, or have a consultant or dealer help you.

Knowing the Secret

A professional magician appeared on television commercials all over the United States for a product called "TV Magic Cards." He'd perform a few tricks, then tell us that it was easy to do these tricks with TV Magic Cards "once you know the secret."

I feel the same way about computers and DOS. Once you know how a command operates, you know "the secret." Learning the secrets of computers is easy. Once you've learned how to use the commands and a little more about how the computer operates, you can imagine what actually goes on when you invoke and use DOS and its commands. Computers are only "mystical" when no one bothers to explain what really happens inside them. I trust that you have gotten some ideas of how your computer operates from this book.

DOS is really a friendly operating system. The best way to become comfortable with DOS is to learn by doing. Just be sure to watch *what* you are doing.

After a while, you will develop *advanced user's syndrome*. Your fingers will fly across the keyboard. You will know exactly what you want to do before you do it. And then you will make an "experienced mistake." You will FORMAT or DISKCOPY the wrong diskette, or COPY the wrong files over good ones. The list goes on.

Even the most experienced users make mistakes. Mistakes occur when you get overconfident or sloppy. You don't check that the proper diskettes are in the disk drives. You don't read the messages completely, or you make a typing error and don't see it. You will get so good at things that you won't notice a mistake until it's too late.

To avoid some of these problems, always proofread your typing and and check your messages. Take the time to be certain. Make sure that the correct diskettes are in the right disk drives. Write-protect important diskettes, even if you plan to remove the tab after you have FORMATted or DISKCOPYed them. Do a DIR to make certain that no useful files will be destroyed with COPY, DISKCOPY, or FORMAT. Label diskettes.

Forgetting to save frequently while you revise a copy of documentation, a spreadsheet, or a program can also be an "experienced mistake." You feel confident that you will not forget to save your information before you are finished, so you keep adding to, editing, or revising the document, spreadsheet model, or program without saving even though the last time you saved a revision to the disk might have been over an hour ago. A troublesome feeling that you should save your revision gnaws at you, but you carry on. This is the time that Murphy strikes.

I worked on a spreadsheet model for more than an hour, and I continued to refine it. Several times I felt the nagging of my subconscious to save my work. I ignored it and continued to refine the model.

True to Murphy's never-ending mischievousness, a one-half second loss of power destroyed the model I was working on. It took only a half hour to restore the model, but this half hour would not have been wasted if I had only taken ten seconds to save the model. Save frequently and often.

Finally, always back up your hard disk and diskettes. It's a cheap form of insurance.

For More Information

User groups are invaluable resources. You may find that you're not the first person to have a problem with a program. Members of user groups can often help each other with problems or projects. Find a group in your area and join it. It will be worth the money.

If you are looking for other programs to use on your computer, catalogs, magazines, and several guides published by Que Corporation can help you discover what is available in hardware and software products.

Finally, try and enjoy. You can learn by doing, as well as from friends, classes, a user group, or a book.

Best wishes to you on using your computer and MS-DOS. I hope the time you have spent with this book was both useful and enjoyable.

Command Summary

Introduction

This section discusses all of the MS-DOS commands. Each command is presented following the same format.

The command name appears first, followed by the version of DOS to which the command applies. Two asterisks (**) indicate that the command's functions are different for the older and newer versions of DOS.

"Internal" and "External" indicate whether the command is built in to DOS (internal) or is disk-resident (external).

The purpose of the command is discussed, followed by the syntax required to invoke the command. The exit codes, if any, are listed for each command.

The rules governing the use of the command are also listed. An asterisk (*) designates a warning.

Examples or sample sessions demonstrate the uses of the commands. The Sample Session shows the exact dialogue between the operator and the computer during a session. Comments appear on the right-hand side of the page.

The Notes section contains additional comments, information, hints, or suggestions on the use of the command.

The Messages section is an alphabetical listing of the messages produced by the command. The following three types of messages may occur:

    1.   INFORMATIONAL - which simply informs or prompts the operator for a response

2. WARNING - which warns the operator of a possible problem

3. ERROR - which informs the operator that an error has occurred; a program terminates after issuing an ERROR message.

In the command summaries that follow, note that certain message designations, such as filename and dirname, will vary as each specific file name and directory name is used.

The common notation used to represent file specifications is

d:path\filename.ext

where

d: is the name of the disk drive holding the file.

path is the directory path to the file.

filename is the root name of the file.

.ext is the file name extension.

If any part of this notation does not appear in the file specification (in the Syntax section), the omitted part is not allowed with this command. For example, the notation **d:filename.ext** indicates that path names are not allowed in the command.

In most cases, a device name may be substituted for a full file specification.

If a notation in the Syntax section appears in **this type face**, it is mandatory and must be entered. If a notation appears in *this type face,* it is optional and is entered only when necessary.

Upper and Lower Case

Letters and words in the Syntax section appearing in upper case must be typed as they appear if you use that portion of the command. Letters and words that appear in lower case are variables. Be sure to substitute the appropriate disk drive letter or name, path name, file name, etc., for the lower-case variable when you type in the command.

Commands, all parameters, and switches typed with the command may be entered in either upper or lower case. The exceptions are SORT and batch commands, where the case of the letters of certain parameters may be important. (See the Batch and SORT commands for further information.)

MS-DOS Commands by Purpose

Note: Names in parentheses are CONFIG.SYS commands.

To execute automatically a batch file:	AUTOEXEC.BAT
To background print:	PRINT
To concatenate files:	COPY
To change the active console:	CTTY
To change the current directory:	CHDIR
To change the current disk drive:	**d:**
To change the date:	DATE
To change the environment:	SET
To change the name of a file:	RENAME
To change the name/location of the command interpreter:	(SHELL)
To change the number of disk buffers:	(BUFFERS)
To change the number of UNIX/XENIX handles:	(FILES)
To change the time:	TIME
To compare files:	FC
To control Ctrl-Break:	BREAK, (BREAK)
To control the verification of files:	VERIFY
To convert an .EXE file to .COM	EXE2BIN
To copy between devices:	COPY
To copy diskettes:	DISKCOPY, COPY
To display the amount of RAM memory:	CHKDSK
To display the contents of a file:	TYPE
To display the date:	DATE
To display the environment:	SET
To display the files on a disk:	DIR, CHKDSK
To display the free space on a disk:	CHKDSK, DIR
To display the subdirectories on a disk:	CHKDSK
To display the time:	TIME
To display the version of DOS:	VER

215

To execute a series of commands: batch
To fix a damaged diskette, hard disk: CHKDSK, RECOVER
To locate a string in a file: FIND
To make a new subdirectory: MKDIR
To move files: COPY
To pause the display: Ctrl-S, MORE
To place the operating system on a disk: SYS, FORMAT
To pipe the output between programs: |
To prepare new diskettes: FORMAT
To prepare the hard disk: FORMAT
To print the video screen: Ctrl-P, >, >>
To reassign the disk drives: ASSIGN
To redirect the input of a program: <, |
To redirect the output of a program: >, >>, |
To remove a file: ERASE
To remove a subdirectory: RMDIR
To restore a damaged directory: CHKDSK, RECOVER
To restore a file with a bad sector: RECOVER
To set the alternative directories for
    commands and batch files: PATH
To set the system prompt: PROMPT
To sort a disk file: SORT
To use a new/changed device: (DEVICE)

Other DOS Messages

When DOS detects an error while reading or writing to a device, including disk drives, the following message appears:

```
type error reading device
```

or

```
type error writing device
```

where `type` is the type of error, and `device` is the device at fault.

Do not remove the diskette from the disk drive. Read the possible causes and actions at the end of this section.

Error Types

The types of errors include:

```
Bad format call
```

An incorrect header length was passed to a device driver. The device driver software is at fault. Contact the dealer who sold you the device driver.

```
Bad command
```

The device driver issued an invalid command to *device*. The problem may lie with the device driver software or with other software trying to use the device driver.

```
Bad unit
```

An invalid submit number has been passed to the device driver. The problem may lie with the device driver software or with other software trying to use the device driver. Contact the dealer who sold you the device driver.

Data

DOS could not correctly read or write the data. Usually the disk has developed a defective spot.

Disk

This is a catch-all error message that is not covered elsewhere. The error usually occurs when you use an unformatted diskette or disk, or if you leave the disk drive door open.

No paper

The printer is either out of paper or is not turned on.

Non-DOS disk

The FAT has invalid information. This diskette is unusable.

Not ready

The device *device* is not ready and cannot receive or transmit data. Check that the connections are correct, that the power is on, and whether the device is ready.

Read fault

DOS was unable to read the data successfully, usually from a disk or diskettte.

Sector not found

The disk was unable to locate the sector on the diskette or hard disk platter. This error is usually the result of a defective spot or defective drive electronics.

Seek

The disk drive could not locate the proper track on the diskette or hard disk platter. This error usually results from a defective spot on the diskette or disk platter, your using an unformatted disk, or drive electronics problems.

Write fault

DOS could not successfully write the data to this device.

`Write protect`

The diskette is write-protected.

Possible Actions

In every case, DOS will display an error message, followed by the line:

`Abort, Retry, Ignore?`

You may type:

A for abort. DOS will end the program that requested the read or write condition.

R for retry. DOS will try the operation again.

I for ignore. DOS will skip this operation, and the program will continue.

The order of responses should be **R**, **A**, then **I**. You should retry the operation at least twice. If the condition persists, you must decide whether to abort the program or ignore the error. If you ignore the error, data may be lost. This is why **I** is the least desirable option.

Batch Command

V1** and V2** - Internal

Purpose: Executes one or more of the commands in a disk file

Syntax: *d:* **filename** *parameters*

d: is the name of the disk drive holding the batch file.

filename is the root name of the batch file.

parameters are the optional parameters to be used by the batch file.

Exit Codes: None

Rules for Executing Batch Files:

1. A batch file must have the extension .BAT.

2. If you do not give a disk drive name, the current disk drive will be used.

3. If the batch file is not in the current directory of the disk drive, DOS will search the directory(ies) specified by the PATH command to find the batch file.

4. To invoke a batch file, simply type its root name. For example, to invoke the batch file OFTEN.BAT, you type **OFTEN**.

5. DOS will execute each command, one line at a time. The specified parameters will be substituted for the markers when the command is used.

6. DOS recognizes a maximum of ten parameters. You may use the SHIFT subcommand to get around this limitation.

7. If DOS encounters an incorrectly phrased batch subcommand when running a batch file, a Syntax error message will be displayed. DOS will ignore the rest of the commands in the batch file, and the system prompt will reappear.

8. You can stop a running batch file by typing Ctrl-C. DOS will display the message:

   Terminate batch job (Y/N)?

If you answer **Y** for yes, the rest of the commands will be ignored, and the system prompt will appear.

If you answer **N** for no, DOS will skip the current command but will continue processing the other commands in the file.

9. DOS remembers which disk holds the batch file. If you remove the diskette that holds the batch file, DOS will prompt you to place that diskette into the original drive to get the next command.

10. DOS remembers which directory holds the batch file. Your batch file may change directories at any time.

11. You can make DOS execute a second batch file, immediately after finishing the first one, by entering the name of the second batch file as the last command in the first file.

12. Batch subcommands are valid only for batch files. The batch subcommands cannot be executed as normal DOS commands.

Rules for the AUTOEXEC.BAT File:

1. The file must be called AUTOEXEC.BAT and reside in the root directory of the boot disk.

2. The contents of the AUTOEXEC.BAT file conform to the rules for creating batch files.

3. When DOS is booted, it automatically executes the AUTOEXEC.BAT file.

4. When AUTOEXEC.BAT is executed after DOS is booted, the date and time are not requested automatically. To get the current date and time, you must put the DATE and TIME commands into the AUTOEXEC.BAT file.

Rules for Creating Batch Files:

1. A batch file contains ASCII text. You may use the DOS command COPY; EDLIN, the DOS line editor; or another text editor to create a batch file. If you use a word processor, make sure that it is in the programming, or nondocument, mode.

2. The root name of a batch file can be one to eight characters long and must conform to the rules for file names.

3. The file name extension must be .BAT.

4. A batch file should not have the same root name as a program file (a file ending with .COM or .EXE) in the current directory. Nor should an internal DOS command, such as COPY or DATE, be used as a root name. If you use one of these root names, DOS will not know whether you want to execute the batch file, the program, or the command.

5. Any valid DOS commands that you can type at the keyboard may be entered. You may also use the parameter markers (%0-%9) and the batch subcommands.

6. You may enter any valid batch subcommand. (Batch subcommands are listed in this section.)

7. To use the percent sign (%) in a command for a file name, enter the percent symbol twice. For example, to use a file called A100%.TXT, you enter A100%%.TXT. This does not apply to the parameter markers (%0-%9).

Notes: For further information on batch files and subcommands, see Chapter 10 of this book.

Batch Commands
ECHO subcommand   V2 Only

Purpose: Displays a message and allows or inhibits the display of batch commands and messages by other batch subcommands as the commands are executed by DOS

Syntax: To display a message:

> **ECHO** *message*

To turn off the display of commands and messages by other batch commands:

> **ECHO OFF**

To turn on the display of commands and messages:

> **ECHO ON**

message is the text of the message to be displayed on the video display.

Rules:

1. To display unconditionally a message on the video screen, use **ECHO** *message*.

2. When ECHO is on, all commands in the batch file are displayed as each line is executed. Any messages from the batch subcommands are also displayed.

3. When ECHO is off, the commands in the batch file are not displayed as they are executed by DOS. In addition, messages produced by other batch subcommands are not displayed. The exceptions to this rule are the Strike any key when ready message by the PAUSE subcommand and any **ECHO** *message* commands.

4. A batch file starts with ECHO ON.

5. An ECHO OFF command is active only while the batch file executes. If one batch file invokes another, ECHO will be turned back on by DOS when the second batch file is invoked.

6. ECHO affects only messages produced by batch subcommands. It does not affect messages from other DOS commands or programs.

Notes: The ECHO message is not the same as the REM message. REM is affected by an ECHO OFF command. The message with the REM subcommand will not be displayed if ECHO is off. The message on the line with ECHO will always be displayed.

Batch Commands
FOR..IN..DO subcommand   V2 Only

Purpose:	Allows iterative (repeated) processing of a DOS command
Syntax:	**FOR %%variable IN (set) DO command**

variable is a single letter.

set is one or more file specifications in the form *d:* **filename**.*ext*. Wild cards are allowed.

command is the DOS command to be performed for each file in the **set**.

Rules:

1. You may have more than one full file specification in the **set**. Each file specification should be separated by a space.

2. **%%variable** becomes each full file specification in the **set**. If you use wild-card characters, FOR..IN..DO will execute once for each file that matches the wild-card file specification.

3. Path names are not allowed. Each file for the **set** must be in the current directory of the disk drive, on either the current or the specified disk drive.

4. FOR..IN..DO commands cannot be nested, and you cannot put two of these commands on the same line. You may use other batch subcommands with FOR..IN..DO.

Batch Commands
GOTO subcommand

V2 Only

Purpose: Jumps (transfers control) to the line following the label in the batch file and continues batch file execution from this line

Syntax: **GOTO label**

label is the name used for one or more characters, preceded by a colon. Only the first eight characters of the label name are significant.

Rules:
1. The **label** must be the first item on a line in a batch file and must start with a colon (:).

2. When the GOTO label is executed, DOS jumps to the line following the label and continues executing the batch file.

3. A label is never executed. DOS uses the label as the jump-to marker for the GOTO subcommand.

4. If you attempt to GOTO a nonexistent label, DOS will issue an error message and stop processing the batch file.

Message: Label not found

ERROR: DOS could not find the specified label in a GOTO command. The batch file is aborted, and the system prompt will reappear.

Batch Commands
IF subcommand   V2 Only

Purpose: Allows conditional execution of a DOS command

Syntax: **IF** *NOT* **condition command**

NOT tests for the opposite of the **condition** (executes the command if the condition is false).

condition is what is being tested. It may be one of the following:

ERRORLEVEL number - where DOS tests the exit code of the program. If the exit code is greater than or equal to the **number**, the condition is true.

string1 == string2 - where DOS tests if the two alphanumeric strings, **string1** and **string2**, are identical

EXIST *d:* **filename.***ext* - where DOS tests if the file *d:* **filename.***ext* is current on the specified (if *d:* is given) or current disk drive

command is any valid command for a DOS batch file.

Rules:
1. For the IF subcommand, if the condition is true, the command is executed. If the condition is false, the command is skipped, and the next line of the batch file is immediately executed.

2. For the IF NOT subcommand, if the condition is false, the command is executed. If the condition is true, the command is skipped, and the next line of the batch file is immediately executed.

3. At present, no Microsoft-supplied programs use exit codes. Using ERRORLEVEL with a program that does not leave an exit code is meaningless.

4. In **string1 == string2**, DOS makes a character-by-character comparison of the two strings, based on the ASCII character set.

5. When using **string1 == string2** with the parameter markers (%0-%9), both strings must not be nulls (empty or nonexistent strings). DOS will give a Syntax error message and abort the batch file.

Batch Commands
SHIFT subcommand
(Shift parameters)

V2 Only

Purpose: Shifts one position to the left the parameters given on the command line when the batch file was invoked

Syntax: **SHIFT**

Rules:
1. When you SHIFT, the command line parameters are moved one position to the left.

2. When you SHIFT, DOS discards the former first parameter (%0).

Batch Commands
PAUSE subcommand   V1 and V2
(Pause execution)

Purpose: Suspends batch file processing until a key is depressed and optionally displays
the user's message

Syntax: **PAUSE** *message*

message is an optional message to be displayed.

Rules: 1. *message* is a series of up to 121 characters. It must be on the batch file
line with the word PAUSE.

2. When DOS encounters a PAUSE subcommand in a batch file, DOS
displays the optional *message* if ECHO is on. If ECHO is off, the
optional *message* will not be displayed.

3. Regardless of ECHO's setting, DOS will display the message Strike a
key when ready....

4. DOS will suspend the processing of the batch file until any single key is
depressed. After the key is depressed, DOS will continue processing the
lines in the batch file. You may enter Ctrl-C to end batch processing.

Batch Commands
REM subcommand
(Show remark)

V1 and V2

Purpose: Displays a message within the batch file

Syntax: **REM** *message*

message is an optional string of up to 123 characters.

Rules:

1. REM must be the last batch file command on the line when used with the IF or FOR..IN..DO subcommand.

2. The optional *message* can be up to 123 characters long and must immediately follow the word REM.

3. When DOS encounters a REM subcommand in a batch file, DOS will display the optional *message* if ECHO is on. If ECHO is off, the optional *message* will not be displayed.

4. The difference between the **ECHO message** and the **REM** *message* is that the message with ECHO is always displayed. IF ECHO is off, the message with REM will not be displayed.

BREAK
(Control Break)   V2 - Internal

Purpose: Tells DOS when to look for a Control Break (Ctrl-C) to stop a program

Syntax: To turn on BREAK:

                BREAK ON

                To turn off BREAK:

                BREAK OFF

                To find out whether BREAK is on or off:

                BREAK

Rules: 1. BREAK is always either on or off.

                2. If BREAK is on, DOS will look for the Control Break when performing any operation.

                3. If BREAK is off, DOS checks for the Control Break only when performing operations with the following equipment:

                        A. The terminal or keyboard/screen

                        B. The printer

                        C. The RS-232 (asynchronous) adapters

                4. When you set BREAK, no other message is displayed.

Notes: The BREAK command tells DOS when to check for Control Break. (Control Break aborts, or stops, the currently running program.) With programs that do very little input and output to the keyboard, screen, or printer (computation-bound programs), you may not be able to stop the program should something go wrong. BREAK ON tells DOS to check for the Control Break before any DOS operation, including using the disk drives.

                BREAK ON has little effect on disk performance. DOS works only 1 to 2 percent slower with BREAK ON.

It is usually safe to have BREAK OFF, unless you are running long programs with little display, keyboard, or printer activity. In these cases, turn BREAK on before running the program and turn BREAK off after the program is finished.

The Ctrl-C command does not work while the computer is "number crunching," but does work when a program is interacting with DOS. Using BREAK ON will not allow Ctrl-Break to stop a CPU-intensive, computative task.

This command is the same as the BREAK command in the configuration file in Chapter 11.

Message: Must specify ON or OFF

WARNING: You gave the BREAK command with some word other than ON or OFF.

CHDIR or CD
(Change directory)   V2 - Internal

Purpose:	Changes the current directory or shows the path of the current directory
Syntax:	To change the current directory:

          CHDIR *d:* **path**

or

          CD *d:* **path**

To show the current directory path on a disk drive:

          CHDIR *d:*

or

          CD *d:*

d: is a valid disk drive name.

path is a valid directory path.

Rules:

1. If you do not indicate a disk drive, DOS will use the current disk drive.

2. When you give a path name, DOS will move you from the root directory to the last directory specified in the **path**.

3. To start your move with the root directory of the disk, the first character in the path must be \; otherwise, DOS assumes that the path starts with the current directory.

4. If you give an invalid **path**, DOS will display an error message, and you will remain in the current directory.

Exit Codes: None

Examples: (Refer to the Sample Hierarchical Directory in Appendix B.)

To move from root to DOS, use

          CHDIR DOS

To move from root to UTIL, use

CHDIR DOS\UTIL

To move from UTIL back to DOS, use

CHDIR ..

or

CHDIR \DOS

These examples illustrate two different ways to move between directories. The first example shows how to move up to a parent directory. DOS does not permit movement by parent directory name when you are in a subdirectory. Therefore, you cannot move up a level from UTIL to DOS by typing the line

CHDIR DOS

In this case, DOS will think that you were trying to move to a subdirectory of \UTIL with the name DOS, rather than trying to move up a level. The only way you can move up one level is by using the parent directory symbol (..).

The second example illustrates how to move from the root directory of the disk to the correct directory. Notice that the first character in the directory name is the path character, the backslash (\). When a backslash is the first character in the path name, DOS returns to the root directory to begin its movement. In this example, we return to the root directory, then move down one level to the DOS subdirectory.

To move from UTIL to BASIC, use

CHDIR ..\BASIC

or

CHDIR \DOS\BASIC

The first example moves you up to the parent directory of UTIL, DOS, then down to the BASIC subdirectory. The second example begins the movement at the root directory, then moves down through DOS to BASIC. Although either method can be used, the first method may be easier to remember.

To move from UTIL to WORDS, use

CHDIR ..\..\WORDS

or

CHDIR \WORDS

Here the first example is almost the same as the one that precedes it. Notice that we move up two directories (DOS and root), then move down to WORDS. The second method, returning to the root directory and moving down one level, is the easier way because it involves typing fewer characters and is easier to remember.

To move from LETTERS to SAMPLES, use

CHDIR ..\\..\\DOS\\BASIC\\SAMPLES

or

CHDIR \\DOS\\BASIC\\SAMPLES

These two examples do the same thing, but the second method is simpler.

Notes: CHDIR, or the shorthand CD, is the command used to maneuver through the hierarchical directories of DOS V2. It is identical to the UNIX/XENIX command in name and use, except for the path separator. (UNIX and XENIX use the slash, /, rather than the backslash, \\.) CD can always be typed in place of CHDIR.

There are two ways to maneuver through the hierarchical directories: (1) you can start at the root (top) directory of the disk and move down, or (2) you can start with the current directory and move up and/or down.

To start at the root directory of a disk, the path must begin with the path character (\\), such as \\ or **B:**\\. When DOS sees the \\ as the first character in the path, DOS will start with the root directory. Otherwise, DOS will assume that you want the current directory.

To start the move with the current directory, use one of the subdirectory names or a parent directory symbol (..). DOS will know that you are starting with your current directory. To move up one level, use the double period (..). DOS will move to the *parent directory* (the directory that holds the name of the current directory). A disk drive name can also precede the (..). Otherwise, use a subdirectory name that appears in the current directory.

To move more than one directory at a time, separate each directory name with a path character (\\). You can have as many directories chained together as you wish, provided that the total number of characters for the path is not more than 63.

You are not restricted to changing directories only on the current disk. For example, if the current drive is A: and your example directory disk is in drive

B:, you can add **B:** in front of each path name, and your examples will work the same way.

Message: Invalid directory

ERROR: A directory you specified does not exist. This error can occur for one of several reasons. Your spelling of the directory name may be incorrect, you forgot or misplaced the path character (\) between the directory names, or the directory does not exist in the path you specified.

CHDIR will abort and remain in the current directory.

CHKDSK
(Check disk)   V1** and V2** - External

Purpose: Checks the directory and file allocation table (FAT) of the disk and reports disk and memory status. CHKDSK can also repair errors in the directories or FAT.

Syntax: **CHKDSK** *d:filename.ext/F/V*

d: is the disk drive name to analyze.

filename.ext is a valid DOS file name. Wild cards are allowed.

Switches: /F   *Fixes* the File Allocation Table, if errors are found

/V   Shows CHKDSK's progress and more detailed information about the errors it finds (*Verbose*)

Rules: 1.   If no disk drive name is given, CHKDSK will use the current disk.

2.   To check a diskette, make sure that the diskette you want to analyze is in the drive before you run CHKDSK.

If you have a one-drive system and want to analyze a diskette that does not have CHKDSK on it, specify the tandem drive (that is, B: instead of A:).

3.   CHKDSK V1.x automatically repairs the FAT. CHKDSK V2.x must be directed to make this repair with the /F switch.

4.   If you give a file name, with or without wild cards, CHKDSK will check the file(s) for continuity.

*5.   Do not use a different version of CHKDSK with a different version of DOS (for example, version 1.1 of CHKDSK with DOS 2). You may lose files if you do.

Examples: A.   **CHKDSK**

analyzes the disk or diskette in the current drive.

B.   **CHKDSK B:**

analyzes the diskette in drive B:.

C. **CHKDSK A: /F**

analyzes the diskette in drive A: and asks permission to repair the file allocation table (FAT) if a flaw is found. When a flaw is found, one of the messages may be

```
xxx lost clusters found in xxx chains
Convert lost chains to files (Y/N)?
```

If you answer **Y** for yes, CHKDSK will convert the lost areas of the disk into files. The files will appear in the root directory of the disk with the name *FILExxxx.CHK*, where *xxxx* is a consecutive number between 0000 and 9999. If these files do not contain anything useful, you may delete them.

D. **CHKDSK /V**

is the verbose mode, which lists each directory and subdirectory on the disk and each file in the directories. This output can be redirected to a file or to the printer.

E. **CHKDSK *.***

checks all files in the current directory on the current drive to see if they are stored contiguously on the disk. If the message

```
All specified file(s) are contiguous
```

appears, you are getting good disk performance. If the message

```
d:path\filename.ext
Contains xxx noncontiguous blocks
```

appears, the specified files are not stored contiguously on the disk. This message will appear for each file. If many files appear, you will probably want to COPY (not DISKCOPY) the files from the analyzed floppy diskette to another one, or, in the case of the hard disk, back up your entire hard disk, reformat it, and restore it. (Check your DOS manual for the programs that back up and restore files on your hard disk.)

What CHKDSK shows:

A. Volume name and creation date (V2 only, if volume label exists)
B. Total disk space
C. Number of bytes used for hidden or system files

    D.   Number of bytes used for directories (V2 only)
    E.   Number of bytes used for user (normal) files
    F.   Bytes used by bad sectors (flawed disk space)
    G.   Bytes available (free space) on disk
    H.   Bytes of total memory (RAM)
    I.   Bytes of free memory

CHKDSK shows that the example directory diskette (in Appendix B) has the following:

```
Volume EXAMPLE_DSK created Jun 23, 1983 11:36a

   362496 bytes total disk space
    25528 bytes in 3 hidden files
     9216 bytes in 9 directories
   323504 bytes in 30 user files
     7160 bytes available on disk

   262144 bytes total memory
   225280 bytes free
```

Because this diskette had no bad sectors, the bytes in bad sectors message was not displayed.

Notes: CHKDSK checks the directory(ies) on the disk and the FAT. The command also checks the amount of memory in the system and how much of that memory is free. If CHKDSK finds any errors, it will report them on the screen before making a status report.

CHKDSK *filename* also checks to see if the specified file or files are stored contiguously on the disk. When you first use a disk, the individual 512-byte sections of the program or data files are stored in contiguous sectors (one after the other). After files have been erased and others added, DOS will attempt to store a new file in any open spot. This means that a large file may be stored in several noncontiguous places on the disk. DOS will slow down when reading this file because DOS must move the disk's recording head many times to read the entire file.

When CHKDSK *filename* is used, DOS reports if any programs are stored noncontiguously and how many different sections the file or files are in.

If CHKDSK reports that many files on a floppy diskette are noncontiguous, you should format a new floppy diskette. Use the COPY *.* (not DISKCOPY) command to consolidate your files from the old diskette to the new one.

Read the chapter on disk storage (Chapter 4) for further information.

Messages: 1.   `All specified file(s) are contiguous`

INFORMATIONAL: The files you specifed are stored in contiguous sectors on the disk, and you are getting the best performance from this diskette.

2.   **filename**
`Allocation error for file, size adjusted`

WARNING: The file **filename** has an invalid sector number in the file allocation table (FAT). The file has been truncated by CHKDSK at the end of the last valid sector.

You should check this file to ensure that all information in the file is correct. If there is a problem, use your backup copy of the file. This message is usually displayed when the problem is in the FAT, not in the file. Your file should still be good.

3.   **filename**
`Contains invalid cluster,`
`file truncated`

WARNING: The file **filename** has a bad pointer to a section on the disk in the FAT. If the /F (fix) switch was given, the file will be truncated at the last valid sector. Otherwise, no action will be taken.

You should check this file to see if all information is intact. If it is, CHKDSK can usually safely correct this problem without any loss of information in the file.

4.   **filename**
`Contains xxx noncontiguous blocks`

INFORMATIONAL: This message informs you that the file **filename** is not stored contiguously on the disk but in xxx number of pieces. If you find a large number of files in noncontiguous pieces, COPY the floppy to another to increase performance.

5.   **dirname**
`Convert directory to file (Y/N)?`

WARNING: The directory **dirname** contains so much bad information that it is no longer usable as a directory. If you respond **Y**, CHKDSK will convert the directory into a file so that you can use

DEBUG or another tool to repair the directory. If you respond **N**, no action is taken.

Respond **N** the first time you see this message. Try to copy any files you can from this directory to another disk. Check the copied files to see if they are usable. Then rerun CHKDSK to convert the directory into a file and try to recover the rest of the files.

6.   `Disk error writing FAT x`

ERROR: This message warns that a disk error was encountered while CHKDSK was attempting to put information into FAT 1 or FAT 2 (as shown by the number **x**).

If this message appears for either FAT on a floppy diskette, copy all of your files from this diskette to another one. Then retire or reformat the bad diskette. If this message appears for the hard disk, back up all files on the hard disk, reformat the hard disk, then restore the files.

If this message appears for both FATs 1 and 2, the diskette is unusable. Copy any files you can to another diskette and retire or reformat the diskette after you have taken off all the information you can from the diskette.

7.   `.`

or

`..`

`Entry has a bad attribute`

or

`Entry has a bad size`

or

`Entry has a bad link`

WARNING: The link to the current directory (**..**) or the parent directory (**.**) has a problem. If you gave the */F* switch, CHKDSK will attempt to repair the problem. This is normally a safe procedure that does not carry the risk of losing files.

8.   `Error found, F parameter not specified`
`Corrections will not be written to the disk`

INFORMATIONAL: An error has been found by CHKDSK. This message tells you that CHKDSK will go through the steps to repair (fix) the disk, but will not actually make any changes to it because you did not give the /F switch.

If you see this message, you can freely answer **Y** to any CHKDSK message, knowing that the disk or diskette will not be changed. You will see what possible actions CHKDSK will take to correct the error it found. However, this message also means that your diskette still has problems. You will have to run CHKDSK with the /F switch to fix the disk.

9. **filename1**
   Is cross linked on cluster x
   filename2
   Is cross linked on cluster x

WARNING: Two files—**filename1** and **filename2**—have an entry in the FAT that points to the same area of the disk (cluster). In other words, the two files "think" that they own the same piece of the diskette.

CHKDSK will take no action to correct this situation. You will have to handle it yourself. You should do the following:

   A. Copy both files to another diskette
   B. Delete the files from the original diskette
   C. Edit the files as necessary

Each file may have some garbage in it.

10. **filename**
    First cluster number is invalid,
    entry truncated

WARNING: The file **filename**'s first entry in the FAT refers to a nonexistent portion of the disk. If you gave the /F switch, the file will become a zero-length file (truncated).

Try to copy this file to another diskette before CHKDSK truncates the file. You may not get a useful copy, however, and the original file will be lost.

11. Insufficient room in root directory
     Erase files from root and repeat CHKDSK

ERROR: CHKDSK has recovered so many "lost" clusters from the disk that the root directory is full. CHKDSK will abort at this point.

Examine the FILExxxx.CHK files. If there is nothing useful in them, delete them. Then rerun CHKDSK with the */F* switch to continue recovering "lost" clusters.

12. **dirname**
    `Invalid subdirectory`

    WARNING: The directory **dirname** has invalid information in it. CHKDSK will attempt to repair this directory. For more specific information about the problem with the directory, do one of the following:

    A. Enter

        CHKDSK /V

    B. Move into the faulty directory, if you can, and enter

        CHKDSK *.* /V

    The verbose mode will tell you more about what is wrong.

13. `Probable non-DOS disk.`
    `Continue (Y/N)?`

    WARNING: The special byte in the FAT checked by DOS indicates that your diskette is a DOS diskette, but the diskette was either not formatted, was formatted under a different operating system, or is badly damaged.

    If you used the */F* switch, answer **N**. Recheck the diskette without the */F* (fix) switch, then answer **Y** to the question. See what action DOS takes. Then, if your diskette is a DOS diskette, run CHKDSK again with the */F* switch.

    If you did not use the */F* switch, answer **Y** and see what action DOS takes. Then decide if you want to rerun **CHKDSK /F** to correct the diskette.

14. `Processing cannot continue,`
    message

    ERROR: This error message indicates that CHKDSK is aborting because of an error. *message* will tell you what the problem is. The likely culprit is lack of enough RAM memory to check the diskette. This message occurs most often with 64K systems.

You may have to increase the amount of memory in your computer or "borrow" another computer to check the diskette.

15.   Tree past this point not processed

WARNING: CHKDSK is unable to continue down the indicated directory path because of a bad track.

Copy all files from the disk to another floppy. The original diskette may no longer be usable, and you may have lost some files.

16.   xxxxxxxxx bytes disk space freed

INFORMATIONAL: CHKDSK has regained some disk space that was improperly marked as *in use*. xxxxxxxxx will tell you how many additional bytes are now available.

17.   xxx lost clusters found in yyy chains

INFORMATIONAL: Although CHKDSK has found *xxx* blocks of data allocated in the FAT, no file on the disk is using these blocks. They are lost clusters, which normally may be safely freed by CHKDSK if no other error or warning message is given.

See the message Convert lost clusters to files and the examples in the Notes section for additional information.

CLS
(Clear screen)   V2 - Internal

Purpose: Erases the display screen

Syntax: **CLS**

Rules:
1. All information on the screen is cleared, and the cursor is placed at the home (upper left-hand corner) position.

2. This command affects only the currently active video display.

3. If you have used the ANSI control codes to set the foreground and background, the colors will remain in effect.

4. If you have not set the foreground/background color, the screen will revert to light characters on a dark background.

5. CLS does not affect memory, disk storage, or anything else.

COMMAND
(Invoke secondary command processor)   V2 - Internal

Purpose:	Invokes a second copy of COMMAND.COM, the command processor
Syntax:	**COMMAND** *d:path /P /C string*

d: is the drive name where DOS can find a copy of COMMAND.COM.

path is the DOS path to the copy of COMMAND.COM.

Switches:

/P   keeps this copy *permanently* in memory (until the next system reset)

/C   passes this set of *commands* (the *string*) to the new copy of COMMAND.COM

A *string* is the set of characters you pass to the new copy of the command interpreter.

Rules:

1. You may load only additional copies of COMMAND.COM.

2. The *string* in the */C* option is interpreted by the additional copy of COMMAND.COM as if you typed it at system level (A:). The */C* must be the last switch used on the line. Do not use the form **COMMAND /C string /P**.

3. You can exit from the second copy of the command processor by issuing the command, **EXIT**, if you have not used the */P* option (permanent).

Notes: COMMAND is an advanced DOS command that is not recommended for use by newcomers or novices. Consult the DOS manual for more information on this command.

COPY
(Copy files)   V1** and V2** - Internal

Purpose: Copies files between disk drives and/or devices, either keeping the same file name or changing it. COPY can join (concatenate) two or more files into another file or append one or more files onto another file. Options allow special handling of text files and verification of the copying process.

Note: The /A and /B switches may not apply to your version of MS-DOS.

Syntax: To copy a file:

> **COPY** /A/B d1:path1**filename1**.ext1/A/B
> d0:path2\\filename0.ext0/A/B/V

or

> **COPY** /A/B d1:path1**filename1**.ext1/A/B/V

To join several files into one file:

> **COPY** /A/B d1:path1**filename1**.ext1/A/B
> + d2:path2**filename2**.ext2/A/B + ...
> d0:path0**filename0**.ext0 /A/B/V

d1:, d2:, and d0: are valid disk drive names.

path1\\, path2\\, and path0\\ are valid path names.

filename1.ext1, **filename2**.ext2, and **filename0**.ext0 are valid file names. Wild cards are allowed (see below).

... represents additional files in the form dx:pathx**filenamex**.extx.

Special Terms: The file being copied from is the *source* file. The names above with *1* and *2* are the source files.

The file being copied to is the *destination* file. It is represented by a *0*.

Switches: /V   Verifies that the copy has been recorded correctly.

The next two switches have different effects for the source and the destination. These switches may not be implemented in your version of MS-DOS.

With source files:

/A   Treats the file as an *ASCII* (text) file. It copies all the information in the file up to, but not including, the end-of-file marker (a Ctrl-Z). Anything after the end-of-file marker is ignored.

/B   Copies the entire file (based on its size, as listed in the directory) as if it were a program file (*binary*). It treats any end-of-file markers (Ctrl-Z) as normal characters and copies them.

With the destination file:

/A   Adds an end-of-file marker (Ctrl-Z) to the end of the file after it is copied. This ensures that the *ASCII* text file has a good end-of-file marker.

/B   Does not add the end-of-file marker to this *binary* file

Notes: The meanings of the /A and /B switches come from their position in the line. DOS will use the /A or /B switch on the file that immediately precedes the switch and on all files after the switch *until* another /A or /B is encountered.

Exit Codes: None

Rules: When you are copying files, if you give both the source and the destination, the following rules apply:

1. The source name will come first, followed by the destination name.

2. If you do not give a drive name, the current drive will be used.

3. If you do not give a path name, the current directory for the disk drive will be used.

4. For the filename:

    A. You must give a file name for the source. Wild cards are permitted.

    B. If you do not give a destination file name, the copied file(s) will have the same name as the source file(s).

5. You may substitute a device name for the complete source or destination name.

6. When copying between disk drives, COPY assumes that binary files are being copied (as if a /B switch were given).

7.   When copying to or from a device other than a disk drive, COPY assumes that ASCII files are being copied (as if the */A* switch were given).

8.   An */A* or */B* switch will override the default COPY settings (Rules 5 and 6).

If you give only one file specification, the following rules apply:

1.   The file specification you give (*d1:path1*\filename1.ext1) is the source. It must have

   A.   A valid file name. (Wild cards are permitted.)

   B.   A drive name, a path name, or both. The drive name, path name, or both must be different from the respective current drive and current path.

2.   The source cannot be a device name.

3.   The destination is the current drive and current directory.

4.   The copied file(s) will have the same name as the source file(s).

5.   COPY assumes that binary files are being copied (as if a */B* switch were given).

When joining (concatenating) files, the following rules apply:

1.   The destination file is the last file in the list, if there is no plus sign (+) before the file name. If you do not specify a destination file name, the first source name becomes the destination name.

2.   If you do not give a drive name, the current drive is used.

3.   If you do not give a path name, the current directory is used.

4.   For the source files:

   A.   You must give a valid file name. Wild cards are permitted but can be dangerous. (See the discussion on COPY in Chapter 12.)

   B.   After the first file name, any additional source file specifications must be preceded by a plus sign (+).

5. For the destination file:

    A. There can be only one destination. If you give a destination without wild cards, only one destination file is used. If you give a destination file name with wild cards, one or more destination files will be used.

    B. If you do not give a destination, the first source file will also be used as the destination, resulting in:

        i. The first file that matches the wild-card file name will be used as the destination file if you gave a wild card as part of the first source name.

        ii. The files to be joined are appended to the end of the first source file.

(See Chapter 12 for examples of how the COPY command is used.)

Message: Invalid path or file name

ERROR: You gave a directory name or file name that does not exist, used the wrong directory name (a directory not in the path), or mistyped a name. COPY will abort at this point. If you used a wild card for a file name, COPY will transfer all valid files before issuing the error message.

Check to see which files were already transferred. Then check your spelling of the directory and file names and that the path is correct, and try again.

CTTY
(Change console)   V2 - Internal

Purpose: Changes the standard input and output device to an auxiliary console and/or back from an auxiliary console to the keyboard and video screen

Syntax: **CTTY device**

device is the name of the device you want to use as the new standard input and output device. This name must be a valid DOS device name.

Exit Codes: None

Rules: 1. **device** should be a character-oriented device capable of both input and output.

2. Do not use a colon after the device name.

3. Programs that are designed to work with the video display's control codes may not function properly when redirected.

4. CTTY does not affect any other form of redirected I/O or piping. For example, the <, the >, and the | work as usual.

Examples: A. **CTTY AUX**

makes the device attached to AUX the new console. The peripheral connected to AUX must be a terminal or a teleprinter (printer with a keyboard). After this command is given, DOS expects normal input to come from AUX and puts anything for the video display to AUX.

B. **CTTY CON**

makes the original keyboard and video display (or terminal) the console. In effect, this command cancels the first example. However, the command must be typed on the currently active console to be effective.

Notes: The CTTY command was designed so that a terminal or teleprinter could be used for console input and output, rather than a built-in keyboard and video screen. This added versatility has little effect on most personal computer users.

You must specify a device that can both input and output characters with the computer system. Using CTTY with a normal printer (one that is output only) is a mistake. DOS will patiently wait forever for you to type commands on the printer's nonexistent keyboard. In other words, the computer will "go west" and will have to be reset before it can be used again.

Message: `Invalid device`

ERROR: You specified an invalid device name. Your spelling may be incorrect, or DOS does not "know" the device. Perhaps you specified a device that is not character oriented or added a colon (:) after the device name.

DATE
(Set/show date)

V1 and V2 - Internal

Purpose: Displays and/or changes the system date

Syntax: **DATE** *mm-dd-yy*

or

DATE *mm-dd-yyyy*

mm is a one- or two-digit month (1 to 12).

dd is a one- or two-digit day (1 to 31).

In the first option:

   yy is a one- or two-digit year (80 to 99; the 19 is assumed).

In the second option:

   yyyy is a four-digit year (1980 to 2099).

Exit Codes: None

Rules:
1. When you enter a correctly phrased date with this command, DOS will set the date and return to the system prompt.

2. If you do not enter a date, DOS will display a date that may or may not be correct. You can do the following:

   A. Enter a correctly phrased date, which DOS will use as the new date, and hit the Enter key.

   B. Hit the Enter key, and DOS will continue to use the same date.

3. You may use either the minus sign (-) or the slash (/) between the month and the day and between the day and the year.

4. Entering an incorrectly phrased or nonsense date (such as 02/29/85, 06/31/83, or 06:03:1983) will cause DOS to display an error message and a request to try again.

Sample Session: _____

A:**DATE 07/31/83**   {The DATE command was run with a
                                    correctly phrased date, July 31, 1983.
A: DOS accepts the date and returns to the
                                    system prompt.}

A:**DATE**   {DATE is invoked, shows the current date, and
                                    allows you to reset the date. When a new
Current Date is Sun 7-31-1983   date is entered, DOS returns to the system
                                    level.}
Enter new date: **8/1/83**

A:

A:**DATE**   {Check to see if DOS did use the new date.}

Current Date is Mon 8-01-1983

Enter new date: **<Enter>**   {In this case, DATE displayed the correct date,
                                    so hit <Enter>. DOS will not change the date
                                    but will return to the system prompt.}
A:

_____

Notes: When you boot DOS, it issues the DATE and TIME command to set
                correctly your system clock. If the AUTOEXEC.BAT file is on the boot
                diskette, DOS will not ask for the date or time. You may include the DATE
                or TIME command if you want these functions to be set when DOS is
                booted.

                Every time you create or update a file, DOS updates the directory with the
                date you enter. The date stamp lets you see which copy is the last revision of
                the file. Some DOS commands provided by the computer's manufacturer
                may also use the date stamp in selecting files to back up.

                The day-of-year calendar uses the time-of-day clock. This means that if you
                leave your system on overnight, the day will advance by one at midnight.
                DOS also knows about leap years and appropriately adjusts its calendar.
                However, you must access this clock once each day, or DOS will not advance

the date properly. If you leave your computer on over the weekend and return Monday, DOS will be one day behind.

The day-of-year and time-of-day clock built in to most computers is a software clock. Its accuracy can vary. If you leave your system on constantly and do not reset it (system boot), the date will usually be accurate, but the time may not be.

Message: Invalid date

ERROR: You gave an impossible date or used the wrong type of character to separate the month, day, and year. This message will also occur if you enter the date with the Personal Computer's keypad when it is in the cursor control mode rather than the numeric mode.

DEL
(Delete files)   V1 and V2 - Internal

Purpose: Deletes files from the disk

DEL is the shorthand form of ERASE. (See ERASE for a complete
description.)

DIR
(Directory)

V1 and V2 - Internal

Purpose: Lists any or all of the files and subdirectories in a disk's directory

The DIR command also shows the following:

> Disk volume name (if any)
> Name of the directory (its complete path)
> Name of each disk file or subdirectory
> Number of files
> Amount, in bytes, of free space on the disk

The DIR command, unless otherwise directed, shows the following:

> Number of bytes occupied by each file
> Date/time of the file's creation/last update

Syntax: **DIR** *d:path\filename.ext/P/W*

d: holds the disk you want to examine.

path is the path name to the directory you want to examine.

filename.ext is a valid file name. Wild cards are allowed.

Switches: */P*   Pauses when the screen is full and waits for a keypress

/W   Gives a *wide* (80-column) display of the names of the files. The information about file size, date, and time is not displayed.

Rules: 1.   If you do not give a drive name, the current drive is used.

2.   If you do not give a path, the current path on the disk is used.

3.   If you do not give a file name, all files in the directory will be displayed.

4.   The DIR command shows the contents of only one directory at a time.

Exit Codes: None

Notes: The DIR command finds the disk files or subdirectories on the disk. This command shows only the files and subdirectories in the specified (or default) directory. To see a list of all of the files on a disk, use the CHKDSK /F command.

If you use the /W (wide) option, the file names and directory names will be listed with five names on a line. The file date and size are not printed, nor is the <DIR> for subdirectories. When you give the **DIR /W** command, you may have trouble deciding which file names refer to actual files and which to directories.

Message: File not found

ERROR: The path or file name you gave does not exist. The path may be incorrect, the file may not exist in the directory, or your spelling may be incorrect.

If you were doing a directory of another directory, you might try moving to the other directory (CHDIR) and trying the command again.

If you still believe that the file should be in the directory, enter **DIR /P** to get the complete directory and check for the file.

Hints:

1. Before you ERASE files, using a wild-card character or characters, do a DIR with the same file name. If files that you do not want to erase are displayed, don't use that file name. Keep experimenting with the DIR command until you get the correct file name for the ERASE command, or issue separate ERASE commands without a wild-card character.

2. I/O redirection is easy with the DIR command. You can print the directory by typing **DIR >PRN**, or put a copy of the directory into a file by typing **DIR >filename**, where **filename** is the name of the file to hold the directory.

(For more information on DIR, see Chapter 12.)

DISKCOPY
(Copy entire diskette)   V1** and V2** - External

Purpose: Copies the entire contents of one diskette to another on a track-for-track basis (carbon copy)

Syntax: **DISKCOPY** *d1: d2:*

d1: is the floppy disk drive that holds the source (original) diskette.

d2: is the floppy disk drive that holds the target diskette (diskette to be copied to).

Switches: None

Your computer manufacturer may add additional switches that will affect DISKCOPY's operation.

Special Terms: The diskette you are copying from is the *source* diskette.

The diskette you are copying to is the *target* diskette.

Rules: *1. If you do not give a drive name, the default disk drive will be used. If this is the hard disk drive, DISKCOPY will attempt to copy the hard disk drive to itself and not give an error message.

2. If you give only one valid floppy disk drive name, it will be used for the copy.

3. Giving the same valid floppy disk drive name twice is the same as giving only one disk drive name.

4. If you have a one-floppy drive system, drive A: will be used regardless of what drive you give.

5. When copying on one floppy disk drive (Rules 2-4), DOS will prompt you to insert the appropriate diskette, then wait for a keystroke before continuing.

6. If you are using one or more floppy disk drives for the DISKCOPY, they must be the same type (microfloppy, minifloppy, or floppy).

7. After copying, DISKCOPY prompts:

```
Copy another (Y/N)?
```

Answer **Y** to copy another diskette and **N** to stop the program. If you answer **Y**, the next copy will be performed on the same disk drive(s) as before.

8. If the target diskette is either not formatted or formatted differently from the source diskette, DISKCOPY will give you an error message. (Some versions of DISKCOPY will format the destination diskette. Check your manual for details.)

*9. DISKCOPY destroys any information previously recorded on the target diskette. Don't use a diskette containing information you want to keep as the target diskette.

Exit Codes: None

Sample Session:

This session involves a two-drive, double-sided system. A double-sided, V2 diskette will be copied onto a formatted but blank diskette.

A:DISKCOPY A: B:
```
Insert the source diskette in drive A:      {Change diskettes before hitting
Insert the target diskette in drive B:      <Enter>.}
Strike any key to begin. <Enter>

Copying 9 sectors per track, 2 side(s)
```

[copying process continues ....]

```
Copy another(Y/N)? N
A:
```

Notes: DISKCOPY makes identical copies of a diskette. It automatically "sizes" the source diskette and makes an exact copy of it on another disk drive.

You should format your target diskettes ahead of time for DISKCOPY. Most versions of DISKCOPY cannot use unformatted diskettes. Also, FORMAT reports any bad sectors. If a diskette has bad sectors, it cannot be used as the target with DISKCOPY. DISKCOPY will still attempt to write to the bad sectors and will not give you a good copy.

Users of computer systems with a hard disk should always give at least one floppy disk drive name with DISKCOPY. If the current disk is the hard disk drive (in this example, drive C) and you type:

C:DISKCOPY

you will see

```
Insert formatted target diskette into drive C
Press any key when ready.
```

Hit Ctrl-C!

DISKCOPY will attempt to copy the hard disk to itself. I did this once and aborted the program just a few seconds into the DISKCOPY. I didn't lose anything, but I don't want to find out if this is a safe mistake. If you always give a floppy disk drive name with DISKCOPY, you shouldn't have a problem.

Hints: 1.   Write-protect your source diskette.

This is particularly important when you make a copy of a diskette using only one floppy disk drive. DOS will periodically prompt you to change the diskette. If the source diskette is write-protected, you cannot damage it if you put it into the drive when DOS tells you to put in the target diskette.

This can also be important for a two-floppy disk drive system in a case where you specified the wrong drives for the copy. An infrequent but fatal mistake is to put the source diskette into drive B:, the target diskette into drive A:, then type:

DISKCOPY A: B:

Now the intended source and target diskettes are reversed. If DISKCOPY is not stopped in time, the information on the intended source diskette is destroyed and replaced by whatever (if anything) is on the old target diskette.

For peace of mind, write-protect the source diskette.

2. If you have a two-floppy disk drive system and didn't write-protect your diskette, watch the disk drive lights and be ready to flip open a disk drive door.

If you don't write-protect your diskette on a two-drive system, watch to see which floppy disk drive light comes on first when the copying starts. The disk holding the source diskette should be the first light to come on. If the wrong disk drive light comes on, **immediately flip the drive door open on the intended source diskette** and let DOS error out (abort). If DOS starts to write to the wrong diskette, it's too late!

Typing the control-abort keystroke(s) does not always work because DOS may not check for this action in time. Nor does flipping the drive door open on the "new" source diskette always work because DOS may have already read enough information on this diskette and be on its way to copying on the wrong diskette.

Flipping open the disk drive door does not hurt either diskette. When DOS starts its copying process, only information from the first diskette is read. It is difficult to damage a diskette from which you are only reading.

3. Have as much free RAM memory available as possible.

When DISKCOPYing, DOS reads into memory as much information from the source diskette as possible. Then DOS copies this information to the target diskette and reads the next batch of information from the source diskette. The more free memory you have, the less time is required to copy a diskette.

4. If you have used a diskette for a long time and have created and deleted many files on it, use COPY *.* rather than DISKCOPY.

DISKCOPY makes a "physical" image (exact copy) of a diskette. A diskette that has had many files created and deleted on it becomes *fragmented,* meaning that a file is stored all over the diskette. This frequently happens with word-processing programs that automatically create a backup copy of files.

The result of this fragmentation is that DOS slows down when using the file because DOS must read your file from all the different places. CHKDSK *.* tells you if this condition is true for a particular diskette.

If CHKDSK *.* tells you that several files are noncontiguous, format a diskette and COPY *.* from the old floppy to the new one to make the files contiguous and speed the search for the file. If you have subdirectories on a diskette, be sure to make the same subdirectories (MD or MKDIR) on the new copy and copy their contents.

**Advanced
User Notes:**   SWITCHAR for this command is always the slash (/).

ERASE
(Erase files)

Purpose:	Removes one or more files from the directory
Syntax:	**ERASE** *d:path\filename.ext*

or

DEL *d:path\filename.ext*

d: is the name of the disk drive holding the files to be erased.

path is the directory of the files to be erased.

filename.ext is the name of the file(s) to be erased. Wild cards are allowed.

Rules:

1. If you do not give a disk drive name, the current disk drive will be used.

2. If you do not give a path name, the current directory on the disk drive will be used.

3. If you give a disk drive name and/or a path name but no file name, DOS assumes the file name is *.* (all files).

4. If you specify *.* or no name (when you have given a disk drive name and/or path name) for the file name, DOS will prompt with the following:

    > Are you sure (Y/N)? _

    If you answer **Y**, all files in the specified directory will be erased.

    If you answer **N**, the files will not be erased.

5. You cannot erase a directory, including the . (current directory) and .. (parent directory) from a subdirectory.

Notes: ERASE, or its shorthand form DEL (delete), removes files. The entry in the directory is altered to mean "not in use," and the space occupied by the file on the diskette or disk is freed.

This activity means that as long as you do not place any more information on that diskette, the file can be recovered by special utility programs not provided with DOS. One such utility is provided with the Norton Utilities. However, RECOVER is not designed for this use and will not recover erased files. Remember, you may not be able to recover erased files if you put any more information on (write to) the diskette.

Hints: Wild cards are useful when you erase a group of files, but inadvertently erasing the wrong file or files is easy to do. Use the DIR command and your intended wild-card file name to test which files will be erased. If a wrong file or files shows up, you must use a different file name. In other words, experiment with the DIR command to find the right file name before you ERASE.

Erasing the wrong file is much easier than recovering the erased file, even if you have the right utility program.

You should also check your typing before you hit Enter. It is very easy to make a typographical error and erase the wrong file.

EXE2BIN
(Change .EXE file into a
.BIN or .COM file)

V1.1 and V2 - External

Purpose:	Changes suitably formatted .EXE files into .COM files
Syntax:	**EXE2BIN** *d1:path1***filename1***.ext1 d2:path2\\filename2.ext2*

d1: is the name of the disk drive holding the file to convert.

path1 is the directory of the file to convert.

filename1 is the root name of the file to convert.

.ext1 is the extension name of the file to convert.

d2: is the name of the disk drive for the output file.

path2 is the directory of the output file.

filename2 is the root name for the output file.

.ext2 is the extension name of the output file.

Special Terms:	The file to convert (*d1:path1***filename1***.ext1*) is the *source* file.
	The output file (*d2:path2\\filename2.ext2*) is the *destination* file.
Exit Codes:	None
Rules:	

1. If you do not specify a drive:

    A. For the source file (*d1:*), the current drive will be used as the source file.

    B. For the destination file (*d2:*), the source drive will be used.

2. When you do not specify a path (*path1* or *path2*), the current directory of the disk will be used.

3. You must specify a root file name for the source file to be converted (**filename1**).

4. If you do not specify a root file name for the destination file (*filename2*), the root file name of the source will be used (**filename1**).

5. If you do not specify an extension:

    A. For the source file (*.ext1*), the extension .EXE will be used.

    B. For the destination file (*.ext2*), the extension .BIN will be used.

6. The .EXE file must be in the correct format (following the Microsoft conventions).

Notes: EXE2BIN is a programming utility that converts .EXE (executable) program files to .COM or .BIN (binary image). The resulting program takes less disk space and loads faster. However, this conversion may be a disadvantage in future versions of DOS. Unless you are using a compiler-based language, you will probably never use this command. For further information on EXE2BIN, see your DOS manual.

FIND
(Find string filter)   V2 - External

Purpose: Displays all the lines from the designated files that match/do not match the specified string. This command can also display line numbers.

Syntax: **FIND** /V/C/N **string** *d:path\filename.ext* ...

string is the set of characters you want to search for. The characters in **string** must bc cncloscd in quotation marks (").

d: is the name of the disk drive for the file.

path is the path to the *filename.ext.*

filename.ext is the file you want to search.

Switches: /V   Displays all lines that do *not* contain **string**

/C   *Counts* the number of times **string** occurs in the file but does not display the actual lines where **string** occurred

/N   Displays the line *number* (number of the line in the file) in front of each line that matches **string**

Rules: 1.   You may use more than one file specification. Each file specification should be separated by a space. All file specifications must appear after **string**.

2.   For each file specification:

A.   If you do not give a disk drive, the current drive will be used.

B.   If you do not give a path name, the current directory will be used.

3.   If you do not give any file specifications, FIND will look for information from the keyboard (standard input).

4.   Switches, if given, must be typed between the word **FIND** and **string**. (Most DOS commands require that switches be placed at the end of the line.)

Sample Session: ─────────────────────

For this example, two files were created: MEN.TXT and GETTY.TXT.

C:dir

```
   Volume in drive C is QUE _ DISK
   Directory of C:\test

   .                 <DIR>        8-01-83     10:27a
   ..                <DIR>        8-01-83     10:27a
   MEN       TXT         72       8-05-83     3:29p
   GETTY     TXT        180       8-05-83     3:31p
         4 File(s)   3981312 bytes free
```

C:type men.txt   {Show what's in the file.}
```
Now is the time for all good
men to come to the aid of
their party.
```

C:type getty.txt   {Show what's in this file.}
```
Fourscore and seven years ago, our
fathers brought forth upon this
continent a new nation conceived in
liberty and dedicated to the proposition
that all men are created equal.
```

C:find "men" men.txt   {Now find the word "men"
                                                    in MEN.TXT.}


```
---------- men.txt
```
                                                    {The file name}

```
men to come to the aid of
```
                                                    {The lines from the file}

C:find "men" getty.txt   {Now do the same thing
                                                    for GETTY.TXT.}

```
---------- getty.txt
that all men are created equal.
```

C:find "men" men.txt getty.txt   {Now find "men" in both files.}

```
---------- men.txt
men to come to the aid of

---------- getty.txt
that all men are created equal.
```

C:find /v "men" men.txt getty.txt   {Now show which lines don't
                                                            have "men."}

```
---------- men.txt
Now is the time for all good
their party.

---------- getty.txt
Fourscore and seven years ago, our
fathers brought forth upon this
continent a new nation conceived in
liberty and dedicated to the proposition
```

C:find /c "men" men.txt getty.txt   {Now count the lines that have
                                                            "men" in them.}

```
---------- men.txt: 1
```
                                                            {The file name and the count}

```
---------- getty.txt: 1
```
                                                            {The file name and the count}

C:find /v/c "men" men.txt getty.txt   {Count the number of lines that
                                                            don't have "men."}

```
---------- men.txt: 3
```

```
---------- getty.txt: 5
```

C:find /n "men" men.txt getty.txt   {Number the lines with "men."}

```
---------- men.txt
[2]men to come to the aid of
```
                                                            {Notice that the count is always
                                                            relative to the file.}

```
---------- getty.txt
[5]that all men are created equal.
```

C:find /v/n "men" men. getty.txt

{Same thing, but lines without "men"}

```
---------- men.txt
[1]Now is the time for all good
[3]their party.
[4]
---------- getty.txt
[1]Fourscore and seven years ago, our
[2]fathers brought forth upon this
[3]continent a new nation conceived in
[4]liberty and dedicated to the proposition
[6]
```

C:find /n "t" men.txt getty.txt

{Now let's search for any line with the letter "t."}

```
---------- men.txt
[1]Now is the time for all good
[2]men to come to the aid of
[3]their party.

---------- getty.txt
[2]fathers brought forth upon this
[3]continent a new nation conceived in
[4]liberty and dedicated to the proposition
[5]that all men are created equal.
```

C:find /n "th" men.txt getty.txt

{I got too many lines. I was actually looking for lines with "th."}

```
---------- men.txt
[1]Now is the time for all good
[2]men to come to the aid of
[3]their party.

---------- getty.txt
[2]fathers brought forth upon this
[4]liberty and dedicated to the proposition
[5]that all men are created equal.
```

C:find /n "the" men.txt getty.txt   {Now I'll look for the word "the."}

---------- men.txt
[1]Now is the time for all good
[2]men to come to the aid of
[3]their party.

---------- getty.txt
[2]fathers brought forth upon this
[4]liberty and dedicated to the proposition

C:find /n "THE" men.txt getty.txt   {How about "THE" ?}

---------- men.txt

---------- getty.txt   {Not in either file}

The last example shows one problem you may encounter when trying to find a string. FIND looks for the exact match to your search string. Upper- and lower-case letters are treated differently. FIND will not locate a lower-case word if it has any capital letters. That's why "the" could be found in the file, but "THE" was not found.

Notes:	FIND is one of several filters provided with DOS V2. This command can find lines that contain **string** as well as lines that do not. It can also number lines and count lines rather than display them.
	This filter is useful when combined with the I/O redirection of DOS V2. The output of FIND can be redirected into a file with the > character. Because FIND lets you name a sequence of files to search, you do not have to redirect the input to FIND.
Messages:	1. FIND: File not found filename
	ERROR: FIND could not find the file named **filename**. The file does not exist, the file is not where you said it should be (wrong drive or path), or the spelling is incorrect. If you give a switch after **string**, FIND will think that the switch is a file name and will give you the above error message.
	2. FIND: Invalid number of parameters

ERROR: You didn't give FIND enough information. You must type at least the following:

FIND "string"

You probably didn't give a string to search for.

3. FIND: Invalid parameter x

    WARNING: You gave FIND an incorrect switch. FIND only recognizes /C, /N, or /V. FIND will print this warning message and continue.

4. FIND: Syntax error

    ERROR: You did not phrase the command correctly. You probably didn't put quotation marks around the string for which you were searching.

FORMAT
(Format disk)

V1* and V2* - External

Purpose: Initializes the disk to accept DOS information and files. The command also checks the disk for defective tracks and optionally places DOS on the diskette.

Syntax: **FORMAT** *d: /O/V/S*

d: is a valid disk drive name.

Switches: */O* Formats an 8-sector diskette (DOS V1.x) and leaves the proper places in the directory for the operating system, *but* does not place the operating system on the diskette

/V Writes a *volume* label on the disk (manufacturer dependent)

/V Does not write a *volume* label on the disk (manufacturer dependent)

/S Places on the disk a copy of the operating *system*, which makes the diskette bootable. The */S* switch must be the last switch given.

Note: Additional switches that affect FORMAT's operation may be added by your computer manufacturer.

Rules:
1. If you do not give a disk drive name, the current disk drive will be used.

2. Before a new diskette can be used, it must be FORMATted.

3. DOS will check the floppy disk drive and format the diskette to its maximum capacity, unless otherwise directed through a switch.

4. You cannot use the */V* or */S* switch with the */O* switch.

*5. FORMAT destroys any information previously recorded on the diskette. Do not FORMAT a diskette with any useful information on it.

6. If you give a volume name, it can be one to eleven characters long and contain any character that is legal in a file name.

7. If you use the */S* switch (place the operating system on the disk) and the current directory does not have a copy of DOS, DOS will prompt you to place a DOS diskette into drive A to get the copy of DOS before formatting the diskette.

Exit Codes: None

Sample Session:

This session covers formatting four diskettes. The first two will only be formatted, the third will have the operating system added (*/S* switch), and the last diskette will have a volume label added. This example assumes that the */V* switch must be given to write a volume label.

A:FORMAT A:

```
Insert new diskette for drive A:
and strike any key when ready
```
{I put a diskette in A: and hit
<Enter>.}

```
Formatting...Format complete

   362496 bytes total disk space
   362496 bytes available on disk
```

```
Format another (Y/N)? Y
```
{Now the second diskette}

```
Insert new diskette for drive A:
and strike any key when ready
```

```
Formatting...Format complete

   362496 bytes total disk space
    15360 bytes in bad sectors
   347136 bytes available on disk
```
{This diskette had several bad sectors.
I can use it for most operations,
but not for DISKCOPY and
DISKCOMP.}

```
Format another (Y/N)? N
```
{To put the operating system on the
next diskette, I must exit FORMAT
and run the program again.}

A:FORMAT A: /S

{Now run the program with the */S*
switch.}

```
Insert DOS disk in drive A:
and strike any key when ready
```
{This message appears only when you
give the */S* switch and the current
disk does not have the operating
system on it.}

```
Insert new diskette for drive A:
and strike any key when ready

Formatting...Format complete
System transferred

    362496 bytes total disk space
     40960 bytes used by system
    321536 bytes available on disk

Format another (Y/N)? N
```

A:FORMAT A: /V
```
Insert new diskette for drive A:
and strike any key when ready

Formatting...Format complete

Volume label (11 characters, ENTER for none)? ACCOUNT DSK

    362496 bytes total disk space
    362496 bytes available on disk

Format another (Y/N)? N
```
A:DIR A:
```
Volume in drive A is ACCOUNT DSK
Directory of A:\

File not found

A:
```

Notes: Every diskette and hard disk must be formatted before it is used. The FORMAT program actually performs several tasks. It sets up each track and sector on the disk to accept information. Special information is recorded, such as track headers (one for each track), sector headers (one for each sector), and CRC bits (cyclic redundancy check) to ensure that the recorded information is accurate.

As DOS completes the formatting of each track of the disk, DOS tests the track. If the track passes the test, DOS moves to the next track. If the track is bad, DOS remembers and marks the track as "reserved" in the FAT. No useful information will be recorded on the bad tracks.

DOS then establishes the area for the disk's root directory and File Allocation Table (FAT). If any bad tracks were found, the FAT is marked appropriately.

The use of the /V switch for volume labels varies among computer manufacturers. Consult your DOS manual to see if /V inhibits or creates a volume label.

Hints: When you use a one-floppy disk drive system, use drive B for formatting. This will prevent the accidental erasure of a good diskette that was inadvertently left in drive A. As you become accustomed to operating your computer, use drive A for formatting, but always check that the proper diskette is in the drive before pressing the key to begin formatting.

With a hard disk system, always give FORMAT a drive name. If you don't, you may inadvertently reformat the hard disk drive. If drive C, the hard disk, is the current disk drive, then

> **C:FORMAT**
> Press any key to begin formatting drive C.

DOS is telling you that when you strike any key, DOS will start formatting the hard disk! Type Ctrl-C immediately, or you will lose all the information on the hard disk! Once FORMAT begins, it is too late. Your information is lost. This possibility necessitates backing up your hard disk frequently.

Messages: 1.   Attempted write-protect violation

WARNING: The diskette you are trying to format is write-protected. On minifloppy diskettes, covering the write-protect notch with a tab protects the diskette. To write-protect 8-inch diskettes, do not cover the write-protect notch.

Check the diskette in the drive. If this is the diskette you want to format, remove the write-protect tab (for minifloppies) or put a write-protect tab over the notch (for 8-inch floppies). If the diskette in the drive was the wrong diskette, put the correct diskette in the drive and try again.

2. `Disk not compatible`

   ERROR: The disk drive or pseudo-disk (RAM disk) drive cannot be used by the DOS FORMAT command.

3. `Disk unsuitable for system disk`

   WARNING: FORMAT detected one or more bad sectors on the diskette where DOS normally resides. Because DOS must reside on a specified spot on the disk and this portion is unusable, the diskette cannot be used to boot (load and start) DOS. You might try to reformat this diskette. Some diskettes format successfully the second time but not the first. If FORMAT gives this message a second time, the diskette cannot be used as a boot diskette.

4. `Format failure`

   ERROR: FORMAT encountered a disk error that it could not handle. This message usually comes after another error message and indicates that FORMAT has aborted.

   One cause of this error may be a diskette that has bad sectors where the boot sector, FAT, or root directory is normally recorded. A diskette or disk with flaws in any of these areas is unusable.

5. `Insert DOS disk in d:`
   `and strike any key when ready`

   INFORMATIONAL: Before formatting a diskette with the /S switch, FORMAT reads into memory the DOS system files IO.SYS, MSDOS.SYS, and COMMAND.COM. However, DOS cannot find these files. To solve this problem, put a DOS diskette containing these three files into drive d: and hit any key to continue.

6. `Invalid characters in volume label`

   WARNING: One or more of the characters in the label name you gave are invalid. Give the name again, making sure that the characters are appropriate for a volume name. The most common mistake is using a period (.) in the volume name. DOS will ask you to try again.

7. `Parameters not compatible`

   ERROR: You gave two or more switches that are not compatible. Check the rules in this section to see which switches can be used together and try running FORMAT again.

8.   `Track 0 bad - disk unusable`

WARNING: Track 0 holds the boot record, the FAT, and the directory. This track is bad, and the diskette is unusable. Try formatting the diskette again. If the error recurs, the diskette is bad and cannot be used.

9.   `Unable to write BOOT`

WARNING: Either the first track of the diskette or the DOS portion of the hard disk is bad. The bootstrap loader (BOOT program) cannot be written to the diskette or disk. The diskette or DOS portion of the hard disk cannot be used. Reformat, and if the error recurs, the diskette or hard disk drive is completely unusable.

MKDIR
(Make directory)

V2 - Internal

Purpose: Creates a subdirectory

Syntax: **MKDIR** *d:path***dirname**

or

MD *d:path***dirname**

d: is the name of the disk drive for the subdirectory.

path is a valid path name for the path to the directory that will hold the subdirectory.

dirname is the name of the subdirectory you are creating.

Exit Codes: None

Rules:
1. If you do not specify a disk drive name, the current disk drive is used.

2. If you do not specify a path name, the subdirectory will be established in the current directory of the specified drive if you gave a disk drive name, or the current disk drive if you did not give a disk drive name.

3. If you use a path name, separate it from the **dirname** with a path character, the backslash (\\).

4. You must specify the new subdirectory name (**dirname**). The **dirname** must be between one and eight characters long with an optional extension, and conform to the rules for directory names.

5. You cannot use a directory name that is identical to a current file in the parent directory. For example, if you have a file named MYFILE in the current directory, you cannot create the subdirectory MYFILE in this directory. However, if the file is named MYFILE.TXT, there is no conflict between the names, and the MYFILE subdirectory may be created.

Notes: MKDIR, or the shorthand form MD, makes subdirectories. You can make as many subdirectories as you like but there is one caution. DOS provides only

63 characters for the path name, including the backslashes. It is possible to make so many levels of subdirectories with long directory names that the path to a directory exceeds the 63-character limit.

You are not restricted to creating subdirectories in the current directory. When you add a path name, DOS will establish a new subdirectory wherever you direct.

Message: `Unable to create directory`

ERROR: The directory you were going to create already exists, one of the path names you gave is incorrect, the root directory of the disk is full, the disk is full, or a file already exists by the same name.

Check the directory in which the new subdirectory was to be created. If a conflicting name exists, change the file name or use a new directory name. If the disk or the root directory is full, delete some files, create the subdirectory in a different directory, or use a different disk.

MORE
(More output filter)   V2 - External

Purpose:	Displays one screenful of information from the standard input device and pauses for a keystroke while displaying the message -- More --
Syntax:	**MORE**
Exit Codes:	None

Rules:

1. MORE displays one screenful of data on the standard output (display).

2. After displaying a screenful of information, MORE will pause and wait for a keystroke. This process is repeated until the input is exhausted.

3. MORE is best used with DOS V2's I/O redirection and piping.

Examples:

A. **MORE <TEST.TXT**

displays a screenful of information from the file TEST.TXT. MORE then displays the prompt -- More -- at the bottom of the screen and waits for a keystroke. When you press a key, MORE continues this process until all information is displayed. MORE will not display the prompt on the final screenful of information.

B. **DIR | SORT | MORE**

displays the sorted output of the directory command, 23 lines at a time.

Notes: MORE is a DOS filter that allows you to display a screenful of information without manually pausing the screen. This command is similar to the TYPE command, except that MORE pauses automatically after each screenful of information.

A screenful of information is based on 80 characters per line and 23 lines per screen. This does not mean, however, that MORE will display 23 lines from the file at a time. When a line exceeds the display width (usually 80 characters), MORE will display the first 80 characters, move down to the next line, display the next 80 characters, and so on, until the complete line from the file is displayed. If one line from the file takes 3 lines to display, MORE will display a maximum of 21 lines from the file. In other words, MORE acts intelligently with long lines and display line widths.

PATH
(Set directory search order)   V2 - Internal

Purpose: Tells DOS to search the specified directories on the specified drives if a
program or batch file is not found in the current directory

Syntax: **PATH** *d1:path1; d2:path2; d3:path3; ...*

d1:, d2:, and *d3:* are valid disk drives names.

path1, path2, and *path3* are valid path names to the commands you want to
run while in any directory.

Rules:
1. If you do not enter a disk drive name for a path, the current disk drive
   will be used.

2. Each path can be any valid series of subdirectories, separated from one
   another by the backslash.

3. If you specify more than one set of paths, the following applies:

   A. Each path set must be separated by a semicolon.

   B. The search for the program or batch file will be in the order of
      the path sets given. First the current directory is searched, then
      d1:path1, followed by *d2:path2,* then *d3:path3,* etc., until the
      command or batch file is found.

4. If you give invalid information (a bad drive name, bad delimiter, a
   deleted path, etc.), DOS will not give an error message. When searching
   the path for a program or batch file, DOS will simply skip a bad or
   invalid path.

5. If the file cannot be found in the current directory and the given paths,
   a Bad command or filename message will be given.

6. PATH affects only the execution of a program (.COM or .EXE file) or
   a batch file (.BAT). This command does not work with data files, text
   files, or program overlays.

Notes: PATH is a useful command with hierarchical directories. Directories that
contain your utility programs, system programs, or batch files can be

established and used from anywhere on the disk. PATH will automatically cause DOS to search these directories to find your programs without your having to type the path each time.

Note that only program files and batch files are eligible for PATH. Once you have invoked a program, it is up to the program, not DOS, to look in other directories for data files, text files, or program overlays. Programs like WordStar need their overlay files in the same directory in which you are working. Future versions of programs will allow you to "install" a path.

To view the current path, use the SET command.

Hints: Specify an absolute path that starts with the root directory of a disk (\), instead of a relative path that starts with the current directory (.\). By specifying an absolute path, you won't be concerned about which current directory you are in.

For example, I keep my DOS programs in a level 2 directory called BIN and a level 3 directory called UTIL. I set the path to

PATH C:\BIN;C:\BIN\UTIL

This command allows me to invoke a DOS command from anywhere on the hard or floppy disk. If I used the PATH command with a relative directory, starting with the current or parent directory, I would have to change the path almost every time I changed subdirectories. In addition, I can be on any disk drive, not just the hard disk, and invoke the DOS commands in BIN and UTIL.

PRINT
(Background printing)

V2 - External

Purpose: Prints a list of files on the printer, while the computer performs other tasks

Syntax: **PRINT** *d1:filename1.ext1/P/T/C d2:filename2.ext2/P/T/C ...*

d1: and *d2:* are valid disk drive names.

filename1.ext1 and *filename2.ext2* are the names of the files you want to print. Wild cards are allowed.

Switches: */P*   Queues up the file (places the file in the line) for *printing*

/T   *Terminates* the background printing of any or all files, including any file currently being printed

/C   *Cancels* the background printing of the file(s)

Exit Codes: None

Rules:

1. If you do not give a disk drive name, the current disk drive will be used.

2. If you do not give a file name, the status of the background printing will be displayed.

3. You may print files only in the current directory. Paths are not allowed.

4. Do not queue more than 10 files. If you do, PRINT will give you the message PRINT queue is full and ignore the command. PRINT will not function correctly until all currently queued files are printed.

5. A switch will affect the file name that precedes the switch and all files that follow until the next switch is found on the line.

6. Entering **PRINT /C** has no effect.

7. The first time you invoke the PRINT command, the message

    Name of list device [PRN]:

    will appear. You may do either of the following:

    A. Press <Enter>. This will send the files to LST:.

B. Enter a valid DOS device name. Printing will be to this device. If you enter a device that is not connected to your system, unpredictable things will happen.

You cannot change the assignment for background printing until the queue (line) is empty; you have changed the current disk drive or directories; and you have issued the PRINT command again.

8. Files are printed in the order in which they were entered. If wild cards are used in the file name, files are printed in the order they are found in the directory.

9. If DOS detects a disk error in the file that it is trying to print, DOS cancels the printing of the file and continues with any other files that are in line to be printed.

Notes: PRINT controls the background printing feature of DOS V2.

Background printing is simply the printing of a disk-based file during the computer's free time. This free time occurs when the computer is not performing a CPU-intensive task.

The word *queue* comes from the Latin word for *tail* or *line*. When you invoke the PRINT command to print a file, you queue this file to be printed, or you add this file to the line of files to be printed. DOS will print each file in the line as free time is available.

Background printing is best used with program files stored in ASCII format. The PRINT command will print any disk file. All characters in the file are transmitted to the printer, including control characters. An exception is made for the tab character Ctrl-I or CHR$(9), which DOS pads with spaces to the next 8-column boundary. If you attempt to background print a .COM or .EXE file, your printer will do strange things.

The position of a switch is important because it affects the file preceding and all files following the switch until another switch is encountered. For example, the command

PRINT LETTER.TXT /P PROGRAM.DOC MYFILE.TXT /C TEST.DOC

will result in the following:

1. Place the files LETTER.TXT and PROGRAM.DOC into the queue to be background printed.

2. Cancel the background printing of MYFILE.TXT and TEST.DOC.

In this example, the **/P** switch affects the files before and after it. The **/C** switch affects the file before it and all files that follow.

If you use the /T switch, all files in the queue, including the file being background printed, will be canceled. Giving the /T switch with a particular file name is unnecessary because all files, including any file names given on the command line, will be canceled.

If you cancel or terminate a file that is being printed, the following occurs:

1. A cancellation message is printed on the printer. If you terminate (/T) all files, the message says: All files canceled by operator. If you cancel (/C) the file currently being printed, the name of the file will appear with the message File canceled by operator.

2. The printer does a form feed.

3. The printer's bell rings.

4. If all files have not been canceled, printing will continue with the next queued file (next file on the list).

If a disk error occurs during the background printing of a file, the following occurs:

1. The current file is canceled.

2. A disk error message appears on the printer.

3. The printer performs a form feed and rings its bell.

4. DOS prints any remaining files in the queue.

Several cautions about the PRINT command should be mentioned. First, when PRINT has control of the printer, don't try to print anything else. Strange things may happen. If you are in BASIC, you will get a printer error message. If you are at the system level or are using some other program, what you attempt to print may be printed in the middle of a background printing task; your output will appear in the middle of the background printout.

Second, if you try to queue more than 10 files, you will not be able to cancel (/C) or terminate (/T) the files if you change to a different directory or to a different disk drive. Once the files have been printed, you may change directories or disk drives without losing the ability to cancel or terminate the print files.

Third, if you are printing files that reside on a floppy disk, don't remove the disk until PRINT is finished printing the files. Also, don't edit, alter, or erase the files being PRINTed. DOS will skip the file if the disk is removed or deleted (as if it had a disk error), or may not print the correct copy of the file (if the file is edited or altered).

Messages:

1. All files canceled by operator

   INFORMATIONAL: You have used the /T switch to terminate all queued files.

2. Errors on list device indicate that it may be off-line. Please check

   WARNING: The device used for PRINT is probably not selected, connected, or turned on. Check your printer and cable, and check to see that all connections are correct.

3. File canceled by operator

   INFORMATIONAL: This message appears on the printout to remind you that because you canceled the printing of this file, the printout is only a partial listing of the file.

4. File is currently being printed
   File is in queue

   INFORMATIONAL: This message tells you what file is currently being printed and what files are in line to be printed. The message is displayed whenever you use PRINT with no parameters or if you queue additional files.

5. List output is not assigned to a device

   ERROR: The device you gave PRINT is not a recognized device. PRINT will abort. To solve this problem, reissue PRINT and give a correct device name when DOS requests it.

6. Print queue is empty

   INFORMATIONAL: No files are currently in line to be printed by PRINT.

7. Print queue is full

   WARNING: You attempted to add too many files to PRINT, exceeding the 10-file limit. Your request to add more files has failed for every file past the 10-file limit in the queue. You must wait until PRINT has processed a file before you can add another one. (See the cautions about PRINT in the Notes section.)

8. `Resident part of PRINT installed`

    INFORMATIONAL: The first time you use PRINT, this message tells you that PRINT has installed itself into DOS and has increased the size of DOS by about 3,200 bytes.

9. `disk-error-type error on file filename`

    WARNING: This message appears on the printer. A disk error (`disk-error-type`) occurred when DOS was trying to read the file **filename**. The procedure for disk errors will be followed.

PROMPT
(Set the system prompt)

V2 - Internal

Purpose: Allows the user to customize the DOS system prompt (the "A:" or "A prompt")

Syntax: **PROMPT** *promptstring*

promptstring is the text to be used for the new system prompt.

Exit Codes: None

Rules:
1. If you do not enter the *promptstring,* the standard system prompt will reappear (A:).

2. Any text you enter for *promptstring* will become the new system prompt. You may enter special characters with the meta-strings listed below.

3. The new system prompt stays in effect until you reset the computer or reissue the PROMPT command.

4. To see the text of PROMPT after it has been set, use the SET command.

5. To start the prompt with a character that is normally a DOS delimiter (blank, semicolon, comma, etc.), precede the character with a null meta-string (a character that has no meaning to PROMPT, such as a **$A**).

Meta-strings: A *meta-string* is a group of characters that is transformed into another character or characters. To use certain characters, you must enter the appropriate meta-string to place the desired character(s) in your *promptstring.* Otherwise, DOS will immediately attempt to interpret the character (for example, the < or > signs).

All meta-strings begin with the dollar sign ($) and are two characters in length (including the $).

Character	What It Produces
$	$, the dollar sign
_ (underscore)	Carriage return, line feed (Move to the first position of the next line.)
b	¦, the vertical **b**ar
e	The **Esc**ape character, CHR$(27)
d	The **d**ate, like the DATE command
h	The **b**ackspace character, which erases the previous character, CHR$(8)
g	>, the **g**reater than character
l	<, the **l**ess than character
n	The current disk drive
p	The current disk drive and path, including the current directory
q	=, the e**q**ual sign
t	The **t**ime, like the TIME command
v	The **v**ersion number of DOS
All other characters	nothing or null; the character is ignored

Examples: A. **PROMPT**

or

B. **PROMPT $n:**

sets the DOS system prompt to the normal prompt (A:). Example A is the default. If you do not specify a prompt string, the standard system prompt is restored. In example B the **$n** is the letter of the current disk drive. The new prompt, if the current disk drive is A:, becomes "A" + ":" or "A:".

C. **PROMPT The current drive is $n:**

sets the new system prompt to:

The current drive is A:

D. **PROMPT $p**

sets the system prompt to the current disk drive and the path to the current directory. If we were using the example disk in drive A and were in the SAMPLES directory, the system prompt in example D would show the following:

A:\DOS\BASIC\SAMPLES

E.   **PROMPT $A;$t;**

sets the system prompt to:

;12:04:12.46;

or whatever the system time is. Note that the semicolon is normally used to separate items on the DOS command line. To make the first character of the system prompt a delimiter, a null meta-string must be used. Because "$A" does not have any special meaning for DOS, it ignores this meta-string but allows the semicolon to become the first character for the new prompt.

F.   **PROMPT $$**

sets the next system prompt to imitate the UNIX prompt

$

Notes: The PROMPT command is a new DOS V2 command that lets users have greater control over their systems—in this case, the system prompt. With the new hierarchical directories, it is helpful to display the current path on your disk drive. For that reason, many DOS V2 users may want to set the system prompt to

PROMPT $p

to display the current disk drive and the current path.

Any text may be used in the prompt, including text you might not normally think of, such as your name. Because I am conscious of time and forgetful of dates, my normal system prompt is

PROMPT $d $t $p $_yes, Chris $

which sets the system prompt to the date, time, and current disk drive and path, then moves to the next line and displays "yes, Chris," as in the following:

Mon 8-15-1983 9:57:13.11 A:\DOS\BASIC
yes, Chris

I used the last dollar sign to ensure that a space would appear between the "s" in "Chris" and whatever I type at this new system prompt. Some text editors "strip" out any spaces after the last printable character on a line. (IBM's Personal Editor does this.) To force the space, I use the dollar sign, which

DOS currently ignores, as the last character. New versions of DOS may force me to use a complete null meta-string like the "$A" instead.

The system prompt has two disadvantages. First, it is a wordy two-line prompt that distracts other people who use my computer. Second, if drive A is the current disk drive, you must always have a floppy in the drive. I use an IBM XT. Normally, the current disk drive is the hard disk, drive C. Whenever I make drive A the current drive, I must have a DOS disk in the drive because every time the system prompt is displayed, DOS reads the disk first to obtain the current path. DOS does this because when you change diskettes, the current directory you were working with before may not exist on the new diskette. If DOS senses that you are working with a different diskette, DOS resets the current directory of the new disk to the root directory.

Another problem with this prompt is that if the drive door is left open or no diskette is in the minifloppy disk drive, I get a "drive not ready" error. If you use the "$p" (drive/path) meta-string in your prompt, expect DOS to read the current disk drive before DOS displays your customized system prompt.

PROMPT is an enjoyable command with which to experiment. You can try it many times without "hurting" anything. Once you have created a prompt that you like, include it in the AUTOEXEC.BAT file, or create a separate batch file that you can execute once DOS has started. To cancel your new prompt and restore the old A-prompt, just reissue the PROMPT without a *promptstring*.

RECOVER
(Recover files or disk directory)

V2 - External

Purpose:	Recovers a file with bad sectors or a file from a disk with a damaged directory
Syntax:	To recover a file:

RECOVER *d:path\filename.ext*

To recover a disk with a damaged directory:

RECOVER *d:*

d: is the name of the disk drive holding the damaged file/diskette.

path is the path name of the path to the directory holding the file to recover.

filename.ext is the file to recover. Wild cards are allowed, but only the first file that matches the wild-card file name will be RECOVERed.

Exit Codes: None

Rules:

*1. Do not use this command on files or disks that do not need it!

2. If you do not give a drive name, the current disk will be used.

3. If you do not give a path name, the current directory will be used.

4. If you give a file name, DOS will recover as much information as possible from the file, skipping over the bad sectors.

5. If you give just a drive name or do not give any names, DOS will attempt to RECOVER the directory of the disk.

6. If you give a wild-card character in the file name, RECOVER will work only on the first file it finds that matches the ambiguous name.

7. RECOVER will not restore erased files.

Notes: RECOVER attempts to recover either a file with a bad sector or a disk whose directory contains a bad sector.

To recover a file with one or more bad sectors, use **RECOVER d:filename.ext**. (DOS gives you a disk error when you try to use the file.)

DOS will read the file, one sector at a time. If DOS successfully reads a sector, DOS places the information into a temporary file. If DOS cannot successfully read the sector, DOS skips the sector but marks it in the FAT so that no other program will use the bad sector. This process continues until the entire file is read. The old file is erased, and the temporary file is renamed with the same name as that of the damaged file. The new file will be in the same directory as the old file.

If the damaged file is a program file, chances are that the program cannot be used. If the file is a data or text file, some information can be recovered. Because DOS reads to the end of the file, make sure that any garbage at the end has been edited out with a text editor or a word processor.

To recover a disk, type the disk drive name after the command. DOS will create a new root directory and recover each file and subdirectory, giving them the name *FILEnnnn.REC* (*nnnn* is a four-digit number). Even good files will be placed in the *FILEnnnn.REC* files. The only way you can determine which file corresponds to which *FILEnnnn.REC* is to type or dump each file and use the last printed directory of the disk—or to have a good memory. If you have a disk editor that can display the ASCII and hexadecimal characters of a file, the editor will be a big help. If you don't have one, type each file and rename it after you are sure what it is. Then try to guess the remaining files.

Remember that subdirectories will also be RECOVERed into *FILEnnnn.REC* files. If you TYPE the file, the first character will be a period (.). About halfway across the screen you will see a double-period (..). When you see these two symbols, you can safely guess that this file is a subdirectory.

RECOVER does not recover erased files. You will need a separate utility program to recover them.

(For more information, see Chapter 12.)

Message: Warning-directory full

ERROR: The root directory on the disk is now full. No more files can be RECOVERed. RECOVER will stop. You should erase or copy the files in the root directory to free more directory space, then rerun RECOVER.

RENAME
(Rename file)

V1 and V2 - Internal

Purpose: Changes the name of the disk file(s)

Syntax: **RENAME** *d:path***filename1**.*ext1* **filename2**.*ext2*

or

REN *d:path***filename1**.*ext1* **filename2**.*ext2*

d: is the name of the disk drive holding the files to be renamed.

path is the path name of the path to the files to be renamed.

filename1.*ext1* is the current name of the file. Wild cards are permitted.

filename2.*ext2* is the new name for the file. Wild cards are allowed.

Rules:
1. If you do not give a drive name, the current disk drive will be used.
2. If you do not give a path name, the current directory will be used.
3. You can give only a disk name and a path name for the first file name.
4. You must give both the old file name and the new file name with their appropriate extensions, if any.
5. Wild-card characters are permitted in the file names.
6. If a file in the same directory already has the new file name (**filename2**.*ext2*), a `Duplicate file name` or `File not found` message is displayed, and no further action is taken.

Notes: RENAME, or the shorthand form REN, changes the name of files on the disk. The form is simply

> **RENAME** *old name new name*

Because you are renaming an established disk file, any drive or path designation goes with the old name. DOS will know which file you are renaming.

Wild-card characters are acceptable in either the old or the new name, but these can be troublesome if you are not careful. For example, suppose that a directory has the following files:

```
LETTER.TXT
LETTER1.TXT
RENAME.DOC
RENAME.TXT
```

If you attempt to rename all .TXT files as .DOC files with the command:

RENAME *.TXT *.DOC

RENAME will stop when it encounters RENAME.TXT because a RENAME.DOC already exists. However, all .TXT files preceding RENAME.TXT will be successfully changed to .DOC files.

Messages:

1. `Duplicate filename or File not found`

   ERROR: You attempted to change a file name to a name that already existed, or the file to be renamed does not exist in the directory. Check the directory for conflicting names. Make sure that the file name does exist and that you have spelled it correctly. Then try again.

2. `Missing file name`

   ERROR: You forgot to enter the new name for the file.

RMDIR or RD
(Remove directory)

V2 - Internal

Purpose:	Removes a subdirectory
Syntax:	**RMDIR** *d:* **path**

or

RD *d:* **path**

d: is the name of the drive holding the subdirectory.

path is the path name of the path to the subdirectory. The last path name is the subdirectory you want to delete.

Exit Codes: None

Rules:

1. If you do not specify a drive name, the current drive will be used.

2. You must give the name of the subdirectory to be deleted. If you supply a path, the subdirectory to be deleted must be the last name in the path.

3. The subdirectory to be deleted must be empty. (The only files allowed are "." and "..".)

4. You cannot delete the current directory or the root directory of a disk.

Notes: RMDIR, or the shorthand form RD, removes subdirectories from the disk. RMDIR is the complement of the MKDIR command (make directory).

When you remove a subdirectory, it must be empty, except for the current directory file (".") and parent directory files (".."). The current directory also cannot be the directory you are using. If you attempt to remove a subdirectory that is not empty or is the current directory, DOS will give you an error message and not delete the directory.

Message: `Invalid path, not directory`
`or directory not empty`

ERROR: RMDIR did not remove the specified directory because you gave an invalid directory in the path, the subdirectory still has files in it other than the "." and ".." entries, or you misspelled the path or directory name to be removed. Check each possibility.

SET
(Set/show environment)

Purpose:	Sets or shows the system environment
Syntax:	To display the environment:

    SET

To add to or alter the environment:

    SET name=*string*

name is the name of the string you want to add to the environment.

string is the information you want to store in the environment.

Special Terms: *Environment* is a reserved area in RAM memory for alphanumeric (string) information that may be examined and used by DOS commands or user programs. For example, the environment usually contains *COMSPEC,* the location of COMMAND.COM; *PATH,* the additional path to find programs and batch files; and *PROMPT,* the string that defines the DOS system prompt.

Exit Codes: None

Rules:

1. If you do not specify a **name** or *string*, SET will display the current environment.

2. To set a string in the environment or to change the string associated with a current name, use **SET name=string**.

3. To delete a **name**, use **SET name=**.

4. Any lower-case letters in **name** will be changed to upper-case letters when placed in the environment.

5. You can also set the system prompt and information for the PATH command with SET, instead of using the PROMPT or PATH commands.

6. You may change the COMSPEC (the location of COMMAND.COM) with SET.

7. If you load a resident program (such as PRINT), DOS cannot expand the environment past 127 characters. If you have not used more than 127 characters, you may add additional information up to that limit. If you have already used 127 characters or more, you cannot add additional information to the envirnoment.

Notes: SET is an advanced DOS command that is seldom used. This command puts information in a safe place in memory for later use by invoked programs. One such use is to store the directory path to some data files or program overlays. When the program is invoked, it can examine the RAM memory where the SET information is stored and issue the proper commands to find the data or program overlays.

SET is a versatile command. It can put almost any information into the RAM memory for the environment. (Remember the restriction stated in Rule 7, however.) Unfortunately, few programs take advantage of the features provided by this versatile command.

SORT
(Sort string filter)

V2 - External

Purpose: Reads lines from the standard input device, performs an ASCII sort of the lines, then writes the lines to the standard output device. The sorting may be ascending or descending, and may start at any column in the line.

Syntax: **SORT** /R /+c

Switches: /R   Sorts in *reverse* order. This means that the letter Z comes before the letter A.

/+c   Starts sorting with the column number, c, indicated

Exit Codes: None

Rules:

1. If you do not give the /R (reverse sort) switch, the file will be sorted in ascending order.

2. If you do not give the /+c switch, sorting will start with the first column (first character on the line).

3. If you do not redirect the input or output, all input will be from the keyboard (standard input), and all output will be to the video display (standard output).

4. SORT uses the ASCII sequence and does not expand any control characters. (See Notes on the significance of this rule.)

5. The maximum file size that SORT can handle is 63K (64,512 characters).

6. SORT sorts the entire physical file, including any information beyond the end-of-file marker.

Examples: A. **SORT <WORDS.TXT**

sorts the lines in the file WORDS.TXT and displays the sorted lines on the video display.

B. **SORT <WORDS.TXT /R**

reverse sorts the lines in the file WORDS.TXT and displays the lines on the video screen.

C. **SORT/+8 <WORDS.TXT**

starts the sorting at the eighth character in each line of the
WORDS.TXT file and displays the output on the video display.

D. **DIR | SORT /+14**

displays the directory information sorted by file size. (The file size
starts in the 14th column.) Unfortunately, other lines, such as the
volume label, are also sorted starting at the 14th column.

Notes: SORT is a "dumb," general-purpose sorting program. Don't let the term
"dumb" deceive you. SORT is a powerful filter, but it has some limitations.

First, SORT uses the ASCII sequence for sorting. Look at the ASCII chart in
Appendix C. Note the relative positions of the numbers, punctuation
symbols, and letters. The first limitation of SORT stems from this chart.

Notice that the upper-case A comes before the upper-case Z, but the lower-
case a comes after the upper-case Z. SORT respects this difference,
sometimes to the chagrin of the user. For example, the word "TEXT" comes
before the words "text," "TEXt," and "TeXT."

A second limitation is that numbers are treated not as numbers but as
characters. Therefore, 1 will always come before 2, 3, or 9. (The 0 comes
before 1, by the way.) The problem is that 11, 123, and 12576 will all come
before 2, 3, 21, or any other number that does not begin with 0 or 1.

For these reasons, SORT is a "dumb" sorting program. The additional
intelligence required to recognize and handle similarly upper- and lower-case
letters and to handle numbers as numbers is not in the SORT filter. Programs
that solve these problems are available. However, these sorting programs are
not provided with DOS. SORT was not intended to handle these problems. It
is simply a good utility program for "standard" sorting and is provided "free"
with DOS.

Control characters are another problem. When you print a Ctrl-I (the tab
character), on the screen or printer, the printer moves out to the next tab
column, usually every ninth character position. Because SORT does not
expand tab characters, the output you expect from SORT may not be what
you get. Some text editors compress extra spaces into tab characters
(Personal Editor, for one). When you sort a file created by Personal Editor,
some lines may appear to be out of order. Loading and resaving the file
without tab characters (Personal Editor has this option), will give you the
correct order when you resort the file.

A thorny problem may arise when you try to sort the output from some text processors or data files created by a few languages. Some text-processing programs (WordStar, for example) put out a series of end-of-file markers, such as Ctrl-Z or CHR$(26), to fill out the last sector when you save a file. Most programs will stop reading more information from the file when they see the end-of-file marker. SORT works with the file's "real" length, the length recorded in the directory. This means that SORT will sort the end-of-file markers.

Look at the ASCII character chart. The Ctrl-Z comes before any printable characters. Therefore, the first line in the newly sorted file is a series of end-of-file markers. When you attempt to edit or type the sorted file, nothing is there because either TYPE or the word-processing program sees the end-of-file marker at the front of the file and thinks that's all there is to the file. Actually, the entire file is there, but it is trapped behind the end-of-file markers.

Some languages store their data in a special, compressed format. When you type a data file, garbage appears on the screen. This kind of file should not be sorted with SORT. The results you get will be unpredictable. The data is not stored as ASCII numbers but as compressed codes, some of which may be control characters. SORT does not have the intelligence to handle these files.

Don't underestimate SORT, however. It can be a very useful filter if you use it correctly. SORT works best when it is used in the "pipeline" with other commands, such as DIR.

SYS
(Place the operating system on the diskette)

V1 and V2 - External

Purpose: Places a copy of DOS on the specified diskette

Syntax: **SYS** *d:*

    d: is the disk drive holding the diskette that will receive a copy of DOS.

Exit Codes: None

Rules:
1. The disk to be SYSed must be:

   A. Previously formatted, using the */S* option (DOS V1 or V2)

   B. Previously formatted, using the */O* option (DOS V2 only)

   C. Completely empty

   D. Formatted with a special program that reserves the proper disk space for the operating system

   If you attempt to SYStem a disk that is not one of the above, a No room for system on destination disk message will appear, and DOS will not perform the operation.

2. A copy of DOS (IO.SYS and MSDOS.SYS) must reside on the current disk.

Notes: The SYS command places a copy of IO.SYS and MSDOS.SYS on the targeted disk. To make the disk bootable (able to load and execute the disk operating system), you must also copy COMMAND.COM.

The SYS command puts DOS on application program diskettes sold without DOS. These SYSed diskettes allow you to boot the computer system from diskettes with the application software. A diskette provided by the program publisher must be specially formatted, or SYS will not work. You should check the instructions that come with the applications program to see if you can SYS the diskette.

There is a small difference between V1 and V2 for SYS. SYS V2 checks the destination disk to see if the proper space is available for DOS. If not, an error message is given. SYS V1 places DOS on the diskette anyway, regardless of whether the proper space is available. Running SYS V1 on a diskette with existing files can garbage some files on the diskette.

To load DOS initially into the computer, the first two entries in the root directory of the boot disk must be IO.SYS and MSDOS.SYS (even though these are system files and hidden from the DIR command). IO.SYS also must reside on consecutive sectors. If either of these two conditions is not true, DOS will not load itself properly from this disk.

Messages:

1. `Insert DOS disk in d:`
   `and strike any key when ready`

   INFORMATIONAL: DOS tried to load itself into memory, but could not find IO.SYS, MSDOS.SYS, or COMMAND.COM. Loading these files into memory is a required step before SYS can place the operating system on a diskette or disk. Put the diskette that holds all three programs into drive **d:** and hit a key.

2. `No room for system on destination disk`

   ERROR: The diskette or disk was not formatted with the necessary reserved space for DOS. This diskette cannot be SYStemed.

TIME
(Set/show the time)   V1.x and V2 - Internal

Purpose: Shows and/or sets the system time

Syntax: **TIME** *hh:mm:ss.xx*

hh is the one- or two-digit representation for hours (0 to 23).

mm is the one- or two-digit representation for minutes (0 to 60).

ss is the one- or two-digit representation for seconds (0 to 60).

xx is the one- or two-digit representation for hundredths of a second (0 to 99).

Exit Codes: None

Rules:
1. If you enter a valid time, it will be accepted, and no other message will appear.

2. If you do not enter the time with the TIME command, the following message will appear:

    ```
    Current time is hh:mm:ss.xx
    Enter new time
    ```

    If you just press Enter, the time will not be reset. If you enter a valid time, the new time will be accepted immediately, and no other message will be displayed.

3. You must enter the correct delimiters between the numbers, as shown above under Syntax (colons between the hours, minutes, and seconds; a period between the seconds and hundredths of a second).

4. You do not have to enter all the information. If you change only the first parts of the time, the remaining portions will be set to 0.

5. If you specify an invalid time or incorrect delimiters, an `Invalid time` message will be displayed, and you will be prompted to enter the time again.

Notes: TIME is used to set the internal, 24-hour software clock of the computer. The time and date are recorded in the directory for every file whenever you create or change it. This directory information can help you locate the most recent version of a file.

The software clock used by most computers is based on the 60Hz power supply. As such, the time usually loses or gains several seconds each day. This is not a fault of the computer, but a minor (and normal) problem with the ac power provided by your power company.

Message: `Invalid time`

ERROR: You entered a nonsense time or did not punctuate the time correctly. Check your typing and try again.

TYPE
(Type file on screen)   V1 and V2 - Internal

Purpose: Displays the contents of the file on the screen

Syntax: **TYPE** *d:path***filename**.*ext*

d: is the name of the disk drive holding the file to type.

path is the DOS path to the file.

filename.*ext* is the name of the file to type. Wild cards are not permitted.

Exit Codes: None

Rules:
1. If you do not give a drive name, the current drive will be used.

2. If you do not give a path name, the current directory will be used.

3. You must provide a file name that matches the name in the directory.

4. All characters in the file, including control characters, are sent to the screen. However, each tab character Ctrl-I, or CHR$(9), is expanded to the next eight-character boundary.

5. You cannot type a directory.

Notes: The TYPE command displays on the video screen the characters in the file. TYPE allows you to see what a file contains.

If you try to TYPE some data files and most program files, you will see strange characters on the screen because TYPE is trying to display the machine-language instructions as ASCII characters.

The output of TYPE, as with most other DOS commands, can be redirected to the printer by adding the line

> PRN

or by typing Ctrl-P. (Don't forget to do a Ctrl-N to turn off the printing.)

However, unpredictable things can happen if you print when you TYPE a program file or some data files that contain control characters. As a rule, if what appears on the video display looks like nonsense, it will look like nonsense—or worse—on your printer.

VER
(Display version number)   V2 - Internal

Purpose:	Shows the DOS version number on the video display
Syntax:	**VER**
Exit Codes:	None
Rules:	None
Notes:	The VER command shows the one-digit version number, followed by a two-digit revision number. The current use of this command is to indicate whether or not you are working with DOS V2. If you type

VER

you will see a message something like this:

MS DOS Version 2.00

If you see a Bad command or file name message, you are working with DOS V1.x.

VERIFY
(Set/show disk verification)   V2 - Internal

Purpose: Sets/shows whether the data written to the disk(s) has been checked for proper recording

Syntax: To show the verify status:

   VERIFY

   To set the verify status:

   VERIFY ON

   or

   VERIFY OFF

Rules: 1.   VERIFY accepts only one of two parameters: ON or OFF.

   2.   Once VERIFY is ON, it remains on until:

   A.   A VERIFY OFF is performed.

   B.   A SET VERIFY system call turns it off.

   C.   DOS is rebooted.

Notes: VERIFY controls the checking of data just written on the disk to ensure that the data has been correctly recorded. If VERIFY is OFF, DOS will not check the data. If VERIFY is ON, DOS will check the data. VERIFY does not affect any other DOS operation.

   Two factors affect the tradeoff between VERIFY ON or OFF. If VERIFY is ON, data integrity is assured. If VERIFY is OFF, you will be able to write to the disk faster. It is usually safe to leave VERIFY OFF if you are not working with critical information (such as a company's accounting figures). It is wise to turn VERIFY ON when backing up your hard disk or making critical copies on the floppy disks.

   The degree of performance lost in verifying the hard disk is different from floppy diskettes. DOS takes only 8 to 9 percent more time to verify information when writing to the fixed disk. DOS takes 90 percent more time when verifying information written to the floppy disk. This difference comes from most hard disks' fast, built-in routines for data verification. As a result, hard disks verify information at a rate faster than that of floppy disks. Also, DOS must do all the work itself when verifying information written to the floppy disk. These factors explain the tenfold difference in verification speed between the hard disk and the floppy disk.

VOL
(Display volume label)

V2 - Internal

Purpose: Displays the volume label of the disk, if the label exists

Syntax: **VOL** *d:*

d: is the optional name of the disk drive whose label you want to display.

Rule: If you do not give a disk drive name, the current disk drive will be used.

Message: Volume in drive d has no label

INFORMATIONAL: The disk or diskette does not have a volume label.

Appendix A
Bugs and DOS V2.1

Known Bugs in DOS V2.0

The following list of known bugs in MS-DOS V2.0 is not complete but covers the major problems. It is very possible that you may never encounter any of these problems.

If your version of DOS is V2.0x or V2.1x or greater, these bugs do not exist in your version.

DOS Input Redirection

DOS does not always find the true end-of-file marker when redirecting input to a program. For example, your redirected program expects an input of 80 characters. Suppose that only 50 characters are left in the file. DOS will read the 50 characters and "wait" forever for the other 30 characters. In other words, if your file does not have enough input to fulfill a program request, DOS will hang. The only remedy for the situation is to turn your system off, then on again. The system reset sequence does not work.

FIND Filter

FIND sorts the entire file line by line, using the file size shown in the directory. Some programs will fill out the last sector of a text file with end-of-file markers. The directory size of the file will be the true file size plus the padding end-of-file markers.

Because end-of-file markers come before any printable characters, FIND will bubble to the top of the file the line containing the end-of-file markers. When other programs, such as TYPE or other text editors, attempt to use the sorted file, the first item they will encounter in the sorted file is the end-of-file marker. These programs will immediately stop reading the file, assuming that they have reached the end; and no useful information will be obtainable from the file.

This is not a bug in FIND, per se, but a caution. The fault lies with the text editors, which pad the text file with extra end-of-file markers, and with FIND.

SWITCHAR

Some MS-DOS programs written by the computer manufacturer do not use SWITCHAR, the switch character that can be set in CONFIG.SYS. This is not a bug in DOS. Microsoft does not document or recommend the resetting of SWITCHAR.

DOS V2.0x versus V2.1x

In early fall, 1983, Microsoft released MS-DOS V2.1. This version is functionally equivalent to V2.0x, with two major differences: (1) all known bugs in DOS V2.0x have been fixed, and (2) the international function call is supported in DOS V2.1.

The international function call allows a country code to be inserted in CONFIG.SYS. Based on the country code, DOS customizes the format of the date and time display for the local country. Programs may also call DOS to get the country code to customize display options and program features, such as using the comma (,) in place of the period (.) for displaying European currency amounts.

MS-DOS V2.1 also has placed the entire prompting text into a fixed area, making the translation of the text into foreign languages easier.

However, the international functions of MS-DOS have little impact on United States or Canadian users of MS-DOS.

Appendix B

Sample Hierarchical Directory

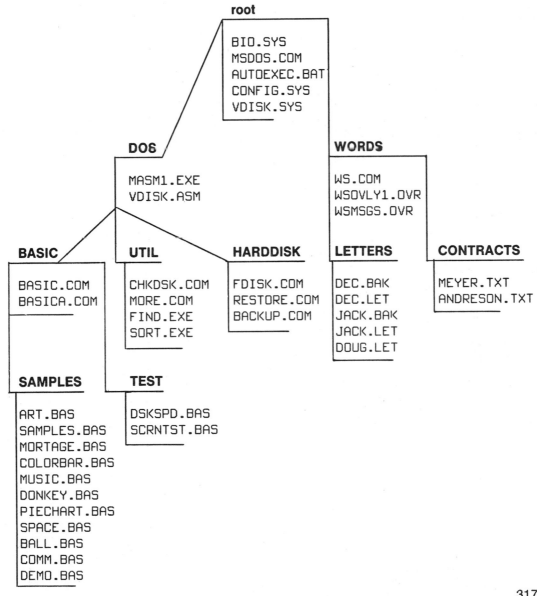

Appendix C
ASCII Codes

The codes for the American Standard Code for Information Interchange, or ASCII, are listed below.

Decimal	Hex	Octal	Binary	ASCII
0	00	000	00000000	(null) NUL
1	01	001	00000001	Ctrl-A SOH
2	02	002	00000010	Ctrl-B STX
3	03	003	00000011	Ctrl-C ETX
4	04	004	00000100	Ctrl-D EOT
5	05	005	00000101	Ctrl-E ENQ
6	06	006	00000110	Ctrl-F ACK
7	07	007	00000111	Ctrl-G (bell) BEL
8	08	010	00001000	Ctrl-H (backspace) BS
9	09	011	00001001	Ctrl-I (tab) horizontal HT
10	0A	012	00001010	Ctrl-J (linefeed) LF
11	0B	013	00001011	Ctrl-K (vertical tabs) VT
12	0C	014	00001100	Ctrl-L (formfeed) FF
13	0D	015	00001101	Ctrl-M (carriage return) CR
14	0E	016	00001110	Ctrl-N SO
15	0F	017	00001111	Ctrl-O SI

16	10	020	00010000	Ctrl-P DLE
17	11	021	00010001	Ctrl-Q DC1
18	12	022	00010010	Ctrl-R DC2
19	13	023	00010011	Ctrl-S DC3
20	14	024	00010100	Ctrl-T DC4
21	15	025	00010101	Ctrl-U NAK
22	16	026	00010110	Ctrl-V SYN
23	17	027	00010111	Ctrl-W ETB
24	18	030	00011000	Ctrl-X CAN
25	19	031	00011001	Ctrl-Y EM
26	1A	032	00011010	Ctrl-Z SUB
27	1B	033	00011011	Escape
28	1C	034	00011100	FS
29	1D	035	00011101	GS
30	1E	036	00011110	RS
31	1F	037	00011111	US
32	20	040	00100000	Space
33	21	041	00100001	!
34	22	042	00100010	"
35	23	043	00100011	#
36	24	044	00100100	$
37	25	045	00100101	%
38	26	046	00100110	&
39	27	047	00100111	'
40	28	050	00101000	(
41	29	051	00101001	)
42	2A	052	00101010	*
43	2B	053	00101011	+
44	2C	054	00101100	,
45	2D	055	00101101	-
46	2E	056	00101110	.
47	2F	057	00101111	/

48	30	060	00110000	0
49	31	061	00110001	1
50	32	062	00110010	2
51	33	063	00110011	3
52	34	064	00110100	4
53	35	065	00110101	5
54	36	066	00110110	6
55	37	067	00110111	7
56	38	070	00111000	8
57	39	071	00111001	9
58	3A	072	00111010	:
59	3B	073	00111011	;
60	3C	074	00111100	<
61	3D	075	00111101	=
62	3E	076	00111110	>
63	3F	077	00111111	?
64	40	100	01000000	@
65	41	101	01000001	A
66	42	102	01000010	B
67	43	103	01000011	C
68	44	104	01000100	D
69	45	105	01000101	E
70	46	106	01000110	F
71	47	107	01000111	G
72	48	110	01001000	H
73	49	111	01001001	I
74	4A	112	01001010	J
75	4B	113	01001011	K
76	4C	114	01001100	L
77	4D	115	01001101	M
78	4E	116	01001110	N
79	4F	117	01001111	O

80	50	120	01010000	P
81	51	121	01010001	Q
82	52	122	01010010	R
83	53	123	01010011	S
84	54	124	01010100	T
85	55	125	01010101	U
86	56	126	01010110	V
87	57	127	01010111	W
88	58	130	01011000	X
89	59	131	01011001	Y
90	5A	132	01011010	Z
91	5B	133	01011011	[
92	5C	134	01011100	\
93	5D	135	01011101	]
94	5E	136	01011110	^
95	5F	137	01011111	_
96	60	140	01100000	`
97	61	141	01100001	a
98	62	142	01100010	b
99	63	143	01100011	c
100	64	144	01100100	d
101	65	145	01100101	e
102	66	146	01100110	f
103	67	147	01100111	g
104	68	150	01101000	h
105	69	151	01101001	i
106	6A	152	01101010	j
107	6B	153	01101011	k
108	6C	154	01101100	l
109	6D	155	01101101	m
110	6E	156	01101110	n
111	6F	157	01101111	o

112	70	160	01110000	p
113	71	161	01110001	q
114	72	162	01110010	r
115	73	163	01110011	s
116	74	164	01110100	t
117	75	165	01110101	u
118	76	166	01110110	v
119	77	167	01110111	w
120	78	170	01111000	x
121	79	171	01111001	y
122	7A	172	01111010	z
123	7B	173	01111011	{
124	7C	174	01111100		
125	7D	175	01111101	}
126	7E	176	01111110	~
127	7F	177	01111111	del, rubout

Index

Assistant to the Managing Editor
Tim P. Russell

Production
Jonathan Mangin
Dennis R. Sheehan

Composed by Que Corporation
in Times Roman, Megaron, and Varityper Digital

More Computer Knowledge from Que

Que Order Line: 1-800-428-5331
Software Support and Maintenance: 1-317-842-7162

All prices subject to change without notice.

BOOKS TO HELP YOU MASTER SOFTWARE AND OPERATING SYSTEMS

Using 1-2-3

by Douglas Cobb and Geoffrey LeBlond

This outstanding best seller is designed to show you how to make the most of the highly popular integrated program, Lotus 1-2-3. Special emphasis is given to keyboard macros, the data base function, and graphics capability. If 1-2-3 is your first experience with an electronic spreadsheet, *Using 1-2-3* contains an introduction to this important tool. Whether you are a beginning or experienced 1-2-3 user, you can benefit from the detailed and clear explanations this book provides.

1-2-3 Tips, Tricks, and Traps

by Dick Andersen and Douglas Cobb

Here's a book designed as a quick reference for both beginning and advanced users of 1-2-3. It offers shortcuts and tips for such procedures as creating macros, producing graphs, and using Data Tables. The traps described in the book offer help with such special problems as transferring data between 1-2-3 and other programs, and handling problems that can arise from the use of particular commands. For anyone who uses 1-2-3, *Tips, Tricks, and Traps* is a must!

1-2-3 for Business

by Douglas Cobb and Leith Anderson

This book presents 15 business models built with the powerful integrated program, Lotus 1-2-3. Included are models for Project Management, Fixed Asset Management, and Lease versus Buy Analysis. Step-by-step instructions help you master 1-2-3 as you build models to manage your business. All the advanced features of 1-2-3, such as macros, data management, and graphics are illustrated in this book. If you use 1-2-3 in your business, this book is an excellent investment.

Using Symphony

by Geoffrey LeBlond and David Ewing

Using Symphony will help you master the exciting new integrated software package from Lotus. This book offers a thorough explanation of the Symphony program, concentrating on the communications tools, word-processing capabilities, and Symphony's Command Language. Be sure to buy *Using Symphony* if you are planning to move up from 1-2-3 to Symphony. Or if Symphony is your first Lotus product, then this is the book you need to get started.

Please send me the following books:

Item	Title	Price	Quantity	Extension
39	Using 1-2-3	$15.95		
127	1-2-3 Tips, Tricks, and Traps	$14.95		
34	1-2-3 for Business	$15.95		
141	Using Symphony	$19.95		
		BOOK SUBTOTAL		
		Shipping & Handling ($1.50 per item)		
		Indiana Residents Add 5% Sales Tax		
		GRAND TOTAL		

Method of Payment:

☐ Check   *Charge My:*   ☐ VISA   ☐ MasterCard   ☐ American Express

Card Number _____ Exp. Date _____

Cardholder Name _____

Ship To: _____

Address _____

City _____ State _____ Zip _____

All prices subject to change without notice.

FOLD HERE

- -

_____

_____

_____

_____

7999 Knue Road
Suite 202
Indianapolis, IN 46250